11-30-59

The Location
of the
Synthetic-Fiber Industry

TECHNOLOGY PRESS BOOKS

Regional Science Studies *edited by Walter Isard*

LOCATION AND SPACE-ECONOMY
By Walter Isard

THE LOCATION OF THE SYNTHETIC-FIBER INDUSTRY
By Joseph Airov

Other Books in the Social Sciences

THE INFLATIONARY SPIRAL: THE EXPERIENCE IN CHINA, 1939–1950
By Chang Kia-Ngau

THE TAO OF SCIENCE: AN ESSAY ON WESTERN KNOWLEDGE AND EASTERN WISDOM
By R. G. H. Siu

SOVIET EDUCATION FOR SCIENCE AND TECHNOLOGY
By Alexander G. Korol

THE ECONOMICS OF COMMUNIST EASTERN EUROPE
By Nicolas Spulber

ON HUMAN COMMUNICATION: A REVIEW, A SURVEY, AND A CRITICISM
By Colin Cherry

SCIENCE AND ECONOMIC DEVELOPMENT: NEW PATTERNS OF LIVING
By Richard L. Meier

MOSCOW AND THE COMMUNIST PARTY OF INDIA
By John H. Kautsky

LANGUAGE, THOUGHT, AND REALITY
By Benjamin Lee Whorf
Edited by John B. Carroll

THE TERMS OF TRADE: A EUROPEAN CASE STUDY
By Charles P. Kindleberger

MACHINE TRANSLATION OF LANGUAGES
Edited by W. N. Locke and A. D. Booth

NINE SOVIET PORTRAITS
By Raymond A. Bauer

THE PROSPECTS FOR COMMUNIST CHINA
By W. W. Rostow and others

LABOR MOBILITY AND ECONOMIC OPPORTUNITY
By Members of the Social Science Research Council

NATIONALISM AND SOCIAL COMMUNICATION
By Karl W. Deutsch

INDUSTRIAL RELATIONS IN SWEDEN
By Charles A. Myers

MID-CENTURY: THE SOCIAL IMPLICATIONS OF SCIENTIFIC PROGRESS
Edited by John E. Burchard

CYBERNETICS: OR CONTROL AND COMMUNICATION IN THE ANIMAL AND THE MACHINE
By Norbert Wiener

The Location
of the
Synthetic-Fiber Industry

A Case Study
in Regional Analysis

by

JOSEPH AIROV

Associate Professor of Economics
Emory University

A SOCIAL SCIENCE RESEARCH CENTER STUDY,
COLLEGE OF SOCIAL SCIENCES, UNIVERSITY OF PUERTO RICO

PUBLISHED JOINTLY BY
The Technology Press of
The Massachusetts Institute of Technology
AND
John Wiley & Sons, Inc., New York

Chapman & Hall, Limited, London

Library of Congress Catalog Card Number: 59-9336

Printed in the United States of America

To Walter Isard

Foreword

The synthetic-fiber industry is among the most rapidly growing industries in the world, and any detailed investigation of it, containing analysis of such high quality as this study, must necessarily be of basic interest to firms in this industry and in the related petrochemical and oil-refinery fields. By the same token, it should be of basic interest to many firms in other industries seeking avenues for diversification and new and varied channels for profitable operations.

This study also relates to such contrasting underdeveloped regions as Puerto Rico and the American South. It explores in fine detail the possibility of an important new industrial development for Puerto Rico and the further growth of the synthetic-fiber industry in the South. The manuscript is thus of significant interest to scholars concerned with industrial planning and economic growth of underdeveloped areas of the world. It also provides valuable information for industrialists and entrepreneurs seeking profitable investment opportunities in such areas.

This study, however, is of still greater moment. In the new emerging field of Regional Science, a number of techniques are being molded for effective application. Some are old techniques that are being reformulated for more vigorous use, such as modern location theory, interregional comparative cost analysis, and interregional input-output models. Others are new techniques that are beginning to fill large gaps in our knowledge and know-how, such as industrial-complex analysis, interregional linear programming, gravity-potential-spatial interaction and similar probability models, and interregional social accounting.

This book is the second in a series of Regional Science Studies projected to develop the field of Regional Science. Volume I of the series, titled *Location and Space-Economy,* presents a modernized version of location theory with important extensions which link location theory with trade, production, and other facets of general economic theory. Volume III, in press, develops a new technique, industrial complex analysis. The present study, Volume II of the series, develops the approach of interregional comparative cost analysis. As a fully detailed case study, this volume is integral to the set of Regional Science Studies and is highly significant for the regional scientist and analyst broadly concerned with regional development and welfare.

WALTER ISARD

Preface

The genesis of this book is my Ph.D. dissertation *Location Factors in the Synthetic-Fiber Industry,* accepted at Harvard University in 1957. My indebtedness to Dr. Walter Isard for supervising its preparation as a doctoral thesis and for editing the manuscript in its transition to this study is simply beyond measure. In a unique way he has fathered the development of modern regional science through his own theoretical and empirical contributions and the stimulation he has provided his students and colleagues.

In addition, I must mention the invaluable assistance of Dr. Eugene V. Schooler of the University of Pennsylvania in preparing the manuscript and molding the content of the book. I have also benefited from the critical comments of Dr. Arthur Smithies and Dr. Leon Moses of Harvard University, who were devil's advocates in the thesis stage.

That this study exists at all was made possible by a grant from the Social Science Research Center of the University of Puerto Rico, which sponsored the project on Economic Relations of Puerto Rico with the Mainland. In this connection I deeply appreciate the far-sighted and constant stimulation provided by Dr. Millard Hansen, Director of the Social Science Research Center. The research was performed at the Section of Urban and Regional Studies, Massachusetts Institute of Technology, where Dr. John F. O'Donnell and Dr. Thomas Vietorisz aided me immeasurably in making chemical engineering estimates.

A host of people in the chemical industry and in engineering firms have helped me by providing information. I am also grateful for permission to reproduce charts, tables, and text passages from the *Daily News Record, Chemistry and Industry, Industrial and Engineering Chemistry, Journal of Chemical Education, Petroleum Processing, Textile Organon,* and publications of the American Association of Railroads, and a map from the American Map Co. I am indebted to Mrs. Richard A. Joyner, Jr., for an excellent job of typing a difficult manuscript.

The findings of this study were presented in a paper, "Location Factors in Synthetic-Fiber Production," published in *Papers and Proceedings of the Regional Science Association,* Volume 2, 1956.

JOSEPH AIROV

Atlanta, Georgia
April 1959

Contents

Summary

This study has three major objectives. The first is to explain the present location pattern of the synthetic-fiber industry in the United States. The second is to forecast the regional distribution of the industry's future growth in terms of both direct employment and capital investment. The third is to evaluate the advantages of Puerto Rico, a low labor-cost area, as a location for synthetic-fiber production.

Synthetic Fibers

The term "synthetic fibers" is defined to include only fibers which are manufactured from synthetic polymers. Representative of such fibers are nylon, Orlon, Acrilan, dynel, and Dacron. These fibers are closely associated with that spectacularly growing sector of the organic chemical industry involving the synthesis of useful materials from basic hydrocarbons. The promise of these fibers, together with the significant effects their production has already wrought in the textile field, justifies a study of their future influence on regional development.

Feasible Locations

In the United States potentially feasible locations for the complex of productive processes leading to synthetic fibers are effectively limited to two sets of regions. One set—the Texas-Gulf Coast area and the West Virginia area—contains sources of the basic hydrocarbon and other chemical raw materials. The second set—*New England,* the *Middle Atlantic* region, the *East South* region (Virginia, North Carolina, and South Carolina), the *Central South*

1

region (Georgia and the eastern parts of Alabama, Tennessee, and Kentucky), and the *West South* region (Mississippi, Louisiana and the western parts of Alabama, Tennessee, and Kentucky)—comprises the markets for synthetic fibers, i.e., the textile manufacturing areas. In addition, Puerto Rico is considered as a synthetic-fiber production location. Puerto Rico cannot be characterized as either a raw-material or a market region, although it is possible that at least some of the basic hydrocarbon raw materials could be supplied by oil refineries on the island. However, Puerto Rico is a low labor-cost area and thereby furnishes an alternative to the location of synthetic-fiber production on the mainland.

The Texas-Gulf Coast region contains a dominant proportion of the continental United States' reserves of crude petroleum and natural gas. The selection of this region reflects the fact that petrochemical materials and processes form the basis for a major part of the chemical-intermediate production required in the synthetic-fiber industry. On the other hand, the West Virginia sector of the Middle Atlantic region possesses a highly developed chemical industry which could furnish some of the required chemical intermediates, produced at least in part from local raw materials. For that reason the West Virginia area is considered as the second principal raw-material region.

The technology of the synthetic-fiber industry comprises two distinct major stages: (*a*) production of chemical intermediates, (*b*) transformation of the intermediates into fibers. Therefore, the location analysis logically considers the following sets of alternatives:

1. Texas-Gulf vs. West Virginia as the *source of raw materials* for chemical-intermediate production.
2. Raw material vs. market regions and Puerto Rico as locations *for chemical-intermediate production.*
3. Raw material vs. market regions as locations *for synthetic-fiber production.*
4. Puerto Rico vs. mainland sites as locations *for synthetic-fiber production.*

Regional Cost Differences

Regional advantage in the production of synthetic fibers is basically dependent upon regional differences in costs of production, including transport costs. Thus the analysis need consider only the elements of cost which exhibit significant regional variation. Those elements which exhibit no pattern of systematic regional variation may be ignored. So may those elements which constitute such a small share of total cost that they lead to insignificant regional differences.

For plants of equal size, in either the chemical-intermediate stage or the synthetic-fiber stage, regional equality may be assumed for capital costs and fixed charges, e.g., plant construction costs, interest charges, depreciation, plant maintenance, insurance, taxes, and land costs. These items are ignored in estimating regional advantage and disadvantage.

Other important costs, however, do exhibit regional differences. For chemical intermediate production these costs cover outlays for (a) major raw-material inputs, (b) utilities, and (c) direct labor. For synthetic-fiber production they cover outlays for (a) major chemical intermediates and solvents, (b) utilities, and (c) direct labor.

Differences in size of plants feasible at different locations can result in significant cost differences. This possibility for regional advantage or disadvantage exists and is evaluated for the production of chemical intermediates. In the synthetic-fiber stage, however, plants of technologically optimum size could be built in any of the regions considered. Thus in the latter stage no regional cost differences arise because of differences in plant size.

Findings of the Study

Chemical Intermediate Production

With respect to the location of chemical-intermediate production, the findings of the study indicate in general that costs are minimized at sites in raw-material regions. It is estimated that 70 to 87.5 per cent of the new chemical intermediate capacity required by the expansion of synthetic-fiber production by 1975 will be located in the Texas-Gulf Coast area. The other 12.5 to 30 per cent can be expected in the West Virginia raw-material region and nearby areas. The above statements hold except for nylon-salt plants. Nylon salt can be produced economically either in multiproduct chemical plants in raw-material regions or in fully integrated nylon operations in the textile area. It is therefore estimated that 50 per cent of new nylon-salt capacity required by 1975 will be in the Texas-Gulf Coast region, 10 per cent in West Virginia and neighboring states, and 40 per cent in the textile South.

Puerto Rico is subject to general disadvantage in the manufacture of chemical intermediates for synthetic fibers. However, from bagasse the island could produce furfural, one of the possible basic raw materials for nylon salt.

Synthetic-Fiber Production

On the mainland costs of synthetic-fiber output tend to be minimized at locations in the fiber-market regions which comprise the textile area. However, location in the West Virginia area is almost as favorable. Furthermore, Puerto Rico exhibits the lowest total costs of all the sites considered for synthetic-fiber production. Accordingly, it is estimated that of the total new synthetic-fiber capacity erected by 1975 80 per cent will be in the textile South and Puerto Rico and 20 per cent in the West Virginia area.

Direct Employment and Capital Investment

For the synthetic fibers examined capacity required by 1975 is estimated at 710 to 830 million annual pounds. The new investment required for plant and facilities is set at $1.1 to $1.3 billion. Direct and indirect labor requirements of these new synthetic fiber plants will provide an estimated 30,650 to 36,225 new jobs. Total new capacity for the required chemical intermediates is estimated at 649 to 783 million annual pounds. The corresponding investment in plant and equipment is set at $238 to $294 million. The direct labor requirements for this additional chemical-intermediate production will provide 950 to 1150 new jobs.

On the basis of these totals and the stated percentage distribution by regions, new investment in chemical-intermediate facilities for the Texas-Gulf Coast region is estimated at $155 to $190 million; the new employment, 630 to 750 jobs. The new investment estimated for West Virginia and nearby areas is $35 to $40 million in chemical intermediate plants and $220 to $265 million in fiber plants. Total new employment for this area is estimated at 6280 to 7420 jobs. New investment in chemical intermediate facilities in the textile South (other than Virginia) is estimated at $50 to $63 million; new employment at 160 to 180 jobs. This region and Puerto Rico will share an estimated new investment in synthetic-fiber plants of $875 million to $1.1 billion and new employment of 24,525 to 28,980 jobs.

There is no firm objective basis for making a separate estimate of the extent to which Puerto Rico will share in the development of synthetic fibers. It can be noted, however, that one typical 60-million-pound-per-year, continuous-filament fiber plant would call for an investment of $150 million and create over 4000 jobs. A staple fiber plant of the same capacity would require an investment of $75 million and would create 1000 jobs.

Chapter 1

Introduction

This book is a case study in regional analysis. The subject to be analyzed is the location of the synthetic-fiber industry.

Man-made fibers as a general category of materials represent a very significant contribution made by chemistry to progress and change in the field of textile manufacture. A *man-made* fiber may be defined as "one that is extruded from a spinning orifice, is collected in an orderly fashion, and is usually used in the textile industry."[1] Chemically speaking, there are two major groups of man-made fibers. One group, consisting of fibers manufactured from *natural* polymers, is dominated by the cellulosic fibers, rayon and acetate, the first man-made fibers. The other group comprises fibers made from *synthetic* polymers and includes nylon, Orlon, Acrilan, dynel, and Dacron.[2] These wholly synthetic fibers, a comparatively recent development, are having a growing impact upon the textile industry as well as upon consumers and the producers of cotton and wool. The analysis of this study is confined to the second group of fibers. As used herein, the term *synthetic fiber* refers only to *fibers made from synthetic polymers* and is not a synonym for man-made fibers.[3]

[1] "Man-Made Fiber Nomenclature," *Textile Organon,* Vol. 28 (August 1957), p. 114.

[2] See pp. 14–15 for details of this classification.

[3] With respect to terminology, industry practices in the United States are not uniform. *Textile Organon* (*op. cit.,* p. 115) reports that the expression *man-made* fiber has been informally adopted to replace the terms *synthetic* or *artificial* fiber. *Textile Organon* uses a threefold classification of man-made fibers: cellulosic, noncellulosic, and textile glass fibers. The fibers termed *synthetic* in this study are included in the noncellulosic group. Both cellulosic and glass fibers are made from natural polymers.

The study has three important objectives.   One is the explanation of the current geographic location pattern of the production of synthetic fibers in the United States.   The second is a forecast of effects of the industry's future growth in terms of regional increments of plant investment and employment.   The third is the evaluation of Puerto Rico, a low labor-cost region, as a possible location for the production of synthetic fibers for U. S. textile markets.[4]

Synthetic-fiber manufacture involves two broad productive stages: (*a*) the derivation of chemical intermediates from basic raw materials and (*b*) the conversion of the chemical intermediates into synthetic fibers.   All the productive processes in the two groups may be located at the same site, or there may exist one or more alternative split-location patterns (e.g., all chemical intermediates produced at one site, the fiber at another site, or primary chemical intermediates produced at one site, advanced chemical intermediates and the fiber at another site, etc.).

The analysis is limited to those processes for chemical intermediates directly and indirectly linked to the manufacture of synthetic fiber and whose locations might be influenced by such manufacture. For example, the location of nylon-salt production is clearly within the scope of this study.   The location of nylon-fiber plants does influence the location of nylon-salt plants.   On the other hand, the location of production of benzene, a raw material in nylon-salt manufacture, is not investigated here.   Benzene is supplied either as a by-product of coke-oven operations or as a product closely associated with large-volume motor-fuel manufacture in petroleum refineries.   The location of benzene is taken as given for the purposes of this study; it is essentially determined by the geographic distribution of steel and refinery capacity.

Data problems limit this location study to the five major general-purpose textile fibers which were in commercial production at the time research was initiated.   The five are nylon 66, Orlon,

---

[4] Such a location study as this may also serve the economic historian in explaining changing location equilibria of industries and consequent regional economic shifts.   Other ends in view in location studies include explanation of interregional or international trading patterns, compilation of data for an economic base study of a region, determination of national policy with respect to plant location in economically distressed areas, or presentation of an optimum location pattern in contrast to some existing pattern which might involve the misallocation of resources.

Acrilan, dynel, and Dacron. However, the results of the study suggest that there is sufficient homogeneity among the several groups of location factors to make the findings applicable, with modifications, to fibers which have been brought into production in the recent past or which may be developed in the future.

The study is developed by means of a number of related analytical procedures. (As indicated in the Plan of Study (pp. 9–10), the supporting materials and discussion are presented in a slightly different order.)

1. A group of regions is selected, each of which is feasible as a location of chemical-intermediate production, fiber production, or both.

2. The various locational alternatives for the production of each fiber are compared by a computation of cost differentials. This procedure identifies the most profitable location alternatives and, in addition, reveals the dominant forces affecting the industry's location pattern.

3. The indicated location pattern is compared with the existing distribution of plants as a further check.

4. The results and implications of the locational analysis are coupled with a long-term forecast of demand for synthetic fibers to estimate the future regional impact of plant location in terms of direct employment and capital investment.

Procedures 1 and 2 require more detailed description.

1. SELECTION OF REGIONS

Identification of regions suitable as locations for the various productive processes depends partly upon information concerning required raw materials and other productive inputs. All the necessary inputs must be available if a region is to be considered. For example, the basic raw materials for most of the chemical intermediates are natural-gas and petroleum (refinery-gas) hydrocarbons. Since most U. S. reserves of natural gas and petroleum are concentrated in the Texas-Gulf Coast area, that area ought logically to be considered as a possible location for the production of the chemical intermediates as well as of the fibers. (The other inputs, such as utilities, capital services, and labor, are also available, as they are generally throughout the United States.)

However, both natural gas and petroleum are transported inter-regionally, and thus many regions come to possess a supply of hydrocarbon raw materials which could support chemical-intermediate and fiber production. Additional information is needed for further limitation of the number of regions to be considered. It is logical, therefore, to identify the location of the synthetic-fiber market. This market coincides with the general textile-producing areas of the United States and is concentrated in the textile South. Accordingly, many regions of the United States in which raw materials are available suffer a disadvantage because of considerable distance from the fiber market. For example, the Chicago area could qualify from the standpoint of raw-material availability but would be clearly at a disadvantage compared to the Texas-Gulf Coast region in the matter of nearness and accessibility to fiber markets.

Such an adversely situated region might still have to be considered as feasible for chemical-intermediate or fiber production if it could supply some required productive input at a significantly lower cost than the other possible regions. For example, Puerto Rico is included as a feasible location for synthetic-fiber production to supply mainland markets because of its marked advantage in the cost of textile-type labor.

Finally, because of the transportability of the basic raw materials and the chemical intermediates location at market-area sites is possible for the synthetic-fiber production processes as well as for one or more chemical-intermediate processes.

Thus possible locations for the synthetic-fiber industry include raw-material-region sites, market-region sites, and low-cost labor sites. The regional framework actually selected for the analysis is developed in detail in Chapter 6.

2. REGIONAL COST DIFFERENCES

When a set of possible regions has been selected, the next step is a comparison of the various locational alternatives to find the most advantageous (profitable) sites. The procedure involves the calculation of cost differentials among the various alternatives. Such calculation in turn requires detailed estimates of the production functions for the various processes as well as estimates of regional differentials in unit prices of the various inputs and outputs.[5] In addition, costs may vary regionally because of differences in the extent to which agglomeration economies may be realized. For the synthetic-fiber industry the significant agglomeration economies are large-scale production economies: integration economies from the output of several chemical products in a multiproduct plant, localization economies from the geographical concentration of chemical production in an area, and external economies from the purchase of raw materials from large-scale producers.

3. PLAN OF STUDY

Chapter 3 discusses the theoretical concepts on which the study is based and identifies the types of costs in the synthetic-fiber industry which tend to vary regionally. This material follows the classification of man-made fibers and the history of the development of synthetic fibers contained in Chapter 2.

In Chapter 4 the detailed production functions for the chemical intermediates are developed from published sources or as original estimates. Chapter 4 also contains an analysis of agglomeration economies and their effect on chemical-plant location. At the end of Chapter 4 is a general summary of the various forces which influence the location of chemical-intermediate plants.

A similar approach—from technology to production functions to general location factors—is followed in Chapter 5, which is concerned with the synthetic-fiber production processes.

Given the variable-input production functions for each stage and the significant agglomeration economies, the analysis turns in Chapter 6 from a physical input to a cost basis. In this chapter the regional framework for the location analysis is described, sites are selected in each region for sample cost computations, and a systematic procedure is developed—in sections on transport, fuel, power, labor costs, and large-scale production economies—for translating variable-input production functions into selected regional differences in production and distribution costs. Sample computa-

---

[5] In this study the detailed production functions are estimated *before* the regional framework is chosen, although strictly speaking the latter task requires only a general knowledge of the raw materials and other inputs required by the various processes.

tions for each stage of the industry are given at the end of the chapter.

The tabulated cost results may be found in Appendices A, B, and C. In Chapter 7 the location analysis is completed by the designation from the cost results of basic regional advantages and disadvantages for each stage, the type of location orientation, and the minimum-cost regions.   In each case the conclusions of the cost model are checked against actual plant locations.   In the final part of Chapter 7 a 1975 forecast of the demand for synthetic fibers is used, together with the findings of the location analysis, to estimate the future regional impact of plant location through added direct employment and capital investment.

Chapter 2

The Development of Fibers
from Synthetic Polymers

Three events have created far-reaching changes in the historical pattern of consumption of textile fibers. In the Industrial Revolution of the eighteenth century cotton displaced wool as the world's principal fiber. The commercial success of rayon and acetate in the first three decades of the twentieth century was the first incursion of man-made fibers into the traditional markets of cotton, wool, and other natural fibers. In this first achievement of the chemical industry artificial fibers were made from cellulose, a naturally occurring polymer. Since the 1930's the textile world has been startled by an innovation whose horizon seems unlimited—the production of man-made fibers from synthetic polymers.[1]

Although the new branch of the man-made fiber industry is still in its infancy, its future is secure enough to be regarded as an integral part of the raw-materials revolution of the twentieth century. In describing the advantageous properties of synthetics in contrast to natural fibers and rayon and acetate, textile chemists stress the striking and important differences which result from dissimilar moisture sensitivity. The older fibers are hydrophilic, i.e., they

---

[1] In the language of chemistry single molecules are *monomers,* the union of *n* molecules, a *polymer.* By chemical structure, cellulose, silk, and rubber are examples of natural substances classified as polymers. Man-made polymers are developed through the synthesis of long, chainlike molecules having properties of the type formerly found only in natural polymers; hence, *synthetic* polymer.

have a high propensity to absorb water, whereas the synthetics are hydrophobic. Quig and Dennison cite the following advantages which are common to the synthetic fibers:

... essentially equivalent wet and dry strength; ability to be heat set and stabilized; retention of pressing, creases, and pleats; dimensional stability to laundering and dry cleaning; retention of shape; easy launderability and quick drying; resistance to chemical degradation; and resistance to moths, mildew and insects.[2]

Because of their outstanding functional properties the synthetics are assured a substantial portion of the fiber market of the future, one which will be attained in part at the expense of existing fibers. The age of synthetics will lessen further man's dependence on nature for his supply of textile fibers and will diminish the importance of wool and cotton in agricultural economies.   In addition, the textile firm of the future will be less specialized than at present. The development of synthetic fibers has contributed to the current merger movement in the textile industry to obtain end-product diversity for survival in the new interfiber competition.   The regional impact of the new industry will find direct expression in the location of fiber plants and chemical plants.

1. CLASSIFICATION OF MAN-MADE FIBERS

A classification of U. S. man-made fibers, as a guide to the area of study which lies ahead, is presented in Table 1.   Man-made fibers are divided into two categories, those produced from natural polymers and those manufactured from synthetic polymers.

From Natural Polymers

Viscose and acetate are the principal cellulosic fibers.   Two other man-made fibers derived from natural polymers are also of commercial significance in the United States: glass fibers and Vicara.

From Synthetic Polymers

In this study the term "synthetic" fiber designates the second group of fibers only, those made from synthetic polymers.

[2] J. B. Quig and R. W. Dennison, "Functional Properties of Synthetics," *Industrial and Engineering Chemistry,* Vol. 44 (September 1952), pp. 2176–2183.

At the time research was initiated on this study the principal general-purpose synthetic textile fibers were nylon 66, Orlon, Acrilan, dynel, and Dacron; and this somewhat homogeneous group of five fibers was selected for the location analysis.[3] Monofilament production, in general, and synthetic fibers with specialized uses, such as saran, polyethylene, and polystyrene, lie outside the scope of this study.[4]

2. MAN-MADE FIBER HISTORY

Although the story of the development of man-made fibers is a fascinating one, only its broad outline is presented here. The idea of man-made fibers is ancient and seems to have been inspired in part by a search for a substitute for silk, the ancient symbol of opulence. In fact, the notion of creating artificial silk was put forward as early as 1664 by the British experimental physicist Robert Hooke in his *Micrographia*. In an account of the silkworm in his *Mémoires pour servir a l'histoire des insects* (1734–1742) the French scientist René Réaumur made a similar suggestion.[5] The inspirations of both men stand in the realm of historical curiosity, as does the century-later effort in 1840 of Louis Schwabe, a silk manufacturer at Manchester who experimented with a machine for producing filaments by drawing various substances through fine

[3] Several new major synthetic textile fibers have reached the stage of commercial significance (pilot or initial full-scale plant) since this study was completed. Nylon 6 is being produced by Allied Chemical and Dye as "Caprolan," by American Enka as "Enka" and "Nylenka," by Industrial Rayon as "IRC," and North American Rayon will also produce a type-6 nylon. New acrylic fibers are American Cyanamid's "Creslan," Dow Chemical's "Zefran," and Tennessee Eastman's "Verel." B. F. Goodrich has introduced "Darlan," a fiber made of vinylidene dinitrile; and a new Du Pont fiber is "Teflon," made of tetrafluorethylene.

[4] Man-made fibers are manufactured in four forms. *Continuous-filament yarn* consists of a number of fine, continuous filaments put up on bobbins with no twist or a light twist; *staple* fiber is made by cutting up the continuous filaments into short lengths and is sold in bales to manufacturers of spun yarn; *tow* is a collection of many parallel continuous filaments grouped in ropelike form and sold to manufacturers with machines designed for direct production of spun yarn from tow. *Monofilaments* are large single filaments with a circular, rectangular, or irregular cross section and are used in the manufacture of bristles, sutures, insect screens, upholstery fabrics, etc.

[5] E. Wheeler, *The Manufacture of Artificial Silk* (New York: D. Van Nostrand Co., Inc., 1931), pp. 1–2.

TABLE 1

CLASSIFICATION OF MAN-MADE FIBERS*

I. From Natural Polymers
- A. Cellulose Base
  - 1. Regenerated cellulose (rayon)
    - a. Viscose
    - b. Cuprammonium
    - c. Saponified cellulose acetate
  - 2. Modified cellulose (esters and ethers)
    - a. Acetate (Celanese)
    - b. Ethylcellulose
    - c. Cellulose acetate butyrate
- B. Protein Base
  - a. Vicara, Zycon
- C. Alginates
- D. Inorganic
  - a. Glass
  - b. Plastic coated glass
  - c. Metal (not a polymer)

II. From Synthetic Polymers
- A. Polyamides
  - 1. Nylon 66
    - a. Chemstrand: Chemstrand nylon (yarn)
    - b. Du Pont: Du Pont nylon (yarn, staple and tow)
    - c. North American Rayon: (yarn)
    - d. Poliafil, Inc.: Poliafil (yarn)
  - 2. Nylon 6
    - a. Allied Chemical & Dye: Caprolan (staple)
    - b. American Enka: Enka, Nylenka (yarn and staple)
    - c. Industrial Rayon: IRC (yarn, staple, and tow)
    - d. North American Rayon: (yarn)
- B. Polyvinyls
  - 1. Polyacrylonitrile
    - a. Du Pont: Orlon (staple and tow)
  - 2. Copolymers
    - a. American Viscose: Avisco Vinyon—vinyl acetate, vinyl chloride. (staple)
    - b. American Cyanamid: Creslan—acrylonitrile, acrylo compounds. (staple and tow)
    - c. Chemstrand: Acrilan—acrylonitrile, vinyl acetate, or pyridine. (staple and tow)
    - d. Dow Chemical: Zefran ("nitrile alloy" fiber)—mainly acrylonitrile. (staple)

  e. Tennessee Eastman: Verel—mainly acrylonitrile. (staple
     and tow)
  f. Union Carbide: Dynel—vinyl chloride and acrylonitrile.
     (staple)
3. Polyvinyl alcohol
4. Vinylidene chloride, vinyl chloride copolymers
  a. Saran, velon, etc.
C. Polyesters
  a. Du Pont: Dacron—polyethylene terephthalate. (yarn,
     staple, tow, and fiberfill)
D. Polyurethanes
E. Others
  1. B. F. Goodrich: Darlan—vinylidene dinitrile. (staple)
  2. Polyethylene
  3. Polystyrene
  4. Tetrafluoroethylene
     a. Du Pont: Teflon (yarn and staple)

---

* Sources: C. S. Grove, Jr. and R. S. Casey, "Fibers," *Industrial and Engineering Chemistry,* Vol. 44 (October 1952), p. 2318; and "U. S. Non-Cellulosic Fiber Producers," *Textile Organon,* Vol. 28, (September 1957), pp. 131-133.

holes. At the 1842 meeting of the British Association in Manchester he exhibited glass threads and cloth woven from them. The threads had been spun from molten glass drawn through a fine orifice, the first recorded use of a crude spinneret, a device which later became a vital part of the process employed in man-made fiber production.[6]

The Development of Rayon and Acetate

Rayon came into existence through progress in the chemistry of cellulose and, circuitously, by way of the discovery of the electric lamp. In Edison's original electric lamp (1879) carbonized bamboo fibers were utilized for the filament but were found to be much too irregular for the purpose. To overcome this defect many substitute materials were examined and tested. In England Joseph W. Swan experimented with an electric lamp almost simultaneously with Edison. In 1883 Swan tried filaments made by squirting nitrocellu-

[6] H. V. Potter, "Synthetic Fibres, an Historical Survey of the Development of some Synthetic Fibrous Materials," *Chemistry and Industry,* Vol. 68 (December 17, 1949), p. 880.

lose solution through a die into a coagulating bath of water and alcohol.[7] The potential use of these nitrocellulose filaments as textile materials was quickly discerned by Swan. Some fine threads were woven and exhibited as "artificial silk" at the Inventions Exhibition in 1885.[8]

But Count Hilaire de Chardonnet was the inventor-entrepreneur who exploited the employment of nitrocellulose fibers for end uses in textile products. His own patents were first published in 1885, and under his direction factories for the production of nitro rayon were opened, first at Besançon in France and later in Belgium, England, Germany, Hungary,[9] and elsewhere in France.

Early nitro rayon was inflammable, and not until Swan developed a denitrating process in 1895 was cellulose nitrate made into a useful yarn. Even so the fiber was weak, especially when wet. Although the process flourished on a small scale, it was gradually superseded by cuprammonium and viscose rayon.

Cuprammonium Rayon

The first patents on cuprammonium rayon were published in France by Louis Despeissis in 1890. As early as 1856 Schweitzer had discovered that cellulose could be dissolved in solutions of cuprammonium hydroxide. German technicians Pauly, Fremery, Bronnert, and Urban made the vital improvements which led to commercial production in 1899, when the Vereinigte Glanzstoff Fabriken were formed. By 1909 cuprammonium rayon was a serious competitor to nitro rayon.[10]

Viscose Rayon

Charles Stearn, a pioneer with Swan in the development of the carbon-filament electric lamp, led a small group of experimental workers to the production of the first skein of viscose rayon yarn in 1898. Stearn's work followed the discovery by C. F. Cross and E. J. Bevan in 1892 that alkali cellulose and carbon bisulphide

---

[7] Cellulose nitrate was discovered by Christian F. Schönbein, a German chemist, in 1846. In 1855 George Audemars of Lausanne, Switzerland, took out the first English patent for the production of artificial silk from a solution of nitrocellulose in an alcohol–ether mixture by drawing out threads from it with a steel pointer and reeling them. Wheeler, *op. cit.*, p. 2.

[8] Potter, *op. cit.*, p. 880.

[9] A. R. Urquart, "Cellulose-Derivative Rayons, Past, Present, and Future," *Journal of the Textile Institute, Proceedings*, Vol. 42 (August 1951), pp. 385–386.

[10] *Ibid.*

react to form cellulose xanthate, a water-soluble ester. Stearn, together with Cross, formed the Viscose Syndicate, Ltd., in 1894 to extrude viscose filaments for carbon lamps and the Viscose Spinning Syndicate in 1898 to produce a textile yarn to compete with nitro rayon. The many difficulties encountered in perfecting viscose, however, were not overcome until 1910.[11]

Cellulose Acetate

In 1894 another result of the fruitful inquiries of Cross and Bevan was a manufacturing process for the production of cellulose acetate, a chemical which had been discovered by Schutzenberger in 1865.

Through the work of Drs. Henry and Camille Dreyfus, the founders of the Celanese companies, cellulose acetate was successfully employed as a raw material for plastics and lacquer and in textile-fiber production. The first undertaking of the Dreyfus brothers was in 1911 at a factory in Basel, Switzerland, which manufactured cellulose acetate plastic (celluloid) and lacquer. During World War I operations were expanded to meet the demand for cellulose acetate for doping airplane wings; for this purpose factories were established in several Allied countries. At the end of the war surplus lacquer capacity was put to a new use—the first production of cellulose acetate yarn.[12]

Growth of Rayon and Acetate Production

In the period from 1885 to 1920—from Chardonnet's nitrocellulose to cellulose acetate yarn—growth of output of the first man-made fibers was slow indeed.[13] Table 2 (U. S. Mill Consumption of Certain Fibers, 1920–1956) shows the rapid expansion of rayon and acetate thereafter. In 1920, 3,180.2 million pounds of textile fibers were consumed by mills in the United States, and the market share for rayon and acetate was less than one per cent. From the outset, rayon had an aesthetic appeal approaching silk and superior to cotton fabrics for intimate apparel. During the 1920's

---

[11] H. J. Hegan, "The Historical Development of and the Outlook for Viscose Fibers," *Journal of the Textile Institute, Proceedings,* Vol. 42 (August 1951), pp. 395–396.

[12] Urquart, *op. cit.,* p. 386.

[13] Nitrocellulose rayon dropped by the wayside with the development of viscose and acetate, and cuprammonium is of minor importance in the United States.

TABLE 2

U. S. MILL CONSUMPTION OF CERTAIN FIBERS BY SELECTED YEARS,
1920–1956*

(millions of pounds)

			Man-Made			
Year	Cotton	Wool	Rayon and Acetate	Other†	Silk	Total
1920	2828.1	314.2	8.7		29.2	3180.2
1925	3074.7	349.9	58.4		66.0	3549.0
1930	2610.9	263.2	119.3		75.6	3069.0
1935	2754.7	417.5	259.2		62.3	3493.7
1940	3953.6	407.9	482.1	4.4	35.8	4883.8
1945	4511.3	645.1	769.9	49.8	0.5	5976.6
1950	4680.1	647.0	1351.6	140.5	8.4	6827.6
1955	4384.2	428.2	1419.2	432.1	7.2	6670.9
1956	4339.1	454.9	1201.1	482.9	7.7	6485.7

* Source: *Textile Organon,* Vol. 28 (March 1957), p. 42.

† Separate figures on the mill consumption of the new synthetic fibers are not available. "Other" man-made fibers include nylon 66, Orlon, Acrilan, dynel, and Dacron—the fibers in this study; the newer synthetic fibers; and, in addition, glass fibers, polyethylene fibers, polystyrene fibers, saran, and Vicara.

a sizable market developed for rayon and acetate in the underwear and dress fields. The early quality of rayon and acetate was not first-rate, and Heckert has noted that "it was not until the 1930's that the industry made a product comparing at all favorably with today's yarn."[14]   More rapid expansion of sales occurred from the 1930's on, especially after rayon and acetate were produced in staple form. Scientists turned out a rayon yarn of high strength and toughness in the same period, and it quickly replaced cotton as a material for tire cord. In 1956 total mill consumption of fibers in the United States was 6,485.7 million pounds, and the market for rayon and acetate had increased to 18.5 per cent.

The Development of Synthetic Fibers

The rapid development of the new synthetic fibers has been made possible by a number of factors.[15]   Perhaps the most important

[14] Winfield W. Heckert, "Synthetic Fibers," *Journal of Chemical Education,* Vol. 30 (April 1953), p. 166.

[15] Joseph B. Quig, "Technical Developments Leading to Present Man-made Fibers," *Textile Research Journal,* Vol. 23 (May 1953), pp. 280–88.

technical development is the fact that fiber synthesis now rests securely on basic advances which have been made in the chemistry of high polymers (a body of fundamental knowledge which also underlies the production of other synthetic materials, such as synthetic rubber, plastics, and finishes). Moreover, technical and market knowledge accumulated through the development of rayon and acetate was at work in paving the way for synthetic fibers. In addition, the significance of the coming of age of a textile science, in which the properties of fibers and fabrics can be measured in a precise way, cannot be overstressed.

Both the chemical and textile industries have been motivated by the necessity of novelty and variety in fibers and fabrics for the maintenance of old markets and the development of new. Inter-fiber price competition has also been instrumental in the search for new fibers, for the high prices of silk in the pre-World War II period and of wool in the postwar period have been a lure to the developers of nylon and the other new synthetics.

Advances in High-Polymer Chemistry

Figure 1, a broad schema of the process for manufacturing synthetic fibers, is designed to facilitate understanding of the technical aspects of the detailed description of the development of synthetic fibers which follows.

Through research in high-polymer chemistry it is now known that (in addition to chemical constitution) the fiber-forming prop-

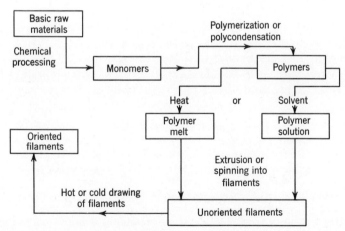

Figure 1. Manufacture of synthetic fibers. Source: H. V. Potter, "Synthetic Fibers, an Historical Survey of the Development of Some Synthetic Fibrous Materials," *Chemistry and Industry,* Vol. 31 (December 17, 1949), p. 880.

erties of chemical compounds depend largely on their molecular weight, i.e., the size of the molecule formed during the reaction and the linear character of the molecule.[16]   Moreover, the molecules of many chemical compounds can combine with themselves to form giant, chainlike molecules via chemical change called *polymerization*.   The molecular weight of the reaction product, a *polymer,* is many times that of the original compound.   Thus, when subjected to polymerization under controlled conditions of heat and pressure, many chemical compounds can be converted into polymers of high molecular weight.   The superpolymers are unlike ordinary polymers, for an extraordinary transformation in physical properties occurs.   Superpolymers produce filaments which can be permanently stretched or drawn after extrusion in a stretching operation (called *orientation*) which causes the molecules to be aligned in an orderly, lengthwise formation.   The tensile strength, elasticity, and pliability of the resulting filament is vastly increased.

Before the 1920's there was no generally accepted theory of fiber-forming molecules.   The theory that the behavior and properties of both natural and synthetic polymers is a consequence of a high molecular structure stems from the work, published in 1922, of the German chemist Staudinger, a 1954 Nobel prize winner.[17]   It seems clear that the new knowledge acquired in the chemistry of high polymers and the prior success of synthetic resins for plastics stimulated the research efforts to yield new manmade fibers.

Use of Vinyl Compounds

From vinyl compounds used initially as raw materials for plastics the first truly synthetic fibers were developed.[18]   Fremon has noted that I. G. Farbenindustrie began experimental production of a polyvinyl fiber in 1931.   The early effort was abandoned in favor of "PeCe" fiber, made from polyvinyl chloride (after-chlorinated

---

[16] This account is based upon Ruth E. K. Peterson, *Nylon and Other Non-cellulosic Synthetic Fibers,* Section II, Project V of *Study of Agricultural and Economic Problems of the Cotton Belt,* hearings of Special Subcommittee on Cotton of the Committee on Agriculture, House of Representatives, Eightieth Congress, First Session, July 7 and 8, 1947.

[17] Rowland Hill (ed.), *Fibres from Synthetic Polymers* (New York: Elsevier Publishing Co., 1953), p. 1.

[18] Plastics made of vinyl-chloride, vinyl-acetate copolymers were introduced in the early 1930's in the United States by Union Carbide under the trademark "Vinylite."

to render it soluble in acetone), which was offered for textile use in small quantities in 1934.[19]

In the United States Union Carbide pioneered in the development of synthetic yarns. From a special grade of Vinylite resin, a copolymer of vinyl chloride and vinyl acetate, synthetic fibers were made and sold under the trade name of "Vinyon."[20] Vinyon fibers were first marketed in 1936.[21]

Although small-scale production of the first vinyl fibers (PeCe and Vinyon) was begun in 1939, both were handicapped by serious limitations for use as wearing-apparel fibers because of low softening points and excessive shrinkage at normal ironing temperatures.

The Development of Nylon 66

In the meantime E. I. du Pont de Nemours & Co., Inc., had started a program of research which lead to the first major venture in synthetic fibers that was a financial success—the manufacture of nylon.[22]

In 1927 Du Pont's chemical director, C. M. A. Stine, sought to augment applied research with a program of pure research in organic chemistry. Wallace H. Carothers, who had been an instructor in chemistry at Harvard University, became the key figure in the search for new fibers. In 1928, together with a small group of highly trained organic chemists, Carothers began his now classic research on the subject of polymerization by condensation and the structure of substances of high molecular weight. The line of exploration proved to be most fertile.

The work of Carothers led to theoretical insight into the theory of the production of linear polymers from simple structures: by the simple conversion of a monomer into a polymer by addition polymerization and by polycondensation.[23] Carothers and his group

---

[19] G. H. Fremon, "Vinyl Fibers," *Technology of Synthetic Fibers,* ed. by Samuel B. McFarlane (New York: Fairchild Publications, Inc., 1953), Chapter VI, p. 135.

[20] Peterson, *op. cit.,* p. 461.

[21] Fremon, *op. cit.,* p. 135.

[22] The account which follows is derived from E. K. Bolton, "Development of Nylon," *Industrial and Engineering Chemistry,* Vol. 34 (January 1942), pp. 53–58.

[23] By *addition polymerization* is meant the union of several molecules with a redistribution of the valency bonds but no splitting off of simple chemical substances; by *polycondensation,* the joining together by the elimination of one structural unit, such as water, hydrochloric acid, or ammonia.

experimented successively with polyesters, polyanhydrides, poly-acetals, and polyamides. The fortunate outcome of an experiment on February 28, 1935, was the synthesis of the polyamide from hexamethylenediamine and adipic acid. Now known as nylon 66,[24] its textile properties first made it an ideal fiber for hosiery production.

Nylon 66 was first evaluated by a number of hosiery manufac-turers from yarn produced in a semi-works unit by a melt-spinning process which was also devised by Carothers. In October 1938 the decision was made to construct a full-scale plant at Seaford, Del. The original capacity, 4 million pounds, was doubled before con-struction of the first unit was completed. In retrospect, it is of interest to note that the 8-million-pound plant capacity for nylon within five years after Carother's laboratory discovery was almost equal to the 8.7 million pounds of rayon and acetate consumed by U. S. mills in 1920, thirty-six years after the first nitrocellulose filaments were made by Swan.

Once the market possibilities of nylon were revealed, additional fiber-producing plants were built by Du Pont at Martinsville, Va., in 1942 and at Chattanooga, Tenn., in 1947.[25]

Other Nylon 66 Producers. The second American concern to enter the nylon 66 market was the Chemstrand Corp., a joint venture of Monsanto Chemical and American Viscose. Production under Du Pont license was begun in 1954 at a plant located at Pensacola, Fla.[26]

Nylon 6

In Germany in 1938 another synthetic fiber of the polyamide class, nylon 6, was developed by Kleine and Schlach[27] and pro-duced under the name of Perlon L.[28]

---

[24] The first digit indicates the number of carbon atoms in the diamine, and the second, the number of carbon atoms in the dibasic acid.

[25] In 1957 Du Pont announced the construction of an additional nylon 66 plant at Richmond, Va.

[26] Production of nylon 66 by North American Rayon is now in the pilot-plant stage at Elizabethton, Tenn., and another producer is Poliafil, Inc., at Scranton, Pa.

[27] G. Loasby, "The Development of Synthetic Fibers," *The Journal of the Textile Institute,* Vol. 42 (August 1951), p. 416.

[28] There are now several American producers of nylon 6. Allied Chemical and Dye makes the fiber under the trade name of Caprolan at Chesterfield, Va.; American Enka, under the trade names of Enka and Nylenka at Enka, N.C.; Industrial Rayon under the trade name of IRC at Covington, Va.; and North American Rayon is in the pilot-plant stage at Elizabethton, Tenn.

Continued Research in Polyvinyls

After the 1930's research in polyvinyls continued. The earliest U. S. patents on the fiber-forming properties of acrylonitrile were those of I. G. Farbenindustrie in 1938. Several American chemical companies including Du Pont, American Cyanamid, and Union Carbide and Carbon, were also at work during World War II on the use of acrylonitrile. The basic problem to be solved was the development of a solvent, and a whole series of patents were issued to Du Pont and other companies for this purpose during the period 1942–1946 until the problem was met by the use of dimethyl formamide.[29]

Orlon.   By 1944 Du Pont had engaged in semi-works production of Orlon at the company's Waynesboro, Va., acetate plant. In 1949 Orlon's discovery was announced, and a plant for its production was completed in 1950 at Camden, S. C.[30]

Dynel.   Union Carbide and Carbon developed a synthetic fiber from acetone-soluble copolymers of vinyl chloride and acrylonitrile, first marketed in continuous-filament form in 1947 as Vinyon N. In 1949 dynel, the staple form, was announced. Dynel is produced at Charleston, W. Va., and Vinyon N is no longer being manufactured.

Acrilan.   Chemstrand's additional venture into the field of synthetic fibers is Acrilan, a copolymer of acrylonitrile and a small amount of vinyl acetate or vinyl pyridine. The Acrilan plant is located at Decatur, Ala.

Other Synthetic Fibers

A host of additional American firms are engaged in research in new synthetic fibers. Among them are American Cyanamid, Dow Chemical, Tennessee Eastman, B. F. Goodrich Chemical, and General Electric.[31]

---

[29] Peterson, *op. cit.,* p. 467.

[30] In 1957 Du Pont announced plans to construct an additional Orlon staple plant at Waynesboro, Va.

[31] Since research on this study was completed, four additional polyvinyl fibers have been introduced. American Cynamid's Creslan is being produced in a pilot plant at Stamford, Conn., and a full-scale plant is being constructed at Pensacola, Fla. Dow Chemical is manufacturing Zefran at a pilot plant in Pittsburg, Calif., and a large plant is under construction at Lee Hall, Va. B. F. Goodrich Chemical is manufacturing Darlan at a pilot plant at Avon Lake, Ohio. Tennessee Eastman's new synthetic fiber Verel is being produced at Kingsport, Tenn. Du Pont has a new tetrafluorethylene fiber, Teflon, in production at Richmond, Va.

Polyester Fibers

The first successful fiber of the polyester class, Terylene (made from polyethylene terephthalate), was discovered by J. R. Whinfield and J. T. Dickson in England.[32]   Carothers had experimented with polyesters as early as 1930, but his efforts resulted in fibers with low melting points.   The English experimenters, working in the laboratories of Calico Printers' Association, Ltd., in Lancashire, solved this difficulty.   In 1947 Terylene's development was turned over to Imperial Chemical Industries, Ltd., and a plant was built at Wilton in Yorkshire for this purpose.

Dacron.   In the United States the right to produce polyethylene terephthalate was acquired by Du Pont, and the fiber is sold under the name of Dacron.   A plant for producing Dacron was built in 1953 at Kinston, N. C., after preliminary output of the fiber at the Seaford, Del., nylon 66 plant.[33]

Growth in the Market for Synthetic Fibers

Separate figures are not available on the consumption history of the new synthetic fibers; however, the astonishing growth of the new synthetics can be demonstrated by figures on plant capacity. In 1938 capacity for nylon 66 output was 8 million pounds.   Table 3 (Estimated Production Capacity for Major Synthetic Fibers, 1954) shows that in 1954 capacity for nylon 66, Orlon, Acrilan, dynel, and Dacron—the five fibers selected for the location study— was approximately 340 million pounds, including plants already built or under construction.

Synthetic fibers have found their way into the industrial market for use in filter cloths, electrical insulation, tire cord, chemical clothing, dye nets, automobile tops and seat covers, sewing thread, etc.   In the realm of home furnishings the synthetics are used in draperies, upholstery, rugs, blankets, awnings, pillows, and other articles.   But the major expansion has been in the apparel field for use in hosiery, in tricot knitted underwear and lingeries, in fabrics (alone or in blends with natural fibers or rayon and acetate), in linings, and in pile and fleece coatings.

---

[32] J. R. Whinfield, "The Development of Terylene," *Textile Research Journal,* Vol. 23 (May 1953), pp. 289–294.

[33] In 1957 Du Pont announced plans to build an additional Dacron plant at Old Hickory, Tenn.

TABLE 3

ESTIMATED PRODUCTION CAPACITY
FOR MAJOR SYNTHETIC FIBERS, 1954*

(millions of pounds)

Type of Fiber	Company	Plant Location	Announced or Estimated Capacity
Polyamides			
Nylon 66	Du Pont	Chattanooga, Tenn.	190
		Martinsville, Va.	
		Seaford, Del.	
	Chemstrand	Pensacola, Fla.	50
Polyvinyls			
Polyacrylonitrile			
(a) Orlon	Du Pont	Camden, S. C.	30.5
Copolymers			
(a) Acrilan	Chemstrand	Decatur, Ala.	30
(b) Dynel	Union Carbide	Charleston, W. Va.	4-5
Polyesters			
Dacron	Du Pont	Kinston, N. C.	35
		Total Capacity:	339.5-340.5

* Sources: *Textile Organon,* monthly issues from January 1952 to June 1955. The Du Pont nylon figure is based on an estimated figure of combined annual production of nylon by both Du Pont and Chemstrand of 240 million pounds for 1953. See J. S. Grove, Jr., J. L. Vodonick, and Robert S. Casey, "Fibers," *Industrial and Engineering Chemistry,* Vol. 43 (October 1951), p. 2235.

Chapter 3

Location Theory and the Synthetic-Fiber Industry

An empirical location study must turn to location theory for a systematic coverage of all factors which might possibly influence the location of an industry and, in general, the geographical distribution of its plants. In this location study of the synthetic-fiber industry an attempt has been made to apply the general substitution approach to the locational equilibrium of the firm.

In this chapter Section 1 records some general considerations relative to the locational equilibrium of the firm. Section 2 shows in detail how the general substitution approach is applied to the synthetic-fiber industry. This approach requires the identification of the items of cost in the industry which vary regionally. These cost items are enumerated in Section 3.

1. THE LOCATIONAL EQUILIBRIUM OF THE FIRM

Underlying the location pattern of an industry are decisions made by business firms. The general area of economic theory which embraces this type of decision-making activity is a branch of microeconomics, the theory of the firm, and, in particular, the locational equilibrium of the firm.

Traditionally, the theory of the firm has been made synonymous with price theory, the postulates of which are inferred through the implications of profit-maximizing behavior of the firm in three roles: first, in the process of production, i.e., the transformation of inputs into outputs; second, as a buyer of inputs; and third, as the seller of a product. Given the familiar data of the problem, including the structure of markets faced by the firm (defined in terms of numbers of buyers and sellers and homogeneity of product), profit-maximizing levels of output can be deduced. Price theory ignores the location problem because buying, production, and selling are looked upon as single-dimension activities, i.e., as occurring at a point. This assumption is abandoned in the theory of the location equilibrium of the firm. As a buyer of inputs, the firm incurs costs in assembling them over space and is also confronted with regional differences in their availability; the impact of site on the technical possibilities of production is recognized; and the selling activity embraces a market area in which transportation costs are also incurred in delivering the product. Thus the attributes of plant-location theory stem from firm behavior in a fourth role as well: that of selecting from an array of geographical possibilities, minimum-cost production, and selling sites; and cost minimization is focused on variations which result from the factor of space.

The Weberian Framework

In his pioneering work Weber's signal contribution was the development of the principal categories of industrial location, largely on the basis of technical empirical knowledge.[1] To Weber, the transportation network of a nation is the basic magnetic field of economic attraction which, through its lines of force, determines the position of industrial particles. He regarded transportation orientation as the basic principle of industrial location. Conceptually, competing magnetic fields are sometimes capable of causing particles to be drawn away from the transportation lines of force to their own. In short, all other types of orientation, such as power or labor, are deviations from minimum-cost transportation sites. Weber also singled out the importance of agglomeration economies in industrial location.

Although his types of location are suggestive for empirical studies, Weber's geometrical approach to the locational equilibrium of the firm, which, for example, requires the solution of location triangles, offers only a rough methodological guide.

[1] Alfred Weber, *Über den Standort der Industrien*, trans., C. J. Friedrich, Alfred Weber's *Theory of the Location of Industries* (Chicago: University of Chicago Press, 1929).

The General Substitution Approach

That the Weberian location categories could be derived by means of the familiar substitution principle of price theory was suggested by Predohl in 1928, but it was not until 1949 that an operational framework was established for the general substitution approach to location theory by Isard.[2] In his work Isard has extended the bounds of traditional production theory to include the locational equilibrium of the firm. Since cost minimization has a spatial dimension, it is specifically recognized by way of transport inputs.[3] Within the enlarged framework the problem of production is that of choosing the right combination of capital, labor, land, *and* transport inputs.

From the most significant cost difference which occurs through variation over space the orientation of an industry can be determined. Isard distinguishes two types of substitution. The exploration of alternative outlays from the use of transport inputs can determine whether costs for a transport-oriented industry are minimized at market or at raw-material sites; and the traditional outlay substitutions of production theory between capital, labor, and land can be used to deduce other types of industrial location such as labor or power orientation.

2. APPLIED GENERAL SUBSTITUTION ANALYSIS AND THE SYNTHETIC-FIBER INDUSTRY

The general substitution approach to the locational equilibrium of the firm provides an effective operational tool for empirical analysis.[4] This approach can be put in simple terms in the case in

[2] A. Predohl, "The Theory of Location in Relation to General Economics," *Journal of Political Economy,* Vol. 36 (June 1928), pp. 371–390; and Walter Isard, "The General Theory of Location and Space-Economy," *Quarterly Journal of Economics,* Vol. 63 (November 1949), pp. 476–506.

[3] Walter Isard, *Location and Space-Economy* (New York: Technology Press of M.I.T. and John Wiley and Sons, Inc., 1956), pp. 77–91; and "Distance Inputs and the Space Economy: Part 1, The Conceptual Framework and Part II, The Locational Equilibrium of the Firm," *Quarterly Journal of Economics,* Vol. 65 (May and August 1951), pp. 181–198 and 373–399.

[4] Empirical location studies which employ the general substitution framework include W. Isard, "Some Locational Factors in the Iron and Steel Industry since the Early Nineteenth Century," *Journal of Political Economy,*

which a given market, or set of markets, is to be served by a plant with given physical inputs per unit of output and is able to draw raw materials from alternative supply areas. As this plant is moved from region to region, the effect on its costs and revenue via the substitution of inputs and of diverse outlays can be determined. Consider, for example, the alternative in the synthetic-fiber industry of producing the chemicals for fiber synthesis at sites in chemical raw-material regions or of manufacturing them in fiber-market regions in the textile area of the United States. Output at a raw-material site requires little outlay on movement of raw materials, but outlays are incurred on the transportation of the finished product and on utilities, labor, etc. At a market site a transportation cost on raw materials is substituted for the cost of moving the finished product, and the market-site utility, labor costs, etc., are substituted for those at the raw-material site. In addition, market-site agglomeration economies are substituted for those at the raw-material site. Substitutions such as these can be used to generate regional cost differences so that the most favorable region for plant location can be uncovered.

The Hypothesis

It is clear that the successful use of the general substitution approach in an empirical location study depends in a large measure upon the extent to which production functions, the physical relationship between various inputs (including transportation inputs) and output, can be obtained or estimated. If, for instance, the location of an ammonia plant is in question, it is necessary to know the raw-material inputs per unit of output, the utility and labor

Vol. LVI (June 1946), pp. 203–217; W. Isard and W. Capron, "The Future Locational Pattern of Iron and Steel Production in the United States," *Journal of Political Economy,* Vol. LVII (April 1949), pp. 118–133; W. Isard and J. Cumberland, "New England as a Possible Location for an Integrated Iron and Steel Works," *Economic Geography,* Vol. 26 (October 1950), pp. 245–259; W. Isard and Eugene W. Schooler, *Location Factors in the Petrochemical Industry* (Washington, D. C.: Office of Technical Services, U. S. Department of Commerce, 1955); and the following unpublished Harvard University Ph.D. dissertations: John V. Krutilla, *The Structure of Costs and Regional Advantage in Primary Aluminum Production,* 1952; J. Robert Lindsay, *The Location of Oil Refining in the United States,* 1954; and Eugene W. Schooler, *Regional Advantage in the Production of Chemicals from Petroleum and Natural Gas,* 1954.

inputs, the manner in which these inputs vary with the size of plant, the manner in which the capital investment varies with size of plant, etc.

The hypothesis in this study of the synthetic-fiber industry is that (a) from an examination of the industry's production functions and market areas a spatial framework of regions which are suitable for plant location can be established, and (b) general substitution analysis can be used to convert the data of the production functions into production and distribution cost differences at selected sites. In this manner basic regional advantages and disadvantages for plant location can be ascertained. The computation of regional differences in production and distribution costs will also point out the basic type of location orientation for each stage of the synthetic-fiber industry as well as the minimum-cost regions among all those tested.

3. COSTS AND LOCATION ANALYSIS

Although in the location analysis of the synthetic-fiber industry it might be desirable to employ all the costs which the chemical engineer or the cost accountant would include, from the standpoint of location theory the estimation of costs, hence the estimation of production functions, can be simplified. All inputs which have a locational significance must be identified, but the cost items which do not vary significantly from region to region can be set aside. Thus the application of the general substitution approach to the synthetic-fiber industry begins with prior determination of relevant cost categories to guide the estimation of production functions.

The basic cost categories in the theory of the firm are variable and fixed costs, and these are applicable in location analysis. With respect to the locational equilibrium of the firm, variable and fixed costs may vary spatially because of interregional differences in achievable agglomeration economies.

Cost Variation

Plants of Equal Size

An examination of specific items in fixed production costs in both the chemical-intermediate and the fiber-producing stages of the synthetic-fiber industry leads to the conclusion that for any given predetermined size of plant regional uniformity in fixed charges can be assumed without doing violence to reality.

The chemical intermediates from which synthetic fibers are produced can be manufactured by more than one process, but the technology of petrochemical production is assumed in almost all cases in this study, since this particular route promises the most locational mobility for the future. In their study of the petrochemical industry Isard and Schooler found the assumption of regional uniformity of fixed costs for plants of given size to be a realistic one, after considering plant construction costs, interest charges, depreciation, plant maintenance, insurance costs, taxes, and land costs.[5] In general, the analysis of the components of fixed charges also applies to the synthetic-fiber stage, even though fiber output is a combined chemical-textile operation.

In the past chemical-plant construction costs in warm-weather regions, such as Texas or California, have tended to be lower than in regions of the North by 10 or 12 per cent because certain structural parts unnecessary in the "outdoor" type of plant were thought to be indispensable in the "indoor" design for northern regions. However, Isard and Schooler note that the recent technical literature of chemical-plant construction points to the feasibility of the cheaper outdoor design for all regions.[6] Plant construction cost inequalities which originate in labor-cost and material-cost variations cannot be systematically forecast and are not considered vital to the location problem in question.

For the large firms engaged in the development of synthetic fibers and their chemical intermediates ready access to the nation's capital market excludes the possibility of interest-cost disparities at different sites; therefore, the United States can be regarded as an area characterized by homogeneous capital availability for the location analysis. In considering the possibility of plant location in Puerto Rico, branch plants of American firms are assumed so that capital-cost uniformity applies to the island as well.

Since depreciation allowances are determined principally by tax legislation at the Federal level, there is little room for regional differences in this item of fixed costs. Plant maintenance has a regional variation and could be expected to be higher for cold-weather regions, but the practice of performing major maintenance work in good weather limits the magnitude of the cost difference.

[5] Isard and Schooler, *op. cit.*, pp. 11–13.
[6] *Ibid.*, p. 12.

Insurance costs are significant in chemical production because of the risk hazard. Manufacture in a raw-material region with plants concentrated at specific sites raises plant insurance costs over areas in which chemical production is dispersed. Since the insurance-cost differences are small and cannot be predicted in their variation with space, they are neglected in the cost analysis.

To account for regional variations in the burden of taxes which enter into fixed charges is a difficult matter. Property taxes are important but are set by legislative bodies and are not amenable to location analysis. Some states offer property-tax exemptions, usually for a five-year period, as an inducement to the location of new industry. The practice is so widespread, however, that its impact on location decisions tends in the long run to become neutralized regionally, although it may be a factor in the selection of a site within a region. For the cost analysis land outlays are assumed to be equal in all regions. The problem of minimizing land outlays in factory construction is not one of choosing the right region but the proper site within a region.

Although interregional equality in fixed charges may be justifiably assumed, in both stages of the synthetic-fiber industry regional differences in variable costs do exist. Computation of the amounts of these differences requires first an estimation of the most important variable physical inputs per unit of output. This aspect of the study is embraced by Chapters 4 and 5. It is sufficient here to indicate the locationally important variable physical inputs—stated in terms of 100 pounds of output in the cost analysis—for each stage of production:

    I. For each chemical intermediate:
        1. Major raw material inputs, pounds.
        2. Utilities:
          a. Steam, pounds.
          b. Water, gallons.
          c. Electric power, kilowatthours.
          d. Fuel gas, cubic feet.
        3. Direct labor, man-hours.
   II. For each synthetic fiber:
        1. Major chemical intermediates and solvents, pounds.
        2. Utilities:
          a. Steam, pounds.
          b. Water, gallons.
          c. Electric power, kilowatthours.

3. Labor:
   a. Direct, man-hours.
   b. Indirect, man-hours.

Agglomeration Economies

For the synthetic-fiber industry the major agglomeration economies are (a) large-scale production economies; (b) integration economies from the output of several chemical products in a multiunit plant—savings are realized, for example, by the utilization of the by-product of one unit as a raw material for another; (c) localization economies from the geographical concentration of chemical plants in a given area—a single large-scale chlorine plant may serve the needs of several users and make it unnecessary for each to construct a small-scale unit; and (d) external economies from the purchase of raw materials from large-scale producers—in Texas, for instance, large-scale oil refineries make available to chemical manufacturers huge streams of waste gas at low prices.

It may be valid to assume that for some products plants of the same predetermined size could be built in any region. In many cases this assumption would imply that agglomeration economies are uniform from region to region. However, if plants of the same predetermined size cannot be built in all regions, then location analysis must evaluate regional differences in variable and fixed costs caused by differences in the extent to which large-scale production and other agglomeration economies can be achieved.

All four of the above-mentioned types of agglomeration economy may be significant in the location of plants in the first stage of synthetic-fiber production, the manufacture of chemical intermediates. Since many of the intermediates have markets in other end uses, there may be regional differences in market potential. A site suitable for fiber manufacture may not draw the chemical stage unless it can serve a market for the excess production over the fiber requirement, for otherwise the chemical unit would suffer a large-scale production economy disadvantage. The other three types of agglomeration economy generally favor raw-material over market regions or, among market regions, those with the most highly developed chemical industries.

In this study agglomeration economies are evaluated for the chemical-intermediate stage through the estimation of the influence of size on fixed and variable costs. The other agglomeration economies—integration, localization, and external—are given qualitative consideration only.

In the second stage of the industry, the manufacture of synthetic fibers, the main agglomeration consideration is large-scale production economies.   The market for each synthetic fiber is spread out geographically over the entire textile area so that the output of a single plant is not sold entirely in a specific region.   For this reason plant size is largely a function of technological and cost considerations common to all fiber producers and is somewhat independent of the region chosen for the location of a plant.   Since the technological and cost considerations permit plants of economic size to be built in any region, agglomeration economies can be eliminated as a factor in the location of synthetic-fiber plants.

Conclusions of Preliminary Cost Analysis

For the first stage of the industry, the output of chemical intermediates, the assumption is made from the foregoing analysis that the location problem can be solved by comparing regional differences in variable costs alone for products for which the assumption is valid that plants of the same predetermined size can be built in any region.   In most cases, however, the comparison of regional differences in variable costs must be augmented by the estimation of the effect on both fixed and variable costs of agglomeration economies.

With respect to the second stage, the manufacture of synthetic fibers from chemical intermediates, the assumption is made that the location problem can be solved by comparing regional differences in variable costs for plants of equal size.

With the theoretical methodology for the location study established and the factors which lead to regional cost differences identified, the analysis turns in the next two chapters to the task of estimating the physical production functions relevant for the selected synthetic fibers and the principal chemical intermediates which are required.

Chapter 4

Chemical Intermediates for Synthetic-Fiber Production

The course marked out for the application of the general substitution approach to the synthetic-fiber industry begins with the estimation of variable-input production functions for the chemical intermediate stage. At the outset, general types of variable inputs in chemical manufacture are set forth in Section 1, along with the technique for evolving production functions in the form required in a location study. Beginning with Section 2, estimated production functions for the chemical intermediates used in making the individual fibers are presented for nylon 66, Orlon, Acrilan, dynel and Dacron. The empirical foundation for the location analysis of the first stage is completed in Section 5, which deals with agglomeration economies in chemical manufacture. 1095282

From the exploration of chemical-intermediate technology, of variable-input production functions, and of agglomeration economies it is possible to identify the general location factors for the first stage of the synthetic-fiber industry, and this is done in the concluding section of the chapter.

1. PRODUCTION FUNCTIONS FOR LOCATION ANALYSIS OF CHEMICAL-INTERMEDIATE STAGE

The technology of chemical manufacture suggests that the most important types of variable physical inputs are (a) raw-material

35

inputs, (*b*) utility inputs (steam, cooling water, electric power, and fuel gas), and (*c*) labor inputs.

Raw-Material Inputs

The chemicals required in the manufacture of synthetic fibers can be produced from more than one hydrocarbon raw-material source. In the development of production functions the petro-chemical source is assumed in most cases because this route domi-nates the construction of new chemical capacity and promises locational mobility.

By one writer's definition, a *petrochemical* is a "chemical compound or element recovered from petroleum or natural gas or derived in whole or in part from petroleum or natural-gas hydrocarbons. . . ."[1] In the United States petrochemical produc-tion is concentrated in the coastal areas of Texas and Louisiana. Here hydrocarbons for chemical manufacture are available in abundance from natural gas, from oil-refinery waste-gas streams, and from petroleum fractions. Since natural gas is mobile, petro-chemical production of chemical intermediates for synthetic-fiber manufacture need not be confined to a raw-material region but may take place at sites on pipelines. A vast pipeline network from the natural-gas fields cuts across the South and up the eastern sea-board, interlacing the textile area, the market for synthetic fibers. Petrochemical processes promise locational mobility in a second way in that manufacture can be based on hydrocarbons from oil-refinery operations located outside raw-material regions.

An example will serve to illustrate how the raw-material inputs are treated in setting up production functions for cost calculations. Acrylonitrile is a chemical intermediate used in the manufacture of Orlon, Acrilan, and dynel. By one route the chemical can be manufactured from hydrogen cyanide and ethylene oxide, and the latter in turn can be reduced to natural-gas equivalents. If acrylo-nitrile is manufactured at a site in a raw-material region, the cost of natural gas will be minimized, but transportation costs will be incurred on the movement of the chemical to fiber plants. If, on the other hand, the chemical is manufactured at a site in the textile region, no cost is incurred on the movement of the intermediate, but the cost of natural gas will be higher at least by the transpor-

---

[1] William F. Bland, "What is a Petrochemical," *Petroleum Processing,* Vol. 7 (April 1952), p. 491.

tation cost from the field.[2]   In each case location analysis requires that the chemical intermediate be reduced to equivalent pounds of petrochemical raw materials.[3]   Then regional variations in material costs which result from the distance factor can be discerned through transportation-cost calculations.

Steam, Fuel, and Electric-Power Costs

Steam and fuel costs depend upon the access of a region to energy resources such as coal or natural gas.   If regions are poorly endowed, distance inputs are necessarily greater in transporting the fuels.   Electric-power costs, too, are fundamentally dependent on natural-resource endowment, and in the absence of data on the future cost of power from atomic energy regional differences are calculated by considering conventional sources only.

Cooling Water

Although the cooling-water requirement is included in each production function the input does not enter into the cost analysis. Water availability exercises a strong permissive influence for chemical manufacture.   For all the regions in the analysis except portions of Texas water is available in abundance.

Labor

In chemical-intermediate manufacture the labor input is not so significant as the other variable inputs.   If the analysis were restricted to the United States, labor could be left out of the cost calculations.   Inclusion is necessary for the purpose of comparing costs in Puerto Rico with costs in the United States, since the island lacks skilled technicians and the latter would have to be attracted from the mainland by higher wage rates than exist in the United States.

Thus, for each chemical intermediate, the following variable physical inputs—stated in terms of 100 pounds of output for the cost analysis—must be estimated:

[2] For Puerto Rico the cost difference can be obtained by comparing the cost of oil-refinery waste gas with natural gas at the source in the United States.

[3] Some chemicals in manufacturing processes under consideration are not made by the petrochemical process, but if alternative site costs are calculated reduction to raw-material equivalents is also required.

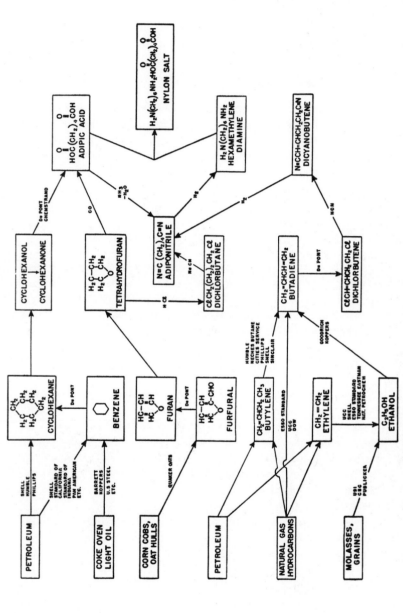

Figure 2.   Process steps in the production of nylon salt.   Source: Howard Bunn, "Cost and Availability of Raw Materials," *Industrial and Engineering Chemistry* (Synthetic Fiber Symposium), Vol. 44 (September 1952), p. 2131.

1. Major raw-material inputs, pounds.
2. Utilities:
   a. Steam, pounds.
   b. Cooling water, gallons.
   c. Electric power, kilowatthours.
   d. Fuel gas, cubic feet.
3. Direct labor, man-hours.

2. PRODUCTION OF NYLON SALT

Nylon salt is the common name of the chemical intermediate (hexamethylene diammonium adipate) from which nylon 66 fibers are made. As shown in Figure 2, nylon salt is obtained by reacting adipic acid and hexamethylene diamine, and there are three general routes to these reactants. In the first, sketched out in the upper portion of Figure 2, cyclohexane—obtained directly from petroleum or indirectly from benzene—is oxidized through cyclohexanol and cyclohexanone to adipic acid, the first reactant; and, in turn, adipic acid can be ammoniated to adiponitrile, which is hydrogenated to yield the second reactant, hexamethylene diamine. In the second route adiponitrile for hexamethylene diamine is not obtained from adipic acid but from furfural—converted to furan, to tetrahydrofuran by hydrogenation, and to dichlorbutane, which, when reacted with sodium cyanide, forms adiponitrile. In the third route adiponitrile is obtained from butadiene by chlorination of the latter to dichlorbutene, conversion to dicyanobutene with hydrogen cyanide, and hydrogenation.

Thus for nylon production the four key raw materials are cyclohexane, benzene, furfural, and butadiene. It should be noted that the location analysis takes the existing centers of production as *given*—including those in the textile area—because the nylon-salt demand alone does not determine their location. Cyclohexane is produced only at oil refineries, and production will follow the geographical distribution of the petroleum industry. Most new butadiene capacity makes use of raw materials recaptured from oil refineries. Benzene is produced both at oil refineries and at centers of steel production. With respect to furfural, the principal raw materials in the United States are corn cobs and oat hulls, and concentrated supply areas are not available in the textile region.

To illustrate the approach, nylon salt for a fiber plant in North

Carolina might be produced there or in a raw-material region such as Texas. If the first general route to nylon salt is used, both of the key raw materials—benzene and cyclohexane—are produced in Texas but not in North Carolina. To calculate the costs of production in North Carolina, transportation outlays on the raw materials might be computed from Birmingham, Ala., where benzene is produced from coke-oven light oil in connection with steel output, or from a petroleum refinery in Texas City, Texas, for cyclohexane. No transportation cost would be entered for nylon salt. If the salt is made in Texas, on the other hand, the cost of assembling the raw materials is minimized, but a transport outlay is entailed in shipping the salt from Texas to North Carolina.

These introductory considerations make it possible to turn to the development of production functions for each general route to nylon salt.

Raw Materials for Nylon-Salt Manufacture

One set of inputs for nylon-salt manufacture can be derived by assuming that the major raw materials are either benzene or 85 per cent petroleum cyclohexane. If benzene is used, the first step in the process is the hydrogenation of the raw material to cyclohexane; the remaining process steps are the same if the starting raw material is petroleum cyclohexane. The cyclohexane is oxidized with air to a cyclohexanol-cyclohexanone mixture. Following this, the unreacted cyclohexane is first stripped from the crude reaction product by steam distillation under a fractionating column and then recycled as feed to the preliminary oxidation step. Cyclohexanol and cyclohexane are recovered as a mixture by further distillation with steam and then separated by vacuum fractionation. The cyclohexanol is further air-oxidized to cyclohexanone, and all of the latter is air-oxidized to adipic acid. In an alternative process the cyclohexane is first air-oxidized, and the partial oxidation product—a mixture of cyclohexanol and cyclohexanone—is put through a nitric-acid oxidation step; from this adipic acid is obtained without separation of the mixture. Finally, a part of the adipic acid is ammoniated and dehydrated to adiponitrile, and the latter is hydrogenated to hexamethylene diamine. Adipic acid is then reacted with hexamethylene diamine to form nylon salt.[4]

[4] For a general description of this aspect of the manufacture of nylon salt see R. J. W. Reynolds, "Polyamides, Polyesters, and Polyurethanes," *Fibres from Synthetic Polymers,* ed. by Rowland Hill (New York: Elsevier Publishing

A second set of inputs can be determined by assuming that nylon salt could be prepared in a second way by obtaining the required adipic acid from benzene or 85 per cent petroleum cyclohexane and the adiponitrile for hexamethylene diamine from butadiene. In this process butadiene is chlorinated to a mixture of dichlorbutenes which is reacted with hydrogen cyanide to form dicyanobutene, and the reaction product is hydrogenated to adiponitrile.

A third set of inputs can be derived by assuming the normal route to adipic acid from benzene or 85 per cent petroleum cyclohexane and adiponitrile manufacture from furfural. In this route furan is prepared from furfural and hydrogenated to tetrahydrofuran. Reaction of tetrahydrofuran with hydrogen chloride forms 1,4-dichlorbutane, and the latter upon reaction with sodium cyanide in the presence of a suitable solvent yields adiponitrile.[5]

Major Raw-Material Inputs per 100 Pounds of Nylon Salt

Since only the broad details of the production of nylon salt have been revealed in the literature, it has been necessary to estimate the major raw-material inputs per 100 pounds from yields published in the technical literature and in patents.[6] Table A, in the technical appendix of this chapter, is a summary of the yields employed, and the footnotes explain how they were derived.

Utility and Direct-Labor Inputs

The chemical engineering procedure for estimating utility and labor inputs for nylon-salt production is described in the footnotes of Table 4, which contains the estimated production functions for a variety of routes to nylon salt.

Production Functions for Nylon Salt, Part I

Since there are two alternative raw materials for adipic acid, benzene and 85 per cent petroleum cyclohexane, two for the

---

Co., 1953), Chapter 6, pp. 115–127; and U. S. Patent 2,439,513 (C. H. Hamblet and Ambrose McAlevy assignors to E. I. du Pont de Nemours Co.), April 13, 1948.

[5] O. W. Cass, "Oat Hulls-Adiponitrile—Nylon," *Chemical Industries,* Vol. 54 (April 1947), pp. 612–613; and A. P. Dunlop and F. N. Peters, *The Furans* (New York: Reinhold Publishing Co., 1953), pp. 31–32 and 690–691.

[6] The writer is deeply indebted to Dr. John F. O'Donnell and Dr. Thomas Vietorisz for invaluable chemical engineering assistance in making the estimates.

TABLE 4

PART I: PRODUCTION FUNCTIONS FOR NYLON SALT
Major Raw Materials, Utilities, and Direct Labor per 100 Pounds of Output

Raw Material Inputs[a]	Plant Types					
	I*	II†	III*	IV†	V*	VI†
Benzene, lb	216	160			135	100
85 per cent petroleum cyclohexane, lb			272	201		
Butadiene, lb					39	39
Furfural, lb						
Ammonia, lb	18	18	18	18	25	25
Chlorine, lb					48	48
Nitric acid, lb		198		198		80
Sodium cyanide, lb						
Process natural gas, cu ft	954	752	176	176	1,526	1,445
Utilities[b]						
Steam, lb	6,838	5,991	3,230	3,005	4,692	4,482
Cooling water, gal	25,676	25,378	15,155	16,866	14,467	15,143
Electric power, kwhr	85	97	52	69	53	59
Fuel gas, cu ft	1,555	1,005	777	429	851	766
Direct Labor[c]						
Man-hours	0.205	0.205	0.195	0.195	0.350	0.350

* Air oxidation of cyclohexane.
† Air, nitric acid oxidation.

[a] Based on the yields given in Table A of the technical appendix of this chapter.

Ammonia. The 18-lb input is for the ammoniation of adipic acid to form adiponitrile. It was assumed that the ammonia required reacts with all the adipic acid introduced and that the excess ammonia is recovered. This estimation made use of Leroy H. Smith (ed.), *Synthetic Fiber Developments in Germany* (New York: Textile Research Institute, Inc., 1946), pp. 584–589.

In the production of adiponitrile from butadiene 55 lb of hydrogen cyanide are required per 100 lb of output. HCN can be manufactured from ammonia and natural gas, and the 25-lb ammonia input is for this purpose. Norman Updegraff, "Hydrogen Cyanide," *Petroleum Refiner,* Vol. 32 (September 1953), is the source of the inputs for HCN production. The HCN requirement has been assumed to be theoretical plus 5 per cent.

Chlorine. The 48-lb input is for the chlorination of butadiene. The amount of chlorine consumed is assumed to be the stiochiometric quantity and the excess chlorine can be recovered and reused. The chlorination step results in by-product hydrogen chloride amounting to about 10 lb per 100 lb of adiponitrile produced.

TABLE 4

PART I (*Continued*)

Raw Material Inputs[a]	Plant Types					
	VII*	VIII†	IX*	X†	XI*	XII†
Benzene, lb			135	100		
85 per cent petroleum cyclohexane, lb	169	126			169	126
Butadiene, lb	39	39				
Furfural, lb			78	78	78	78
Ammonia, lb	25	25				
Chlorine, lb	48	48	46	46	46	46
Nitric acid, lb		80		80		80
Sodium cyanide, lb			50	50	50	50
Process natural gas, cu ft	1,036	1.036	682	648	239	239
Utilities[b]						
Steam, lb	2,625	2,537	4,803	4,475	2,670	2,531
Cooling water, gal	8,833	10,027	14,482	14,523	8,409	8,882
Electric power, kwhr	35	41	52	57	32	39
Fuel gas, cu ft	361	357	1,066	892	781	607
Direct Labor[c]						
Man-hours	0.340	0.340	0.450	0.450	0.440	0.440

Eighty-nine lb of hydrogen chloride are consumed in the production of 100 lb of adiponitrile from furfural. The 46-lb chlorine input is for this purpose. In "Anhydrous Hydrogen Chloride Process," *Petroleum Refiner*, Vol. 27 (September 1949), p. 340, it is estimated that 100 lb of hydrogen chloride can be made from 97.5 lb of chlorine and 2.87 lb of hydrogen.

Nitric acid. The net nitric-acid consumption in the two-step oxidation of cyclohexane is based on Smith, *op. cit.*, pp. 566–583.

Sodium cyanide. Ninety-six lb of sodium cyanide are required per 100 lb of output of adiponitrile from furfural.

Process natural gas. Hydrogen is required in the production of cyclohexane from benzene, in the hydrogenation of adiponitrile to hexamethylene diamine, and in obtaining adiponitrile from dicyanobutene. The stiochiometric quantity is incorporated in the estimates on the assumption that the excess hydrogen used is recycled. Hydrogen can be made from natural gas and steam. Via the Hygirtol process 4700 cu ft of natural gas is required per 100 lb of hydrogen. Raw materials and utilities per 1000 scf of hydrogen are given in *Petroleum Refiner*, Vol. 27 (September 1948), p. 356.

It has been assumed that there is no net hydrogen consumption in the production of adiponitrile from furfural. The carbon monoxide released by decomposition of the furfural reduces the steam to form carbon dioxide and hydrogen, and it is supposed that the hydrogen by-product can be used in the hydrogenation of furan to tetrahydrofuran.

separate production of adiponitrile, butadiene and furfural, and two oxidation processes in obtaining adipic acid from cyclohexane, twelve different nylon production units are technologically conceivable and are designated "Plant Types" in Table 4. In Table 4 estimated major raw materials, utilities, and direct-labor requirements are given for the alternative ways of producing 100 pounds of nylon salt.

Plant Types I to IV are based on the assumption that adipic acid is the sole source of adiponitrile; Plant Types V to VIII can be derived on the supposition that all the required adiponitrile is made from butadiene; and IX to XII, on the supposition that all the adiponitrile is obtained from furfural. The odd-numbered plant types employ air oxidation of cyclohexane; the even-numbered, the two-step oxidation process (air followed by nitric-acid oxidation).

Twenty and three tenths lb of hydrogen per 100 lb of nylon salt is the estimated requirement via the benzene, air-oxidation-of-cyclohexane route; 16 lb via the air-nitric-acid-oxidation process. From 85 per cent petroleum cyclohexane the requirement is 3.7 lb. In the production of adiponitrile from furfural hydrogen is again required for the hydrogen chloride. As indicated, 2.87 lb of hydrogen and 97.5 lb of chlorine are needed to make 100 lb of hydrogen chloride, and the natural-gas equivalent of the hydrogen is included in the process natural-gas figure.

Finally, natural gas is also required for the production of hydrogen cyanide. The process natural-gas figure includes this requirement in the appropriate plant unit column.

[b] The utilities estimates are based on similar processes adjusted for differences in yields and process conditions.

Plant Types I to IV. Hydrogenation of benzene to cyclohexane is based on the hydrogenation of phenol to cyclohexanol, as given in Smith, *op. cit.,* p. 605; the manufacture of cyclohexanone from cyclohexanol, p. 607, was used as the basis for estimating the utilities required for the air oxidation of cyclohexane.

Utility requirements for the ammoniation of adipic acid to adiponitrile are based on those used in the production of ethanolamines from ethylene oxide and ammonia in Walter Isard and Eugene W. Schooler, *Location Factors in the Petrochemical Industry* (Washington, D.C.: Office of Technical Services, U. S. Department of Commerce, 1955), p. A-4. The reference in the preceding paragraph was employed for the hydrogenation of adiponitrile to hexamethylene diamine. And for the reaction for nylon salt it is estimated that the only utility required would be 0.5 kwh electricity per 100 lb of the salt.

In the nitric-acid oxidation of cyclohexanol-cyclohexanone to adipic acid use was made of G. C. Mustakas, R. L. Slatter, and R. L. Zipf, "Potassium Acid Saccharate by Nitric Acid Oxidation of Dextrose," *Industrial and Engineering Chemistry,* Vol. 46 (March 1954), pp. 427–434.

Part I of Table 4 contains the basic data needed for one set of comparative regional cost calculations, but many of the inputs—ammonia, chlorine, nitric acid, sodium cyanide—can be reduced to their basic raw-material equivalents. Units to produce these chemicals may also be considered to be within the framework of the location analysis.

Production Functions for Nylon Salt, Part II

Table 4, Part II, shows the same twelve basic plant types and, in addition, an alternative set of inputs to include the manufacture of some of the minor chemicals used in nylon-salt manufacture. The utilities and labor inputs have been adjusted appropriately.

The inputs required for the production of ammonia, chlorine, and nitric acid are given in *Location Factors in the Petrochemical*

Utilities for the production of hydrogen from natural gas and steam are given in the reference article in (*a*).

Plant Types V to VIII. Utilities for the chlorination of butadiene to dichlorbutenes are based on those given for the production of ethylene dichloride and methyl chloride in Isard and Schooler, *op. cit.,* p. A-15. For the conversion of dichlorbutenes to dicyanobutene with HCN comparison was made with the production of vinyl chloride from ethylene dichloride, *ibid.,* p. A-12. The requirements for making adiponitrile from dicyanobutene are based on the hydrogenation of phenol to cyclohexanol in Smith, *op. cit.,* p. 605.

Other utilities requirements are given in the appropriate reference articles in (*a*) under ammonia.

Plant Types IX to XII. The utilities employed in the production of hydrogen from natural gas and steam were used to estimate those required for the production of furan from furfural. Utilities consumed in the hydrogenation of furan to tetrahydrofuran were compared with the hydrogenation of phenol to cyclohexanol. Reaction of tetrahydrofuran with hydrogen chloride to form 1,4-dichlorbutane has been compared with the production of methyl chloride from methanol in Isard and Schooler, *op. cit.,* p. A-15; and for the conversion of 1,4-dichlorbutane to adiponitrile by reaction with sodium cyanide, the production of vinyl chloride from ethylene dichloride, referred to in Plant types V–VIII above. Other utilities are given in the reference articles in (*a*), chlorine.

[c] Direct labor was estimated by using the method of Henry E. Wessel, "New Graph Correlates Operating Labor Data for Chemical Processes," *Chemical Engineering,* Vol. 59 (July 1952), pp. 209-211. This method is based on the correlation of operating labor in man-hours per ton per processing step with the size of the plant in tons of product per day, without regard to the particular process. A 330 working-day year and an annual output of nylon salt of 100 million lb were assumed in the computations. Labor for hydrogen production is assumed to be proportional to the size of the nylon salt plant.

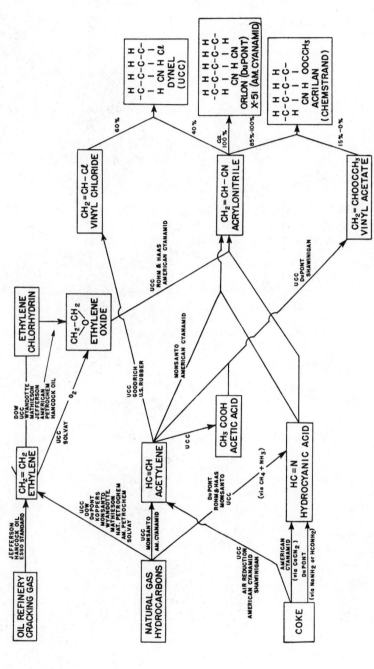

Figure 3. Process steps in the production of chemical intermediates for polyvinyl fibers. Source: Howard Bunn, "Cost and Availability of Raw Materials," *Industrial and Engineering Chemistry* (Synthetic Fiber Symposium), Vol. 44 (September 1952), p. 2130.

Industry.[7]   Ammonia can be manufactured from natural gas; and the production of nitric acid—from natural gas and ammonia—has been reduced to an input of natural gas.   In making chlorine the inputs are for the electrolytic process in which chlorine and caustic soda are produced jointly and the minor chemicals are ignored. One hundred pounds of sodium cyanide can be produced from 55 pounds of hydrogen cyanide and 82 pounds of 100 per cent caustic soda.[8]   The HCN in Table 4, Part II, is also reduced to natural gas via ammonia.

3. CHEMICAL INTERMEDIATES FOR POLYVINYL FIBERS

In Figure 3 the process steps for the production of chemical intermediates for the polyvinyl fibers, Orlon, Acrilan, and dynel, are outlined.   Orlon is made from a synthetic polymer which is 100 per cent acrylonitrile.   On the other hand, Acrilan and dynel are copolymers, Acrilan of acrylonitrile, in the main, and a small vinyl acetate or vinyl pyridine component; and dynel of acrylonitrile (40 per cent) and vinyl chloride (60 per cent).   The exposition will be facilitated if Orlon is taken first because acrylonitrile is also used in the other two fibers.

Production Functions for Acrylonitrile

Acrylonitrile can be produced in two ways: from hydrogen cyanide and either ethylene oxide or acetylene.[9]   For both routes the major chemical inputs and the utilities and direct-labor requirements have been published.[10]

Table 5 contains several production functions for acrylonitrile output differentiated by process and raw materials.

[7] W. Isard and Eugene W. Schooler, *Location Factors in the Petrochemical Industry* (Washington, D.C.: Office of Technical Services, U. S. Department of Commerce, 1955), pp. 26, A-4, A-16.

[8] O. P. B. No. 516, *German Carbide, Cyanamide, and Cyanide Industry* (Washington, D. C., U. S. Department of Commerce, 1946), pp. 32-35; B.I.O.S. Final Report No. 260, Item 22, *I. G. Farbenindustrie: Liquid Sulphur Dioxide and Cyanides* (London: H.M.S. Stationery Office, 1945), pp. 26-31.

[9] R. F. Messing and R. L. James, "Acrylonitrile," *Chemical Industries Week,* Vol. 68 (January 27, 1951), pp. 19-24.

[10] Isard and Schooler, *op. cit.,* p. A-3.

TABLE 4
PART II: PRODUCTION FUNCTIONS FOR NYLON SALT
Major Raw Materials, Utilities, and Direct Labor per 100 Pounds of Output

Raw-Material Inputs	Plant Types					
	I*	II†	III*	IV†	V*	VI†
Benzene, lb	216	160			135	100
85 per cent petroleum cyclohexane, lb			272	201		
Butadiene, lb					39	39
Furfural, lb						
Salt, lb (for chlorine)					82	82
Process natural gas, cu ft	1,260	2,027	482	1,451	1,903	2,213
Utilities						
Steam, lb	6,904	6,266	3,296	3,280	4,751	4,625
Cooling water, gal	26,171	28,994	15,650	18,928	15,197	17,134
Electric power, kwhr	94	134	61	106	143	170
Fuel gas, cu ft	1,155	1,055	777	429	803	718
Direct Labor Man-hours	0.208	0.375	0.208	0.375	0.450	0.510

* Air oxidation of cyclohexane.
† Air, nitric-acid oxidation.

Acrylonitrile is produced from acetylene and HCN in Plant Type I, and the HCN has been reduced (via ammonia) to its natural-gas equivalent. Of the two principal routes to acetylene the one embodied in Plant Type I is the petrochemical route rather than the traditional calcium carbide route. To produce acetylene in the petrochemical manner various hydrocarbon feedstocks can be employed in high-temperature, pyrolytic operations, using variations of the partial combustion process.[11] Typical feedstocks are natural gas, ethane, and propane; in Plant Type I the feedstock for acetylene is natural gas. The production possibility represented by Plant Type II differs from I only in that acetylene is produced from ethane stripped from natural gas.[12]

[11] Marcel J. P. Bogart, G. R. Schiller, C. J. Coberly, "The Wulff Process for Acetylene from Hydrocarbons," *Petroleum Processing,* Vol. 8 (March 1953), pp. 377–382.
[12] The content of natural gas is about 95 per cent methane, and in the remaining 5 per cent some ethane is present. Under existing practices a producer at a market site in the United States would have to purchase natural

TABLE 4

PART II (*Continued*)

Raw-Material Inputs	Plant Types					
	VII*	VIII†	IX*	X†	XI*	XII†
Benzene, lb			135	100		
85 per cent petroleum cyclohexane, lb	169	126			169	126
Butadiene, lb	39	39				
Furfural, lb			78	78	78	78
Salt, lb (for chlorine)	82	82	78	78	78	78
Process natural gas, cu ft	1,413	1,804	1,797	2,214	1,354	1,715
Utilities						
Steam, lb	2,688	2,680	4,947	4,703	2,814	2,759
Cooling water, gal	9,563	12,018	17,115	18,416	11,042	12,775
Electric power, kwhr	125	152	149	174	130	156
Fuel gas, cu ft	313	309	1,003	829	718	554
Direct Labor						
Man-hours	0.430	0.500	0.620	0.690	0.620	0.680

* Air oxidation of cyclohexane.
† Air, nitric-acid oxidation.

In Plant Type III the manufacture of acrylonitrile from HCN and ethylene oxide is visualized. Ethylene oxide is produced either by direct oxidation of ethylene in the presence of a catalyst or by the chlorhydrin route.[13] In turn (see Figure 3) ethylene can be obtained from oil-refinery cracking gas or from natural-gas hydrocarbons. For Plant Type III it is assumed that ethylene is obtained from ethane stripped from natural gas and that ethylene oxide is produced via the oxidation process. Plant Type IV is identical with III, except for the assumption that ethylene oxide is shipped to the hypothetical regional production sites from existing centers of production to be combined with HCN made at the hypothetical sites.

---

gas to obtain the small ethane content. The technological alternative open to the operator of a natural-gas pipeline is to strip from the gas the ethane content alone and sell it for use as a chemical raw material.

[13] W. E. Kuhn and J. W. Hutcheson, "Ethylene Petrochemicals Today and Tomorrow," *Petroleum Processing,* Vol. 6 (October and November 1951), reprint, p. 5.

TABLE 5

PRODUCTION FUNCTIONS FOR ACRYLONITRILE*

Major Raw Materials, Utilities, and Direct Labor per 100 Pounds of Output

Raw-Material Inputs	Plant Types					
	I	II	III	IV	V	VI
Chlorine, lb					171	
Salt, lb						291
Ethylene oxide, lb				102		
Ethane, lb		135	157		100	100
Process natural gas, cu ft	8,498	2,802	2,165	2,165	2,165	2,165
Utilities						
Steam, lb	4,029	3,335	2,205	1,094	1,941	2,035
Cooling water, gal	17,902	11,779	16,444	5,548	13,423	14,671
Electric power, kwhr	87	82	83	75	82	374
Fuel gas, cu ft	−2,324	−627	795	250	412	412
Direct Labor						
Man-hours	0.360	0.360	0.450	0.300	0.390	0.700

* Source: Isard and Schooler, *op. cit.*, p. A-3.

Plant Type V again makes use of the route to acrylonitrile via ethylene oxide and HCN, but the supposition is made that ethylene oxide is manufactured, via the chlorhydrin process, from chlorine shipped to the hypothetical production sites from existing centers. Plant Type VI merely changes the latter set-up to provide for an integrated unit including chlorine production.

Acrilan

Because the vinyl acetate or vinyl pyridine component of Acrilan is very small it is ignored in the cost calculations. Instead, the location results obtained by costing the acrylonitrile for Orlon are used. This procedure does not do violence to reality because the transport cost on vinyl acetate or pyridine is the same as that of acrylonitrile.

**Production Functions for Joint Output of
Acrylonitrile and Vinyl Chloride**

Dynel is a copolymer of vinyl chloride (60 per cent) and acrylonitrile (40 per cent). In Figure 3 two general methods of producing vinyl chloride are sketched: first, from acetylene, and second, from ethylene dichloride.

To test the possibility of producing acrylonitrile and vinyl chloride at dynel plant sites as an alternative to their production in raw-material regions, seven production functions, incorporating the estimates in *Location Factors in the Petrochemical Industry* of the raw-material inputs, utilities, and direct labor for vinyl chloride,[14] are given in Table 6.

In Plant Type I acrylonitrile is made from natural gas via acetylene and HCN, and vinyl chloride is made from natural gas via acetylene. For the second plant type the only change is the production of acetylene from ethane.

TABLE 6

PRODUCTION FUNCTIONS FOR DYNEL*

Major Raw Materials, Utilities, and Direct Labor per 100 Pounds of Output

	Plant Types						
Raw-Material Inputs	I	II	III	IV	V	VI	VII
Acrylonitrile, lb						40	
Vinyl chloride, lb							60
Chlorine, lb	40	40	46		114	40	
Ethane, lb		107	87		64	53	54
Ethylene oxide, lb				41			
Ethylene dichloride, lb				63			
Process natural gas, cu ft	5,681	1,177	866	866	866	56	1,121
Utilities							
Steam, lb	2,510	1,960	1,010	511	905	626	1,334
Cooling water, gal	15,860	11,078	8,266	2,705	7,804	6,366	4,712
Electric power, kwhr	47	43	34	31	34	10	33
Fuel gas, cu ft	−1,783	−441	444	187	291	−190	−215
Direct Labor							
Man-hours	0.210	0.210	0.280	0.170	0.256	0.070	0.140

* Source: Table 5 and Isard and Schooler, *op. cit.*, p. A-12.

Plant Type III incorporates the production of acrylonitrile from ethane and natural gas, via ethylene oxide (oxidation process) and HCN, and the manufacture of vinyl chloride from ethane, via ethylene dichloride. In Plant Type IV the process provides for the production of acrylonitrile from ethylene oxide and natural gas via HCN, whereas vinyl chloride is produced from ethylene dichloride. In this case both the ethylene oxide and ethylene

[14] Isard and Schooler, *op. cit.*, p. A-12.

dichloride are assumed to be shipped into the producing unit from an outside source.

For Plant V acrylonitrile is produced from ethane and natural gas, this time with ethylene oxide made via the chlorhydrin process and HCN, and vinyl chloride from ethane by way of ethylene dichloride. For Plant VI the assumption is made that acrylonitrile is produced in a separate geographical locality and shipped to the producing unit which makes only the vinyl chloride component via acetylene from ethane. Finally, in Plant Type VII the reverse is assumed, with acrylonitrile being made from ethane and natural gas via acetylene and HCN.

4. CHEMICAL INTERMEDIATES FOR DACRON

The raw materials for the manufacture of polyethylene terephthalate, the synthetic polymer from which Dacron polyester fiber is made, are ethylene glycol and dimethyl terephthalate, as depicted in Figure 4.

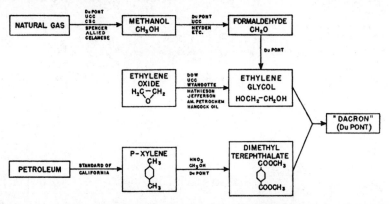

Figure 4. Process steps in the production of chemical intermediates for dacron. Source: Howard Bunn, "Cost and Availability of Raw Materials," *Industrial and Engineering Chemistry* (Synthetic Fiber Symposium), Vol. 44, (September 1952), p. 2131.

Ethylene Glycol

For the cost calculations the petrochemical route to ethylene glycol is utilized from ethylene oxide produced either by direct oxidation of ethylene or by the chlorhydrin route. Ethylene can be obtained from ethane stripped from natural gas and, for Puerto Rico, from hydrocarbon content of oil-refinery cracking gases. Data on the major raw materials, utilities, and labor requirements per 100 pounds of ethylene glycol are available from *Location Factors in the Petrochemical Industry.*[15]

Dimethyl Terephthalate

The paucity of data on the production of dimethyl terephthalate in the technical journals made it necessary to use the patent literature to make estimates of the raw-material inputs.

Major Raw-Material Inputs per 100 Pounds of Dimethyl Terephthalate

As Figure 4 shows, the key raw material for the production of dimethyl terephthalate is paraxylene made by oil refineries. In the manufacturing process paraxylene is first oxidized to terephthalic acid either by nitric-acid oxidation or by a two-stage, liquid-phase oxidation, in which paraxylene is air-oxidized to paratoluic acid in the presence of an oxidation catalyst, followed by noncatalytic oxidation to terephthalic acid by means of oxygen. In the final step terephthalic acid is esterified with methanol to yield dimethyl terephlate.[16]

Table B in the technical appendix of this chapter is a summary of the yields used in estimating the paraxylene input by the two alternative production processes, as derived from the patent literature.

---

[15] Isard and Schooler, *op. cit.,* pp. 14, 16.

[16] Peter W. Sherwood, "Phthalic Acids—Petrochemicals of the Future," Part II, "Commercial Operations," *Petroleum Refiner,* Vol. 32 (April 1953), pp. 155–158; H. R. Mauersberger, *Synthetic Fiber Handbook* (New York: Textile Book Publishers, 1952), p. 336; Howard Bunn, *op. cit.,* pp. 2129–2130; "Manufacture of Terephthalic Acid," *Chemical Age,* Vol. 68 (June 6, 1953), pp. 855–856; V. S. Swaminaton, "I. C. I. Wilton Works to Make Petroleum-Derived Terylene," *Oil and Gas Journal,* Vol. 50 (June 7, 1951), pp. 86–87; R. E. Kirk and D. F. Othmer (eds.), *Encyclopedia of Chemical Technology* (New York: Interscience Publishing Co., 1949), Vol. 10, pp. 600–607; and Hill, *op. cit.,* pp. 144–150.

Production Functions for Joint Output of Ethylene Glycol and Dimethyl Terephthalate

For 100 pounds of Dacron polymer (polyethylene terephthalate) it is estimated that 101 pounds of dimethyl terephthalate and 32 pounds of ethylene glycol are required.[17]   Table 7 contains a series of production functions with the major raw materials, the utilities, and labor inputs per 100 pounds for the joint output of ethylene glycol and dimethyl terephthalate.

In Plant Types I and II dimethyl terephthalate is produced from paraxylene via the air-oxidation route to terephthalic acid; in Plant Type I ethylene glycol is produced via the oxidation process; and in Plant Type II, via the chlorhydrin process. For Plant Types III and IV the only change is the nitric-acid oxidation route from paraxylene to terephthalic acid in the manufacture of dimethyl terephthalate.

Plant Types V to VII represent split production possibilities. Plant Type V assumes that dimethyl terephthalate is transported from a raw-material region to a fiber plant which makes only one intermediate for Dacron, ethylene glycol. In VI and VII the reverse is assumed, with Plant VI manufacturing dimethyl terephthalate via air oxidation of paraxylene and VII, via nitric acid oxidation.

5. AGGLOMERATION ECONOMIES IN CHEMICAL-INTERMEDIATE MANUFACTURE

Both location theory and the economics of chemical manufacture point to the importance of agglomeration economies in industrial plant location.

Large-Scale Production Economies

In general, large-scale production economies are a concentrating force in plant location, and the less significant they are, the more production can be localized. Large-scale production economies are extremely significant in the early stages of chemical manufacture.

---

[17] U. S. Patent 2,465,319 (J. R. Whinfield and J. T. Dickson, assignors to E. I. du Pont de Nemours & Co.), "Polymeric Linear Terephthalic Esters," March 22, 1949.

TABLE 7

PRODUCTION FUNCTIONS FOR DACRON POLYMER*

Major Raw Materials, Utilities, and Direct Labor per 100 Pounds of Output

Raw-Material Inputs[a]	Plant Types						
	I*	II*	III†	IV†	V	VI*	VII†
Dimethyl terephthalate, lb					101		
Ethylene glycol, lb						32	32
Ethane, lb	35	25	35	25	35		
Paraxylene, lb	69	69	60	60		69	60
Methanol, net lb	7	7	7	7		7	7
Nitric acid, lb			118	118			118
Chlorine, lb		42		42			
Utilities[b]							
Steam, lb	27	−25	1288	1239	399	−307	957
Cooling water, gal	4573	3977	6573	5977	3212	2656	4656
Electric power, kwhr	56	77	29	50	3	53	26
Fuel gas, cu ft	347	283	205	141	121	283	141
Direct Labor[c]							
Man-hours	0.19	0.18	0.17	0.16	0.06	0.15	0.13

*Air oxidation of paraxylene.

† Nitric acid oxidation of paraxylene.

[a] U. S. Patent 2,465,319 (J. R. Whinfield and J. T. Dickson, assignors to E. I. du Pont de Nemours & Co.), "Polymeric Linear Terephthalic Esters," March 22, 1949.

Ethane. For ethylene glycol per 100 lb, Isard and Schooler, *op. cit.,* p. 14 (oxidation process) and p. 16 (chlorhydrin process).

Paraxylene. Based on yields given in Table B, technical appendix of this chapter.

Methanol. For the esterification of terephthalic acid to dimethyl terephthalate. Terephthalic acid and methanol are reacted in the presence of sulfuric acid, and it is assumed that $\frac{1}{10}$ of the methanol removed with the water bleed stream is lost and that $\frac{9}{10}$ is recovered.

Nitric acid. Along the lines suggested in British Patent Specification 17,883 of July 6, 1949, a weight ratio of nitric acid to paraxylene of 2 to 1 was assumed in calculating the nitric-acid consumption, and it is further assumed that all of the nitric acid is consumed.

Chlorine. Required for producing ethylene glycol by the chlorhydrin process.

[b] Utilities for the production of ethylene glycol are given in Isard and Schooler, *op. cit.,* pp. 14 and 16.

For dimethyl-terephthalate production the utilities were estimated by comparison with similar processes, with adjustment for differences in reaction, etc. In the production of terephthalic acid by the air oxidation of paraxylene the basis for the estimate is the production of pthalic-anhydride from orthoxylene,

In this case the basic advantage of a large-scale plant over a small-scale plant is in the lower capital cost per unit of capacity.

For the synthetic-fiber industry one of the questions to be investigated is whether production of chemical intermediates is raw-material or market-oriented. A large-scale plant in a raw-material region could serve many fiber plants located in the textile area. Small-scale plants integrated with fiber output at sites in the textile area or in Puerto Rico would have a scale-economy disadvantage (this might be offset by transport-cost savings). Another factor of importance is that for many of the chemical intermediates the synthetic-fiber use is a small part of total output, so that regional differences in market potential also influence plant size and plant location.

Integration Economies

The typical chemical plant is a multiproduct plant composed of many production units. A single large-scale unit within the plant may produce from a basic feedstock a raw material for a number of smaller units, each producing a particular chemical product. Integration of many units at the same site also enables the manufacturer to utilize a by-product in one process as the raw material for another. In addition, many chemical processes yield joint products.

If intermediates for synthetic fibers are manufactured in multiproduct plants, then production is likely to occur in raw-material regions or regions with well-established general markets for chemicals. On the other hand, a decision to manufacture synthetic fibers need not be a decision to build a multiproduct chemical plant so that manufacture of intermediates can take place in the textile area.

Localization Economies

The plants of an industry may be concentrated in a particular area because of the pool of skilled labor, the location of service

---

ibid., p. A-8. For the nitric-acid process use was made of utilities given in Mustakas, Slatter, and Zipf, *op. cit.* The process step from terephthalic acid to dimethyl terephthalate was compared with the production of methyl chloride from methanol in Isard and Schooler, *op. cit.,* p. A-15.

[c] Direct labor requirements were estimated by using the method presented in Wessel, *op. cit.* A 330 working-day year and an annual output of polyethylene terephthalate of 100 million lb were assumed in the computations.

industries and suppliers, etc. Thus the more highly developed the chemical industry of a region, the greater is its advantage over other areas.

External Economies

In petrochemical production—the main route assumed in this study—external economies have a considerable influence on plant location. In Texas, for example, large-scale oil refineries make available at low prices huge streams of waste gas which are often delivered by pipeline to nearby chemical plants.

6. GENERAL FACTORS IN THE LOCATION OF CHEMICAL-INTERMEDIATE PLANTS

The general factors which determine the location of chemical-intermediate plants (the first stage of the synthetic-fiber industry) can be deduced from the technology of chemical manufacture and the role of agglomeration economies.

Hydrocarbon Raw Materials

Availability of hydrocarbon raw materials is a prime requisite, of course, in chemical-plant location, so that regions with coal, petroleum, natural gas, etc., have obvious attractions. But via the petrochemical route the choice is not limited to location at the source of the raw material.

Natural gas is one of the major feedstocks in petrochemical manufacture, and the price is cheapest at the source. In addition, before natural gas is transported by pipeline the heavier hydrocarbons (or "natural" gasoline) are removed, and in the process natural gasoline plants take off some lighter hydrocarbons and provide another raw material for chemical manufacture. But with a pipeline network for transporting natural gas it may be cheaper to locate on a pipeline in a market region and to substitute the lower cost of transporting gas for the cost of transporting the chemical product from the raw-material region.

Another important feedstock for petrochemicals is the waste gas from cracking operations in the refining of petroleum. The greatest concentration of refineries in the United States is at the raw-material source, but there is also a considerable number of market locations, especially in areas of high population density. Another refinery raw-material source is the reforming process for upgrading gasoline, which creates aromatic hydrocarbons for the manufacture of chemicals, such as benzene, toluene, and xylene, as well as hydrogen for the manufacture of ammonia. Even crude oil and distillate stocks are used in petrochemical manufacture; moreover, liquefied petroleum gas (LPG) is a chemical feedstock which contains raw materials such as propane and butane.

Agglomeration Economies

The four agglomeration phenomena which influence chemical-plant location are large-scale production, integration, localization, and external economies.

Transportation Costs

The costs of assembling raw materials and of transporting finished products enter into chemical-plant location. Important factors in the economics of chemical transportation costs include rates at the raw-material stage vs. rates at the finished stage, water vs. rail or truck transportation costs, the need of special equipment for corrosive chemicals or chemicals that must be transported under pressure—and the effect on transportation costs, and the role of weight-losing processes.

Regional Differences in Power and Fuel Costs

The significance of regional differences in power and fuel costs for the chemical intermediates under consideration can be deduced from the variable-input production functions.

Water

The typical chemical manufacturing process requires a very large input of cooling water and/or process water, so that regional differences in water supply or in water properties exercise an influence on plant location.

Regional Differences in Labor Costs

Since, in the main, chemical manufacture is capital intensive and characterized by a high degree of automation, regional differences in labor costs are not so significant in plant location as the other factors.

TECHNICAL APPENDIX

TABLE A
YIELD BASIS FOR ESTIMATING MAJOR RAW-MATERIAL INPUTS FOR NYLON-SALT PRODUCTION

Process Step	Assumed Yield (per cent of theoretical)
Nylon Salt from Benzene or 85 per cent Petroleum Cyclohexane[a]	
Benzene to cyclohexane	99.0
Cyclohexane to adipic acid:	
(a) Air oxidation	40.0
(b) Air followed by nitric acid oxidation	54.0 based on the cyclohexane
Adiponitrile from adipic acid, reaction and purification	74.2
Hexamethylene diamine from adiponitrile	91.0
Nylon salt from hexamethylene diamine and adipic acid	100.0
Adiponitrile from Butadiene[b]	
Butadiene to dichlorbutenes	85.0
Dichlorbutenes to dicyanobutene	82.9
Dicyanobutene to adiponitrile	96.0
Adiponitrile from Furfural[c]	
Furan from furfural	87.5
Tetrahydrofuran from furan	90.0
1,4-dichlorbutane from tetrahydrofuran	80.0
Adiponitrile from 1,4-dichlorbutane	95.0

[a]All patents referred to are assigned to E. I. du Pont de Nemours & Co., unless otherwise indicated.

Benzene to cyclohexane. U. S. Patent, 2,373,501 (M. D. Peterson) "Preparation of Cyclohexane," April 10, 1945; and U. S. Patent 2,391,283 (A. G. Weber and M. D. Peterson) "Process for the Hydrogenation of Benzene," December 18, 1945.

Cyclohexane to adipic acid, air oxidation. The over-all yield of 40 per cent is given in U. S. Patent, 2,439,513 (C. H. Hamblet and Ambrose McAlevy) "Adipic acid Process," April 13, 1948.

Cyclohexane to adipic acid, air followed by nitric acid. The adipic acid yield is based on U. S. Patent, 2,557,281 (C. H. Hamblet and F. S. Chance) "Oxidation of Petroleum Cyclohexane," June 19, 1951; and U. S. Patent 2,557,282 (C. H. Hamblet and F. S. Chance) "Adipic Acid Process," June 19, 1951.

Adiponitrile from adipic acid. See Smith (ed.), *op. cit.,* pp. 584–589 in which adiponitrile manufacture by I. G. Farbenindustrie at Ludwigshaven is described. This account was augmented by U. S. Patent 2,144,340 (W. A. Lazier), January 17, 1939, which covers a continuous vapor-phase catalytic process to produce adiponitrile from adipic acid. U. S. Patent 2,305,103 (W. V. Osgood), December 15, 1942, relates to a method for purification of nitriles.

Hexamethylene diamine from adipic acid. U. S. Patent 2,284,525 (A. W. Larchar and H. S. Young) "Process for Hydrogenation of Adiponitrile," May 6, 1942.

Nylon salt from hexamethylene diamine and adipic acid. See U. S. Patent 2,163,584 (W. H. Carothers and George D. Groves), June 22, 1939, which covers the preparation of polyamides from diamines and dicarboxylic acids; and U. S. Patent 2,130,947 (W. H. Carothers) "Diamines-dicarboxylic Acids and Preparing Same," September 20, 1938; and Hill (ed.), *op. cit.*, p. 125.

[b] *Butadiene to dichlorbutenes.* See British Patent 661,806, "Improvements in or relating to the Production of Dichlorbutenes," November 28, 1951. Additional information is provided in Robert F. Taylor and G. H. Morey, "Vapor Phase Chlorination of Butadiene," *Industrial and Engineering Chemistry*, Vol. 40 (March 1948), pp. 432–435.

Dichlorbutenes to dicyanobutene. In the chlorination of butadiene an isomeric mixture of 1,4-dichlorbutene-2 and 3,4-dichlorbutene-1 is produced by the reaction. U. S. Patent 2,477,617, "Preparation of 1,4-dicyanobutene-2 from 3,4-dihalo-1-butene and mixtures containing Same," August 2, 1949, indicates that both 1,4-dichlorbutene-2 and 3,4-dichlorbutene-1 will yield the desired dicyano derivative (1,4-dicyanobutene-2) to the complete exclusion of the 3,4-dicyano isomer if the nitrilation is carried out in acid medium. Hence 1,4-dicyanobutene-2 can be obtained fom the dichlorbutene mixture obtained directly by the chlorination of butadiene.

Peter W. Sherwood in "Hydrogen Cyanide," *Petroleum Processing,* Vol. 9 (April 1954), p. 351, notes that: "Different investigations have reported different proportions of isomeric dichlorbutenes in the products. However, in each case, 3,4-dichlorbutene-1 and 1,4-dichlorbutene-2 are predominant, and in approximately equal amounts." That these isomers are obtained in approximately equal amounts is also reported by Taylor and Morey, *op. cit.,* p. 433, and in British Patent 661,806. Hence patent examples employed to estimate the yield in this step are those employing a dichlorbutene mixture of the isomers in approximately equal proportions. The yield selected, 82.9 per cent, is based on U. S. Patent 2,518,608, "Atmospheric Pressure Cyanation of Dihalobutenes in the Liquid Phase," August 15, 1950, where the crude dichlorbutene mixture contains 62.5 per cent of 1,4-dichlor-2-butene.

Dicyanobutene to adiponitrile. See U. S. Patent 2,532,311, "Gas Phase Hydrogenation of Dihydromucononitrile to Adiponitrile," December 5, 1950; and U. S. Patent 2,532,312, "Hydrogenation of Dicyanobutene to Adiponitrile," December 5, 1950. The first of these patents covers the gas phase hydrogenation of dicyanobutene, and the second, the liquid phase in the presence of a solvent. In either case yields of adiponitrile are almost quantitative, and the chemical requirement is based on gas phase hydrogenation.

[c] *Furan from furfural.* The assumed yield of 87.5 per cent is based on U. S. Patent 2,374,149, "Method of Preparing Furan," April 17, 1945, in which the furfural is vaporized and mixed with steam before passage over a catalyst consisting of a mixed chromite of zinc and either manganese or iron.

Tetrahydrofuran from furan. British Patent 428,940 of November 22, 1933;

and U. S. Patent 2,033,292 of March 10, 1936, both of which cover the liquid phase hydrogenation of furan.

1,4-dichlorbutane from tetrahydrofuran. U. S. Patent 2,491,834, "Production of 1,4-dihalobutenes," December 20, 1949. Tetrahydrofuran is reacted with hydrogen chloride in the presence of an amine salt catalyst.

Adiponitrile from 1,4-dichlorbutane. U. S. Patent 2,414,261, "Production of Nitriles," February 4, 1947. The conversion of 1,4-dichlorbutane to adiponitrile is carried out by reaction with sodium cyanide in the presence of a solvent.

TABLE B

YIELD BASIS FOR ESTIMATING PARAXYLENE INPUT FOR
DIMETHYL TEREPHTHALATE PRODUCTION

Process Step	Assumed Yield (per cent of theoretical)
Paraxylene to Terephthalic Acid	
(a) Nitric-acid oxidation[a]	93.0
(b) Air oxidation[b]	80.0
Terephthalic Acid to Dimethyl Terephthalate[c]	100.0 based on the terephthalic acid

[a] See British Patent 655,074 (L. A. Burrows, R. M. Cavanaugh, Wesley M. Nagle, and E. I. du Pont de Nemours & Co.), "An Improved Process for the Preparation of Terephthalic Acid," July 11, 1951; and British Specification 17,883 of July 6, 1949, an addendum to the above patent.

[b] British Patent 666,709 (California Research Corp.), "Preparation of Aromatic Paradicarboxylic Acids," February 20, 1952; and U. S. Patent 2,531,173 (W. O. Toland, Jr., assignor to California Research Corp.), November 21, 1950. These patents describe a two-stage oxidation process in which paraxylene is first air-oxidized to paratoluic acid and then the latter is oxidized to terephthalic acid by means of oxygen. The reported yield is approximately 70.0 per cent of theoretical based on the paraxylene. In addition, British Patent 623,836 (C. H. Bowden, et. al., and Imperial Chemical Industries, Ltd.) of May 24, 1949, covers the direct oxidation of paraxylene to terephthalic acid by means of air, in the liquid phase, and in the presence of an oil-soluble salt of cobalt as catalyst. In this patent it is claimed that overall yield of terephthalic acid can be boosted to as much as 95 per cent of theory (based on the paraxylene) by recycling all partial oxidation products to the reaction stage.

In the absence of direct information on yields obtained in the commercial practice and in view of the yield of 70 per cent reported in the California Research patent (B. P. 655,074) a yield of 80 per cent has been assumed in the calculations, but it was also assumed that the California Research two-step technique is employed.

U. S. Patent 2,479,067 (W. F. Gresham assignor to E. I. du Pont de Nemours & Co.) August 16, 1949, also covers the production of terephthalic acid from paratoluic acid.

[c] U. S. Patent 2,459,014 (R. M. Cavanaugh and J. E. Lufkin, assignors to E. I. du Pont de Nemours & Co.), January 11, 1949.

Chapter 5

Production of
Synthetic Fibers

To complete the underlying framework of the study, this chapter is devoted to the estimation of variable-input production functions for synthetic-fiber output. In preparing the way for the individual production functions the general technology of synthetic-fiber manufacture is explored in Section 1, and in Section 2, the manufacture of the individual fibers. Section 3 contains production functions for nylon 66, Orlon, dynel, Acrilan, and Dacron.

The technology of fiber production and the estimated variable-input production functions point to the general factors which determine the location of synthetic-fiber plants, the topic of the last section of the chapter.

1. GENERAL TECHNOLOGY OF SYNTHETIC-FIBER PRODUCTION

In the manufacture of any synthetic fiber three general process steps are required to produce a finished product: (a) chemical intermediates are polymerized; (b) filaments are spun from the polymers; and (c) the untreated filaments are processed to prepare them for use by the textile industry.

Polymerization

Chemical compounds which serve as raw materials for synthetic fibers do not possess the fiber-forming property until they first undergo a chemical reaction called *polymerization.* To "polymerize" is to change a chemical compound, by union of two or more molecules of the same kind, into a higher molecular-weight compound having different physical properties. The product of the reaction is called a *polymer.*

Polymers of low or average molecular weight cannot be made into commercially usuable fibers; rather, the fiber-forming polymers consist of molecules of very high molecular weight, often called "macromolecules." How such large molecules can be built up is generally explained by the theory that monomer (single) molecules are joined together in long chains. Thus it can be said that in the first step in fiber output polymers with long chainlike molecules are synthesized.

Before it becomes a polymer a chemical intermediate is a *monomer,* the term for the simple unpolymerized form of a compound. Thus it can also be said that the first step in synthetic-fiber manufacture is to make polymers out of monomeric raw materials. To establish a link between the material in Chapter 4 on chemical intermediates and the general technology of fiber production, Table 8 lists in summary form the monomer or monomers for each fiber. Also included in the table is the chemical designation of the derived polymers.

TABLE 8

MONOMERS AND POLYMERS FOR SYNTHETIC FIBER PRODUCTION*

Fibers	Monomers	Polymers
Nylon 66	Hexamethylene diammonium adipate (nylon salt)	Polyhexamethylene adipamide
Orlon	Acrylonitrile	Polyacrylonitrile
Acrilan	Acrylonitrile and vinyl acetate (or pyridine)	Copolymers of acrylonitrile vinyl acetate or pyridine
Dynel	Acrylonitrile and vinyl chloride	Copolymers of acrylonitrile vinyl chloride
Dacron	Ethylene glycol and dimethyl terephthalate	Polyethylene terephthalate

* Source: Rowland Hill (ed.), *Fibres From Synthetic Polymers* (New York: Elsevier Publishing Co., 1953), pp. 62, 74, 120, 145.

In the manufacturing plants there is an area, usually designated the "polymer" area, in which the conversion is carried out as a batch or as a continuous process. Quantities of the monomeric raw materials are fed into polymerization reactors under pressure, temperature, and duration conditions which vary with the monomers.

The Spinning Step

Three spinning technologies are used to make filaments from synthetic polymers: dry spinning, wet spinning, and melt spinning. In all these methods filaments are formed by forcing a viscous polymer through a *spinneret,* a small dielike plate with many fine holes. In the preparation of the polymer for spinning and in the solidification of the newly formed filaments the spinning methods differ in detail.

Dry Spinning

In *dry* spinning the polymer is dissolved in an organic solvent to form a spinning solution which is extruded through a spinneret into a long tubular spinning cell through which hot air is circulated. The filaments are solidified by the evaporation of the solvent.

Wet Spinning

For *wet* spinning a solution is prepared in the same way, but it is extruded through a spinneret into a spinning bath capable of coagulating the filaments.

Melt Spinning

In the production of synthetic fibers which can be "melt" spun the preparation of a spinning solution is unnecessary. Molten polymer is forced through the holes in the spinneret by pump action, and the filaments solidify upon contact with a stream of cold air.

The *spinning* area of a synthetic-fiber plant contains several spinning machines or spinning *batteries,* each with multiple cells for filament production.

Processing the Filaments

After the polymers are spun, the process steps depend on the output mix of the fiber plant. In the production units under consideration here man-made fibers are produced in three different forms for sale to the textile industry—as *continuous-filament yarn,* as *staple* fiber, or as *tow.*

Synthetic-filament yarn consists of a number of fine continuous filaments. For sale to ultimate users it is put up on bobbins with no twist or a light twist.[1]

Staple fiber is made by cutting up the continuous filaments into short lengths and is sold in bales to the textile industry for the manufacture of *spun* yarn.[2]

Spun yarn can also be made from tow, the third form in which synthetic fibers are sold. Textile spinners with traditional spinning equipment must use staple fiber in spun-yarn manufacture. Tow is a collection of many parallel continuous filaments, grouped together in ropelike form and put up into packages without twist. It is sold to manufacturers who have special machines designed for the direct production of spun yarn from tow. The tow is mechanically broken up into short lengths, and the yarn is prepared by methods which eliminate many of the steps in the staple-to-yarn process.[3]

At the present time nylon 66, Orlon, and Dacron are produced in all three forms, but Acrilan and dynel are being manufactured only as staple fiber and as tow. How the various forms of synthetic fiber are made is dealt with in the sections devoted to the manufacture of each fiber.

[1] To the textile industry, continuous-filament yarn is a *raw* yarn because it has to be thrown and uptwisted before it can be used in weaving or knitting operations. In "throwing" continuous-filament yarn two or more strands are combined to form one of heavier weight. Twist is given to the yarn in conventional equipment to the extent required by the end use. Herbert R. Mauersberger (ed.), *American Handbook of Synthetic Textiles* (New York: Textile Book Publishers, Inc., 1952), p. 479.

[2] Yarn spinners with worsted, woolen, cotton, or spun-silk equipment can process staple fiber, for it can be cut into lengths suitable for each spinning system. The yarn spinner receives the staple as a tangled mass of highly compressed fibers. In the initial step of spun-yarn manufacture the mass is torn apart and fluffed up. Mechanical blenders mix the fluffy staple from several bales to provide yarn uniformity; they can also be used to mix synthetic staple and a natural fiber if the end product is of the blend variety. In any event, the fluffy staple is converted into a uniform web called a *picker lap,* which is wound up on paper tubes. The paper tubes are transferred to carding equipment designed to transform the still-tangled fibers of the picker lap into a *sliver,* a loose, soft, untwisted rope in which all the fibers are more or less parallel to one another. Drawing equipment is then employed for the purpose of improving fiber parallelism in the sliver and to improve the uniformity of the blend. Drawn sliver is made into a yarn of very low twist, called *roving,* from which a fine yarn can be made with the right amount of twist to produce whatever effect is desired in the final yarn or fabric. *Ibid.,* pp. 411–416.

[3] *Ibid.,* p. 215.

2. MANUFACTURE OF THE INDIVIDUAL FIBERS

A considerable lag always exists between the marketing of a new product and the publication of specific details about its manufacture. Of the five fibers under consideration, excellent accounts of the production steps are available for nylon 66 only, a product which has been on the market for almost twenty years. For the other fibers, all of very recent origin, broad pictures of the process of production, but not the details of the individual steps, can be obtained. Therefore, the nature of the technical literature on the subject should be made clear. The published accounts employed are surveys, based on the patent literature and the literature of chemistry, of alternative approaches to each general process step. Since only the general steps are important for the identification of the locationally strategic inputs, no pretense is made that the accounts which follow are of any firm's actual manufacturing operation.

Production of Nylon 66

As specified in Table 8, the monomer from which nylon 66 is made is hexamethylene diammonium adipate, commonly called *nylon salt*. If fiber manufacture is separate from chemical intermediate manufacture, the salt is made into a water solution to facilitate handling and shipment to yarn plants.[4] In conversion into nylon 66 fiber the salt is first run from storage tanks into evaporator kettles where it is concentrated. Acetic acid is added as a viscosity stabilizer in polymer formation. From the evaporator kettles a 60 per cent solution of the salt is run into autoclaves where polymerization takes place. If a delustered yarn is wanted, an

---

[4] For descriptions of nylon 66 production see "Nylon Production Flow Chart," *Chemical and Metallurgical Engineering,* Vol. 53 (March 1946), pp. 148-151; C. L. Hilton, "Engineering Aspects of the New Nylon Yarn Factory at Pontypool," *Proceedings of the South Wales Institute of Engineers,* Vol. 67, No. 2 (1951), pp. 63-91; James A. Lee, "Nylon Production Technique is Unique," *Chemical and Metallurgical Engineering,* Vol. 53 (March 1946), pp. 96-99; R. M. Lodge, "Fibres by Melt Extrusion," *Fibres from Synthetic Polymers,* Hill, *op. cit.,* pp. 363-377; Leonard Mauer and Harry Wechsler, *Man-Made Fibers* (New York: Rayon Publishing Corp., 1953), pp. 20-25; Herbert R. Mauersberger, *op. cit.,* pp. 235-295; Peterson, *op. cit.,* pp. 437-479; and R. J. W. Reynolds, "Polyamides, Polyesters, and Polyurethanes," Hill, *op. cit.,* pp. 115-164.

aqueous suspension of titanium dioxide is added to the reaction mass soon after it begins to boil. When polymerization is completed, nitrogen pressure is applied to force the polymer, a sirupy material, to flow out through a slot in the bottom of the autoclave.

Nylon 66 is spun by the melt-spinning process. Several steps are required to prepare the polymer for melt spinning.[5] From the autoclave a ribbon of the polymer flows onto a casting wheel, where it is hardened by sprays of water and cooled with streams of air. Then a mechanical cutter reduces the ribbons of polymer to small flakes; these flakes are conveyed to a blender and then transferred to supply hoppers which ride (via an overhead rail) over the spinning machines. Specially designed spinning machines, consisting of batteries of spinnerets, are used to extrude the polymer. From an overhead supply hopper the flaked polymer is fed into funnel-shaped, nitrogen-filled melt chambers which, in turn, feed one or more spinnerets. In the melt chamber a heated grid melts the polymer, which can then be pumped directly to the spinnerets. The holes of the spinnerets vary in size and number according to the size of the filaments and yarn desired.[6]

From the lower face of the spinneret the viscous filaments pass down through the orifices into a cooling chimney and are subjected there to an air blast to aid in solidification. A converging guide gathers the filaments into a bundle of yarn. To prevent elongation and to keep the yarn from loosening and slipping in a subsequent winding operation, it is passed through a chamber and humidified with steam. After the steam treatment, the yarn is passed over glass finish rollers which apply an oil emulsion as a lubricant for other operations. At the bottom of the spinning unit the yarn is wound up in undrawn and untwisted form on bobbins.[7] At this point the remaining process steps depend on the form in which the yarn is to be sold.

Continuous Filament

To make continuous-filament fiber, bobbins of yarn are conveyed to the textile area of the plant. Most nylon 66 filament is sold as low-twist yarn. In preparing the untreated yarn the filaments are

---

[5] Lee, *op. cit.,* p. 96.

[6] Ruth E. K. Peterson, *Nylon and Other Noncellulosic Synthetic Fibers,* Section II, Project V of *Study of Agricultural and Economic Problems of the Cotton Belt,* pp. 450–451.

[7] Lodge, *op. cit.,* pp. 368–372.

twisted together—on conventional textile machinery—with about one or two twists per inch.   Then the yarn is rewound on bobbins for a cold-drawing process on machines which stretch it to about four times the original length by passing it through sets of rollers moving at different speeds.[8]   From the viewpoint of chemistry the molecules of the undrawn filaments have random orientation only. After drawing, the linear molecules are aligned parallel to the fiber axis, a change which gives the yarn its particular physical properties.   After the yarn has been drawn, it is wound on bobbins, the typical put-up, and is inspected and packaged for shipment.

Staple and Tow

For the manufacture of nylon 66 staple thousands of continuous-filament fibers are combined into a rope or tow.   The tow is drawn and then crimped by mechanical means to give the yarn the loftiness associated with natural fibers such as wool.   The crimped ropes of yarn are set with steam and then cut into the desired length by staple cutters.   At the end of this operation the staple is dried and baled for shipment.   If tow is to be sold, it is packaged after being drawn.

Production of Orlon

Orlon is made from monomeric acrylonitrile, and Morgan suggests that for a large-scale operation polymerization can best be carried out as a continuous process.   A water-soluble catalyst, such as ammonium persulphate, and a reduction agent, such as sodium bisulphite or sodium thiosulphate, can be used.   In the suggested continuous process streams of acrylonitrile and aqueous solutions of the catalyst and reducing agent are fed into a reactor.   Low rates of conversion of the monomer to polyacrylonitrile make it necessary, after filtration of the slurry issuing from the reactor, to recover unconverted acrylonitrile by fractional distillation so that it may be recycled.   As the polyacrylonitrile is formed, it precipitates in fine granular form which can be readily filtered.[9]

Lessing, in writing on the development of Orlon, notes that in the experimental production of filaments both the wet- and dry-spinning processes were employed but that the latter method

[8] Peterson, *op. cit.,* p. 451.
[9] R. B. Richards, L. B. Morgan, and I. Harris, "Fibre-Forming Vinyl Polymers: Preparation," Hill, *op. cit.,* pp. 62-63.

proved best.[10]   In either event a spinning solution must be prepared by dissolving the dry polymer in an organic solvent.   For Orlon manufacture polyacrylonitrile is dissolved in dimethyl formamide.[11] If a delustered yarn is desired, an agent such as titanium dioxide is introduced into the spinning solution, or *dope.*

Once prepared, the solution for dry spinning must be carefully filtered for the removal of foreign matter and gels of undissolved material.   Each batch of polymer solution can be processed through conventional filter presses.[12]

In a typical dry-spinning process sketched by Fremon the filtered dope is stored in tanks which feed the cells of the spinning units. Spinning dope is pumped into the top of each cell by metering pumps.   As the polymer is forced through the spinneret, filaments are formed and solidified as the solvent in the solution is evaporated by hot air.   The volatized solvent can be drawn off from an aperture in the cell by air flows and conveyed to a solvent recovery unit, a vital operation in the economics of the process.[13]   As the new filaments are gathered together in each cell by wind-up devices at the bottom, they are passed over a roller which applies a protective lubricant and wound up on spools for further processing.[14]

Fibers produced by the dry-spinning process are hot-stretched rather than cold-drawn as in the case of nylon.   The stretching operation may be preceded by a washing treatment in which the yarn is passed through a bath to remove solvent residue.   Frey and Sippel point out three alternative hot-stretching methods.   First, the yarn may be drawn between two or more sets of rollers, moving at different velocities, through a hot bath consisting of a nonsolvent for the fiber or of hot air.   In the second approach hot drawing is made possible by passing the yarn through heated rollers or over hot plates.   Finally, they note that for polyacrylonitrile fibers the yarn may be stretched in special steam tubes.[15]   To stabilize the molecular arrangement brought about by stretching

[10] Lawrence P. Lessing, "Orlon: Case History of a New Fiber," *Fortune,* Vol. 42 (October 1950), p. 109.

[11] "Small but Hopeful," *Chemical Week,* Vol. 59 (September 12, 1953), pp. 71–72.

[12] W. Frey and A. Sippel, "Fibres by Dry Spinning Processes," Hill, *op. cit.,* p. 398.

[13] G. H. Fremon, "Vinyl Synthetics—Orlon, Dynel, and Acrilan," McFarlane, *op. cit.,* p. 1952.

[14] Frey and Sippel, *op. cit.,* pp. 399–402.

[15] *Ibid.,* p. 502.

and to relieve the strains in the drawn fibers, the yarn may be "relaxed" by a heat treatment in an annealing oven.[16]

Continuous-filament Orlon is sold with low twist or none at all, so that the final operation is to wind the yarn on bobbins or to give it a low twist and then put it up. In describing the production of Orlon staple Mauersberger cites a seven-step operation. Filaments are gathered together to form a tow which is drawn and then passed through mechanical devices which put a crimp in the fiber. A relaxing step follows, and the yarn is cut into staple fiber. The cut staple is dried and put up into bales for use by the textile industry.[17]

Dynel Output

Dynel, the vinyl fiber of the Union Carbide and Carbon Corp., is made of a copolymer of vinyl chloride (60 per cent) and acrylonitrile (40 per cent). Harris describes an emulsion polymerization procedure for the preparation of constant composition copolymers of vinyl chloride-acrylonitrile containing the monomers in the proportion 60/40. The step is carried out by mixing vinyl chloride and acrylonitrile in water containing a water-soluble catalyst and an emulsifier. At the end of the reaction the polymer is a resin in powder form.[18]

The published literature shows that dynel is made by the wet-spinning process.[19] Although none of the wet-spinning methods used in the production of vinyl fibers has been described in detail, the general nature of the operation is known from viscose rayon production.[20] Just as in the case of dry spinning, a solution is prepared by dissolving resinous polymer in a suitable solvent. For dynel production acetone is used. The solvent, the resin powder, and a viscosity stabilizer are mechanically mixed to form the spinning dope. To prepare it for use in spinning, the solution is filtered.

[16] Fremon, op. cit., p. 153.

[17] H. R. Mauersberger, Matthews' Textile Fibers (New York: John Wiley and Sons, Inc., 6th Edition, 1954), pp. 973–974.

[18] Richards, Morgan, and Harris, op. cit., p. 75.

[19] Mauer and Wechsler, op. cit., p. 31; P. A. Koch, "Co-Polymer Fibres," Fibres, Vol. 10 (May 1955), p. 174; and Mauersberger, op. cit., p. 988.

[20] J. M. Preston, "Fibres by Wet-Spinning Processes," Hill, op. cit., pp. 379–388.

In the wet process the spinning apparatus lies horizontal, submerged in a liquid-bath medium. The spinning solution is extruded into the liquid, and filaments are formed by coagulation. As indicated in the introduction, dynel is manufactured in the form of staple and tow only. Fremon has described a wet-spinning process for making synthetic staple which provides a glimpse of the general steps which follow filament formation. After the fiber in tow form emerges from the coagulating medium it can be taken to a second bath where it is washed and stretched. In the next step the tow is dried in an oven and is also annealed to stabilize the molecular structure brought about by stretching. From the annealing oven the tow is passed through a mechanical crimper and then can be cut into staple form and baled. In an alternative approach the tow can first be dried to low moisture content, cut, and then passed through a device known as a *tunnel* dryer. The air temperature of the dryer is maintained as high as possible without injury to the yarn, and the fiber shrinks unevenly, taking on a crimp.[21]

Acrilan Manufacture

Few details have been released by the Chemstrand Corp. on the manufacture of Acrilan, its vinyl fiber. Production so far has consisted of staple and tow only. Like dynel, the fiber is a copolymer. Acrilan is made principally of acrylonitrile (85 to 90 per cent), and the other component has been most frequently identified in the technical accounts as vinyl acetate or vinyl pyridine.[22] Morgan notes that copolymers of acrylonitrile containing small amounts of a second monomer, such as vinyl pyridine, can be manufactured in a manner similar to the process described in the Orlon section for the polymerization of acrylonitrile. The second monomer can be mixed in with the acrylonitrile stream.[23]

In the most recently published account Mauersberger has described the general steps for the manufacture of Acrilan.[24] He reports that the spinning process employed is the wet method. Whatever solvent is used to prepare the spinning solution of the powdered copolymer has not been specifically identified.

[21] Fremon, *op. cit.,* pp. 155–157.
[22] *Ibid.,* p. 137.
[23] Richards, Morgan and Harris, *op. cit.,* p. 63.
[24] Mauersberger, *op. cit.,* p. 1008.

Dacron Production

Dacron, Du Pont's polyester fiber, is the condensation product of dimethyl terephthalate and ethylene glycol. A commercial route used in the production of the polymer, polyethylene terephthalate, has been described by Reynolds.[25] Ester interchange between dimethyl terephthalate and excess ethylene glycol yields a condensate which is heated in a vacuum to effect removal of the excess glycol and to give a polymer of high molecular weight. Ester interchange requires a catalyst such as magnesium or zinc borate. As the temperature of the reaction mixture is raised, methanol forms and is removed by distillation. Pressure filtration can be used to purify the initial condensate product before it is transferred to a polymerization reactor. In the polymerization step excess ethylene glycol is evolved which presumably can be recycled. The molten polymer is released from a heated extrusion valve at the base of the vessel by the application of nitrogen pressure.

Dacron is melt-spun, and the manufacturing steps are reported to be very similar to the general procedure followed in the production of nylon. The molten polymer emerges from the polymerization reactor as a solid ribbon, which is run onto a casting wheel, cooled by water sprays, and cut into flakes for the spinning operation. Again, if a delustered yarn is desired, titanium oxide is used and it can be added to the condensate mixture as a dispersion in the ethylene glycol.

The fiber is produced as continuous-filament yarn without twist and as staple and tow. Since the remaining steps in a fiber plant with a melt-spinning process were described for nylon, the details are assumed to apply in an approximate way for Dacron.

3. PRODUCTION FUNCTIONS FOR SYNTHETIC-FIBER OUTPUT

From the technology of synthetic-fiber manufacture the important inputs for the production functions are

1. Major chemical intermediates and solvents, pounds.
2. Utilities:
   a. Steam, pounds.
   b. Water, gallons.
   c. Electric power, kilowatthours.

[25] Reynolds, *op. cit.,* pp. 146–150.

3. Labor:
   a. Direct, man-hours.
   b. Indirect, man-hours.

As a result of discussions with engineers familiar with the production of man-made fibers, the general conclusion was reached that the magnitude of the inputs is more nearly related to the output mix of a fiber plant than to process differences which are a function of the type of fiber produced, i.e., polyamide, polyvinyl, or polyester. For this reason two sets of estimated variable-input production functions are given for each fiber. Table 9 contains production functions for plants specializing in staple-fiber output, and Table 10, for continuous-filament yarn.

TABLE 9

PRODUCTION FUNCTIONS FOR STAPLE FIBER MANUFACTURE
Selected Variable Inputs per 100 Pounds of Output

	Nylon 66	Orlon	Dynel	Acrilan	Dacron
Major Chemical Inputs	(1)	(2)	(3)	(4)	(5)
Nylon salt, lb	250				
Acrylonitrile, lb		100			
Dimethyl formamide, net lb		15–30			
Vinyl chloride, lb			60		
Acrylonitrile, lb			40		
Acetone, net lb			20–40		
Acrylonitrile, lb				85–90	
Vinyl acetate or pyridine, lb				10–15	
Solvent, net lb				20–40	
Dimethyl terephthalate, lb					101
Ethylene glycol, lb					32
Utilities					
Steam, lb	5,000	5,000	5,000	5,000	5,000
Water, gal	12,300	12,300	12,300	12,300	12,300
Electric power, kwhr	120	120	120	120	120
Labor					
Direct, man-hours	6.9	6.9	6.9	6.9	6.9
Indirect, man-hours	2.8	2.8	2.8	2.8	2.8
Total, man-hours	9.7	9.7	9.7	9.7	9.7

TABLE 10
PRODUCTION FUNCTIONS FOR CONTINUOUS FILAMENT YARN MANUFACTURE
Selected Variable Inputs per 100 Pounds of Output

	Nylon 66	Orlon	Dynel	Acrilan	Dacron
Major Chemical Inputs	(1)	(2)	(3)	(4)	(5)
Nylon salt, lb	250				
Acrylonitrile, lb		100			
Dimethyl formamide, net lb		15–30			
Vinyl chloride, lb			60		
Acrylonitrile, lb			40		
Acetone, net lb			20–40		
Acrylonitrile, lb				85–90	
Vinyl acetate or pyridine, lb				10–15	
Solvent, net lb				20–40	
Dimethyl terephthalate, lb					101
Ethylene glycol, lb					32
Utilities					
Steam, lb	5,500	5,500	5,500	5,500	5,500
Water, gal	12,300	12,300	12,300	12,300	12,300
Electric power, kwhr	150	150	150	150	150
Labor					
Direct, man-hours	14.6	14.6	14.6	14.6	14.6
Indirect, man-hours	6.2	6.2	6.2	6.2	6.2
Total, man-hours	20.8	20.8	20.8	20.8	20.8

The procedure and basis for estimating the magnitude of each selection input is given by considering in turn the major chemical, utilities, and labor requirements.

Major Chemical Inputs

From the general technology of fiber production it seems clear that chemical-intermediate requirements per pound of output do not differ between the staple form and the continuous-filament form. This conclusion stems from the fact that the process steps are identical through the polymerization stage for each type.

As a general rule minor chemical requirements, such as catalysts and stabilizers, have been omitted. No basis is provided in the literature for estimating the chemicals employed in coagulating baths in the wet-spinning process or for estimating the amounts of lubricating oils used in protecting fibers during manufacture.

Nylon 66

Two different sources indicate that 250 pounds of nylon salt in solution are shipped for the production of 100 pounds of nylon 66 fiber. First, Taylor reports that, "It is reliably stated that it requires two and one half pounds of nylon salt to produce one pound of nylon yarn"; and Norman, in describing nylon 66 production, states that, "This nylon salt solution is 60 per cent water and 40 per cent nylon intermediate when it arrives."[26]

Polymer loss during the melt-spinning operation is negligible.[27] Peterson has noted that in the highly efficient nylon operation of Du Pont at Seaford, Del., there is only about 3 per cent yarn loss in the manufacturing process.[28] Therefore, the figures suggest that about 250 pounds of nylon salt are required for 100 pounds of fiber output.

Orlon

For Orlon production there may be a small loss of acrylonitrile in the polymerization process, but it is ignored. The 100-pound acrylonitrile input is deduced from the known fact that Orlon is a 100 per cent acrylonitrile fiber.

The solvent consumption estimate was obtained in the following manner. Frey and Sippel state that in all dry-spinning processes three to five times as much solvent as polymer is used, based on the yarn produced, and that without solvent recovery dry spinning is not economically feasible. In addition, they cite a patent (U. S. 2,404,714) in which the concentration (percentage polymer of weight) in the spinning solution of polyacrylonitrile and dimethyl formamide is 25 per cent.[29] If this is so, then gross consumption of

[26] W. L. Taylor, *Group 8: Synthetic Fibers, Raw Silk* (Washington: Railroad Committee for the Study of Transportation, Subcommittee for Economic Study, Association of American Railroads, 1945), p. 70; and John T. Norman, "Synthetic Fiber Production in the South, Part I," *Daily News Record,* February 28, 1948, pp. 4-7, 11.

[27] Letter from C. L. Hilton, British Nylon Spinners, Ltd., October 9, 1953.

[28] Peterson, *op. cit.,* p. 451.

[29] Frey and Sippel, *op. cit.,* pp. 401 and 404.

dimethyl formamide per 100 pounds of yarn would be 300 pounds. If the solvent loss is 5 per cent, as suggested by an article on the use of dimethyl formamide, then the net consumption of the solvent would be 15 pounds per 100 pounds of fiber produced.[30] The second figure, 30 pounds, was obtained by assuming that the loss might be as high as 10 per cent.

Dynel

For dynel manufacture the fact that the copolymer is 60 per cent vinyl chloride and 40 per cent acrylonitrile is the basis for the chemical-input estimate.   Again, some losses undoubtedly occur in the polymerization step.   The net acetone consumption was obtained in an indirect way, since no details on the recovery of solvent in the wet spinning of vinyl fibers have yet been released.   However, in a discussion of the advantages of dry spinning Frey and Sippel observe that solvents are more readily recovered in dry than in wet spinning.[31]   For this reason it was estimated that for dynel between 20 and 40 pounds of acetone would be required for 100 pounds of finished product.

Acrilan

In the case of Acrilan the inputs are based on published accounts of the chemical composition of the fiber.[32] Since Acrilan and Orlon are so similar from the standpoint of chemical requirements, no separate cost calculations for location analysis are necessary for Acrilan.   Although the specific solvent for Acrilan is not known, the net magnitude of the input is assumed to be about the same as for dynel because wet-spinning processes are employed for the manufacture of both.   All chemical solvents can be transported at about the same freight rate, and this makes it possible to deduce the forces in the location of Acrilan production from an examination of Orlon.

Dacron

For Dacron the estimated requirements of dimethyl terephthalate and ethylene glycol per 100 pounds are based on the "master"

---

[30] "Small but Hopeful," *Chemical Week,* Vol. 60 (September 12, 1953), pp. 71–72.

[31] Frey and Sippel, *op. cit.,* p. 412.

[32] See p. 46, Figure 3.

patent for the production of polyethylene terephthalate, the polymer from which the fiber is made.[33]

Utility Inputs

The production of continuous-filament yarn requires twisting
and wind-up operations which are not part of synthetic-staple
manufacture. An effort is made, therefore, to distinguish between
the higher utility requirements of continuous-filament as compared
with staple output. Within this framework no effort is made at
all to determine how the utility inputs vary between one type of
continuous-filament yarn and another or one type of staple fiber
and another. In short, a homogeneous set of utility inputs is employed for all the continuous-filament production functions and
another for all the staple-fiber functions.

Three technical observations must be made before the utility
estimates are explained. The general tendency in the construction of new synthetic-fiber plants has been to rely on purchased
power, and the steam input makes this assumption. No attempt is
made to ascertain the steam input for a plant with its own power
installation, a set-up which makes it possible for process steam to
be recycled to the power unit. Second, synthetic fiber plants must
operate on a twenty-four-hour, seven-day-week schedule, and in
making all the utility estimates a 365-day year is assumed.
Finally, steam, water, and power inputs per pound do not seem to
vary significantly with the size of the fiber plant, so that estimates
obtained for plants of different scales can be combined to arrive at
final figures.

In the paragraphs which follow utilities are first explained for
staple-fiber production in Table 9 and then for continuous-filament
yarn in Table 10.

Steam

Three different sets of data were used to make the estimate of
the steam required per 100 pounds of staple output. First, in its
company publication, *Heat Engineering,* the Foster Wheeler Corp.
has described the steam plant at Chemstrand's Acrilan factory at

[33] U. S. Patent 2,465,319 (J. R. Whinfield and J. T. Dickson, assignors to
E. I. du Pont de Nemours & Co.), "Polymeric Linear Terephthalic Esters,"
March 22, 1949.

Decatur, Ala.[34]   There are three steam generating units, each with a per hour capacity of 100,000 pounds of steam. The efficiency of the generators is reported to be in excess of the 86 per cent, when operating at full capacity, and 87 per cent, at 75 per cent of capacity; the steam produced is 275 psig with a temperature of 500° F. Built primarily for generation of process steam, the boiler plant has only one 20-kilowatt, turbine-driven electric generating unit which starts automatically on power failures. It is further stated that bituminous coal having a Btu value of 12,500 is used in the steam plant.

Without describing the plant installation, an engineer provided the basis for a second steam input estimate in stating that for a 40-million-pound-per-year *acrylic* staple plant the coal input for the steam plant would be 264 tons per day of 12,500 Btu coal.[35]   A second engineer estimated that for a 30-million-pound-per-year staple plant a steam installation of three boilers, each of 80,000 pounds per hour capacity would be sufficient—with two boilers to carry the normal load and one for winter use.[36]

From the three sets of data the steam required per output of 100 pounds of staple fiber was estimated in the following way:

1. 1259 Btu of heat are required to produce one pound of steam at 500° F., 275 psig.[37]

2. From the information that 264 tons of 12,500 Btu coal per day would be required for a 40-million-pound-per-year staple plant a steam output of 220,000 pounds per hour is obtained if we assume the steam is also 500° F., 275 psig. This is so because a ton of 12,500 Btu coal has the heat equivalent of 20,000 pounds of steam on this basis, and 264 tons of coal is the equivalent of 5.28 million pounds of steam per day, or 220,000 pounds of steam per hour.

3. The reported capacity of the Acrilan plant is 30 million pounds per year. The Foster Wheeler units could operate at 85 per cent of capacity and at 85 per cent efficiency and produce 216,750 pounds of steam an hour.

4. If the capacity and efficiency percentages used above are applied to the third bit of information, i.e., a three 80,000-pound-per-hour boiler plant for a 30-million-pound staple factory, then steam production would be 173,400 pounds per hour.

[34] " 'Acrilan' a New Industry," *Heat Engineering,* Vol. 27 (October 1952), pp. 156–161.
[35] Mr. C. P. Wood, Lockwood Greene Engineers, Inc., New York, interview.
[36] Mr. R. W. Logan, Charles T. Main Co., Boston, Mass., interview.
[37] John H. Perry (ed.), *Chemical Engineers' Handbook* (New York: McGraw-Hill Book Co., Inc., 1934), p. 2018.

If it is assumed that in all three cases the fiber plants operate at full capacity, twenty-four hours a day over a 365-day year, then three estimates can be obtained of steam consumption per 100 pounds of fiber produced:

Plant Capacity (million lb)	Steam Plant Output (lb per hr)	Steam Input per 100 lb of Fiber
40	220,000	4,818 lb
30	216,750	6,329 lb
30	173,400	5,013 lb

For the production functions for staple-fiber output in Table 9 the round sum of 5000 pounds of steam per 100 pounds of fiber was selected as a representative figure.

Electric Power

In obtaining data for an estimate of the power input for staple-fiber production a confidential source furnished the information that for a 30-million-pound-per-year plant a monthly electricity purchase of 3.2 million kilowatthours would be required. A second source indicated that a steady load of 6000 kilovolt-amperes would be needed for the power input.[38] With engineering assistance, a 70 per cent load or diversity factor was applied to convert the 6000 kilovolt-amperes to a 4.2 million kilowatthour requirement.[39] A third figure suggested is a steady load of 4000 kilovolt-amperes for a plant with annual capacity of 40 million pounds, or a monthly need of 2.8 million kilowatthours, if the load factor is also 70 per cent.[40]

Each estimate can be multiplied by twelve to get the annual power consumption and divided by the full plant capacity in each case to obtain estimates of power consumption per 100 pounds of fiber:

Plant Capacity (million lb)	Annual Power Consumption (million kwhr)	Power Input per 100 lb of Fiber
40	32.6	81 kwhr
30	50.4	168 kwhr
30	38.4	128 kwhr

[38] Mr. R. W. Logan, Charles T. Main Co., Boston, Mass., interview.
[39] Mr. R. J. Potter, Lockwood Greene Engineers, Inc., Boston, Mass., interview.
[40] Mr. C. P. Wood, Lockwood Greene Engineers, Inc., New York, interview.

Since the differences in the estimates may be partially attributable to the spinning process used, i.e., wet, dry, or melt spinning, the middle figure rounded off to 120 kilowatthours per 100 pounds of output was selected as representative of the power requirement for all staple-fiber production.

Cooling and Process Water

The water input for synthetic-fiber production is a vital one from the standpoint of the selection of an exact site for an operation. Manufacture can take place only at a river or lake site with an abundance of water for the chemical process steps and for fiber production. Engineers weigh alternative sites until one is chosen where the fixed costs of the pipes, the pumping installation, and the filtering equipment, as well as the power input to operate the pumps, are minimized.

Three estimates were obtained of the amount of water required in staple-fiber manufacture. A confidential source thought that the water requirement could range from 9720 to 15,270 gpm for a 30-million-pound plant. In a second case, for a 40-million-pound unit, the estimate was 6400 gpm (3200 for filtered process water and 3200 for cooling water).[41] From a third person three different estimates were obtained for a 30-million-pound-per-year plant on the basis of three different assumptions about the temperature of the water and the extent to which the water can be recycled:[42]

1. High temperature water, no recycling: 12,000 gpm.
2. Normal temperature water, no recycling: 7000 gpm.
3. Normal temperature water, with recycling of all water except the filtered process water: 2700 gpm.

The figure of 7000 gpm in the third estimate for normal temperature water with no recycling was selected as a typical figure for fiber production without regard for variations which depend on the spinning process used. For a plant of 30-million-pound capacity operating around the clock the water plant output of 7000 gpm amounts to an input of 12,300 gallons per 100 pounds of staple fiber produced.

Utility Inputs for Continuous-Filament Plants

From the general technology of synthetic-fiber production it appears that the steam input would not vary much between staple

---

[41] Mr. C. P. Wood, Lockwood Greene Engineers, Inc., New York, interview.
[42] Mr. William E. Stanley, Professor of Civil Engineering, MIT, interview.

and continuous-filament production. If there is any variation, it is assumed that it would be in the direction of a slightly higher input for the production of filament yarn. Therefore, the steam for a plant devoted solely to the production of yarn was raised by 10 per cent over the amount required in staple production so that an input of 5500 pounds of steam per 100 pounds of yarn appears in the production functions in Table 10.

The power input for continuous-filament production was obtained by increasing the 120-kilowatthour input in staple production by 25 per cent to make the figure 150 kilowatthours in Table 10. This was done to allow for the use of more power in the twisting and winding operations in making continuous-filament yarn.

As to the water requirement, there is no information that indicates that the need would depend on the final output of the plant, i.e., continuous filament or staple fiber. Hence the same input, 12,300 gallons per 100 pounds, is used for both, and this figure also appears in the production functions of Table 10.

Labor for Synthetic-Fiber Production

As in the case of utilities, separate estimates of labor inputs were made for staple-fiber and continuous-filament yarn production, but no attempt was made to distinguish labor inputs for each class of synthetic fibers. Although utilities for continuous-filament production were developed from information about staple output, the reverse is true of the labor estimates.

Continuous Filament

For the production of filament yarn one of the main determinants of the amount of labor required per pound of output is the denier of the yarn produced. The *denier* of yarn, or a filament, is a measure of its fineness or coarseness and is the weight in grams of a length of 9000 meters. Low denier yarns are fine yarns, and high denier yarns are coarse. To illustrate the point, one pound of 20-denier yarn contains 223,224 yards; a 40-denier yarn, 111,612 yards; and an 800-denier yarn, 5581 yards per pound. In the stage of manufacture of continuous-filament yarn in which the filaments are wound on bobbins the machine and labor time at equal machine speeds required for fine denier yarn is greater than for the coarse variety.

Since the amount of labor required in continuous-filament yarn manufacture is related to the denier produced, the labor input estimate is based on the output mix of a "typical" plant. An esti-

mate was obtained of the number of laborers employed in a typical yarn plant with a capacity of 35 to 40 million pounds per year
and is given here:[43]

Operation	Per cent	Number of Employees
Polymer and spinning	15.0	375
Textile area	55.0	1375
Administrative and general services	30.0	750
Total	100.0	2500

On the supposition that each employee works eight hours a day
and the plant operates 365 days a year, an estimate can be made
of the man-hours required to produce 100 pounds of continuous-
filament yarn. By combining the polymer and spinning labor with
the textile-area labor, a direct labor requirement of 14.6 man-hours
per 100 pounds of yarn output is obtained. From the administrative and general services figure an indirect labor requirement of 6.2
man-hours can be computed. These figures are included in the
production functions in Table 10.

Because of the short experience of producers with staple-fiber
production and the intensity of interfirm competition estimates of
the labor force needed to operate a staple-fiber plant could not be
obtained directly from any producer. From the technological differences, however, it is clear that far less labor is required in staple
than in continuous-filament production. This is so because staple-
fiber manufacture does not require the textile labor needed for the
twisting and winding operations of continuous-filament yarn output. The labor input for staple may also vary with the denier, but
a very limited range of deniers is sold.

The labor input per 100 pounds of staple fiber was estimated in
the following way. When the Du Pont company announced the
construction of its 30-million-pound capacity Orlon staple plant at
Camden, S. C., it was stated that "the new unit will add 1000 to
the number of employees required" over the labor force already
employed in the company's continuous-filament unit there.[44]

[43] Letter from Charles H. Rutledge, Manager, Product Information, E. I.
du Pont de Nemours & Co., Wilmington, Del., June 15, 1954.
[44] "Du Pont to Build Unit to Make Orlon Staple," *Daily News Record,* April
21, 1950, p. 24.

From a confidential source an estimate of 900 to 1000 employees was obtained as the labor force needed for a 30-million-pound staple operation. Since the announced capacity of the Du Pont staple plant at Camden is also 30 million pounds, it was decided that approximately 1000 employees would be needed to man staple plant of economic size.

Since the technology of polymer and spinning does not vary much as between continuous-filament and staple production, it was assumed that 375 workers would also be required in polymer and spinning, the figure given for continuous-filament yarn manufacture. By assuming that administrative and service personnel also make up 30 per cent of the labor force, 300 workers would be required in this category for staple output. The balance, 325, would therefore be needed for processing steps in staple production, such as cutting, crimping, drying, and baling.

By adding together 375 workers in polymer and spinning and 325 for fiber processing, a direct labor force of 700 was estimated. Given an eight-hour day and a plant operation of 365 days a year for a 30-million-pound plant, the direct labor input in staple-fiber production turns out to be 6.9 man-hours per 100 pounds. In the same manner 300 employees in administrative and general service jobs can be converted to an indirect labor input of 2.8 man-hours. These figures are found in the appropriate place in Table 9, where the production functions which incorporate the variable inputs for staple-fiber manufacture are given.

4. GENERAL FACTORS IN THE LOCATION OF SYNTHETIC-FIBER PLANTS

The reader will recall that the preliminary analysis of Chapter 3 led to the conclusion that the location of synthetic-fiber plants is determined by regional differences in production and distribution costs and that agglomeration economies are not a significant factor. For this reason the general location factors can be inferred from the technology of synthetic-fiber production as revealed particularly in the variable-input production functions.

Labor

Synthetic-fiber production is many times as labor intensive as the output of chemical intermediates (the first stage of the industry); and manufacture of continuous-filament yarn is more labor intensive than manufacture of staple fiber. In addition to managerial and clerical personnel, fiber plants require chemical workers in the polymer and spinning areas; there are textile occupations in some of the steps in making continuous-filament yarn; and many plants have laboratories for research and testing which require chemists and laboratory technicians. Thus all of the factors which enter into regional differences in labor costs are significant in plant location.

Regional Differences in Power and Fuel Costs

Sizable power and fuel inputs are consumed in the manufacture of synthetic fibers. All plants are built with at least emergency power-generating facilities; beyond this there are installations for generating all power, or the normal power requirement is purchased. In addition to the normal use of steam, some process steps in the manufacture of synthetic fibers employ steam. Regional differences in power and fuel costs are thus another factor in plant location.

Transportation Costs

Two sets of transportation costs enter into fiber plant location decisions: the cost of shipping raw materials or chemical intermediates and of shipping fibers to textile mills. Either rail or water transportation can be used to assemble the chemical raw materials or chemical intermediates; and for water transportation regional sites with access to raw-material regions via intercoastal canal or chemical tanker are important in plant location. For the delivery of fibers to textile mills rail and truck transportation costs, as well as the question of location in areas of heavy textile mill concentration or on the perimeter of such areas, must be considered.

Water

As the variable-input production functions show, synthetic-fiber manufacture involves a very large water input, so that regional differences in water supply, sites on rivers and lakes, water properties and temperature, and the consequent cost of processing and pumping facilities, etc., are important factors in plant location. The waste-disposal problem is minor, say, in comparison with rayon manufacture.

Chapter 6

The Regional Cost Model
for the Location Analysis of
the Synthetic-Fiber Industry

By means of location analysis and examination of the technology of both stages of the synthetic-fiber industry the factors which are strategic for plant location have been identified. For chemical-intermediate production a prime consideration is the availability of hydrocarbon raw materials. Transportation costs are significant in both stages, in assembling raw materials for chemical manufacture or the transportation of intermediates to fiber plants and in the shipment of fibers to textile mills. Labor costs are of vital importance in the synthetic-fiber stage but less important in chemical manufacture except in areas with a short supply of technically trained personnel. In both stages of the industry other location factors are regional differences in fuel and power costs and in the availability of water. All the foregoing factors affect variable production and distribution costs. In addition, a consideration of great importance for the chemical stage concerns regional differences in agglomeration economies.

The location factors serve as a guide in selecting general types of geographic areas in which plant location might take place, such as raw-material, fiber-market, or low-cost labor regions. To complete the analysis, cost comparisons must be made for two purposes: first, to select from many regions of the same general type the lowest cost areas; and second, to determine the orientation of each stage of production through the operation of the dominant location factors.

In Section 1 the regions which qualify in a general way as sites for the location of chemical-intermediate facilities and/or synthetic-fiber plants are selected. Section 2 is concerned with the development of data which serve as parameters for the generation of regional differences in variable production and distribution outlays through transportation, fuel, power, and labor costs. The technique for judging the significance of the agglomeration factor in the chemical stage is presented in Section 3 in a description of a method for calculating large-scale production economies. The complete costing procedure is illustrated in Section 4 by the computation of sample sets of costs in both stages of the synthetic-fiber industry.

1. THE REGIONAL FRAMEWORK

The regions of the United States whose economies can benefit directly from the investment and employment impact of the development of synthetic fibers are those which make up the textile manufacturing area and the centers of intensive chemical production.

Since consuming plants in the textile area constitute the national market, the attraction of sites in this area for the production of synthetic fibers is perfectly clear. One consideration—but by no means the only one—in locating a plant in the textile area is the cost of serving a widely dispersed sales territory. The varying degrees of concentration in the geographical distribution of the textile industry makes it possible to divide up the national market for fibers into a number of regional markets and to assign to each a sales potential. In this way it is possible to assess the cost of distributing synthetic fibers from hypothetical sites in the textile area, from points outside it in raw-material areas of chemical manufacture, or from Puerto Rico.

Fiber-Market Regions

In determining the regional markets the first consideration is the pattern of end uses for synthetic fibers. If all these fibers were used in blends with wool alone, then the matter would simply become a question of measuring the distribution of wool plants in the United States. But the fibers are consumed by all types of textile producers. Table 11 (End Uses of Man-Made Fibers, 1951) covers rayon and acetate as well as the synthetic fibers then in produc-

tion. Separate figures are not available on the current markets for
the five fibers under consideration—nylon, Orlon, Acrilan, dynel,
and Dacron. In any event, such figures would not cover all the
possible uses for the new fibers, so that the data for all man-made
fibers represents the potential market for the synthetics as well.

TABLE 11

END USES OF MAN-MADE FIBERS, 1951*

(millions of pounds)

End Use	Yarn	Staple	Total
Men's and Boys' Apparel: Total	47.1	97.8	144.9
Outerwear	16.1	66.8	82.9
Shirts	16.3	24.1	40.4
Underwear and nightwear	1.8	0.6	2.4
Hosiery	6.3	5.2	11.5
Furnishings	6.6	1.1	7.7
Women's and Misses' Apparel: Total	261.5	102.2	363.7
Outerwear	84.3	99.8	184.1
Blouses and shirts	21.0	0.7	21.7
Intimate wear	117.9	0.4	118.3
Hosiery	25.0	1.2	26.2
Accessories and misc.	13.3	0.1	13.4
Children's and Infants' Apparel: Total	18.6	10.5	29.1
Outerwear	7.1	9.7	16.8
Blouses and shirts	0.7	---	0.7
Underwear and other	10.8	0.8	11.6
Household Uses: Total	78.0	80.0	158.0
Bedding and blankets	10.5	19.0	29.5
Linens	4.6	0.7	5.3
Carpets and rugs	16.4	32.7	49.1
Curtains	18.4	0.1	18.5
Upholstery, draperies, etc.	26.2	27.5	53.7
Misc.	1.9	---	1.9
Other Consumer-Type Products: Total	114.7	16.1	130.8
Linings and piece goods	91.8	15.0	106.8
Narrow woven goods	14.7	---	14.7
Yarn and thread	0.1	0.6	0.7
Industrial Uses: Total	409.5	16.2	425.7
Transportation uses	31.5	14.1	45.6
Rubber industry	340.0	---	340.0
Other	0.1	0.6	0.7

* Source: "Textile Inter-Fiber Competition, 1951," *Textile Organon,* Vol. 24
(August, 1953) pp. 134–139.

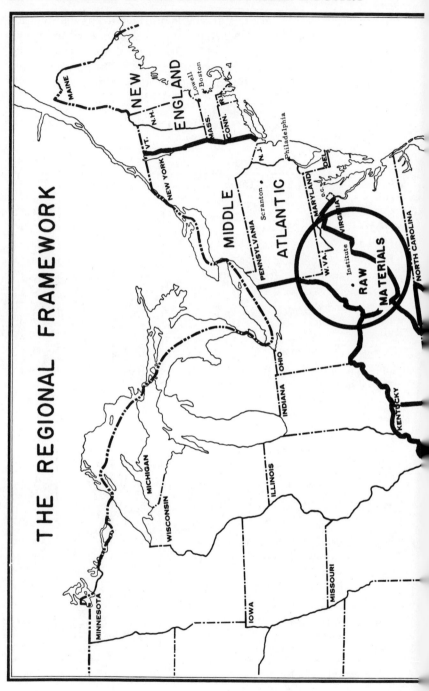

THE REGIONAL FRAMEWORK

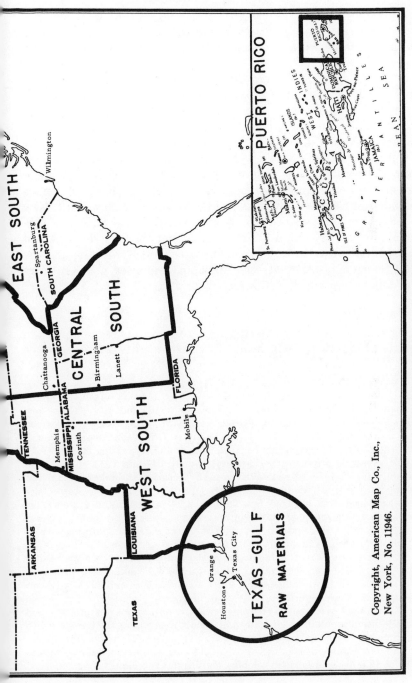

Copyright, American Map Co., Inc.,
New York, No. 11946.

Figure 5. The Regional Framework.

Judging from the end-use pattern in 1951, the industry sector of the *Census of Manufactures,* which most nearly represents an enumeration of *initial* consuming mills for synthetic fibers, is Industry No. 22, Textile Mill Products.[1] To split up the national market for synthetic fibers into regional markets with different degrees of sales potential, the distribution of employment in 1947, 1951, and 1952 of the Textile Mill Products sector was used as an index. The employment figures by states and census regions are incorporated in Table 12. Guided by the data, the national market for synthetic fibers was divided into the five regional markets shown in Figure 5, The Regional Framework.[2] The New England market is made up of Maine, Vermont, Massachusetts, Rhode Island, and Connecticut; the Middle Atlantic, of New York, New Jersey, Pennsylvania, and West Virginia; the East South, of Virginia, North Carolina, and South Carolina; the Central South, of Georgia and eastern Alabama, Tennessee, and Kentucky; and the West South market, of western Alabama, Tennessee, and Kentucky and Mississippi and Louisiana.

Market Weights

By taking into account continuing trends in the regional shift in textile production, each market is given weight to represent the

---

[1] *Census of Manufactures, 1947.* Vol. II, Statistics by Industry (Washington: U. S. Government Printing Office, 1949), pp. 153–154. Industry Group 22 includes the following components of the textile industry: *Woolen and Worsted Manufactures.* Industry Group 2212, yarn mills, wool, except carpet. *Yarn and Thread Mills, except Wool.* Industry Group 2222, yarn-throwing mills (establishments primarily engaged in throwing or twisting filament yarn of silk, rayon, or other synthetic fiber); Industry Group 2233, thread mills (establishments primarily engaged in manufacturing thread of cotton, silk, rayon, or other synthetic fiber); Industry Group 2224, yarn mills, cotton system (establishments engaged in spinning yarn on the cotton system from cotton, wool, silk, rayon, or other synthetic staple fibers); and Industry Group 2235, yarn mills, silk system (establishments engaged in spinning yarn on the silk system from silk, rayon, or other synthetic staple fibers. *Knitting Mills.* Industry Groups 2251, full-fashioned hosiery mills; 2252, seamless hosiery mills; 2253, knit outerwear mills; 2254, knit underwear mills; 2255, knit glove mills; 2256, knit fabric mills; 2259, knitting mills, nec.; and 2271, wool carpets, rugs, and carpet yarn.

[2] The regional markets are groupings of states or portions of states relevant to the location problem under study and are not the same as the Census region groupings in Table 12. In addition, the minor activity of the textile industry indicated by employment in the East North Central and Pacific States regions in Table 12 is disregarded in developing textile market regions.

estimated percentage of future national fiber sales which will accrue to each:

Fiber-Market Region	Market Weight
New England	12%
Middle Atlantic	20%
East South	36%
Central South	22%
West South	10%

Sites for Sample Cost Computations

Figure 5 also shows the hypothetical production sites selected in each fiber-market region for the purpose of obtaining sample costs to represent the whole region:

Fiber-Market Region	Hypothetical Production Sites
New England	Boston, Mass.
Middle Atlantic	Institute, W. Va.
East South	Wilmington, N. C.
Central South	Mobile, Ala.
	Chattanooga, Tenn.
	Birmingham, Ala.
West South	Memphis, Tenn.

These sites were chosen with an eye toward the use, wherever possible, of water transportation in the movement of chemical intermediates from raw-material regions to fiber plants.

In addition, Figure 5 shows some typical consuming centers for synthetic fibers selected to obtain the cost of transporting fibers from production sites to market concentrations: New England, Boston, Mass.; Middle Atlantic, Philadelphia, Pa.; East South, Spartanburg, S. C.; Central South, Lanett, Ala.; and West South, Corinth, Miss.

To handle the cost of transporting fibers from Puerto Rico to the United States, ports of entry were chosen for each fiber-market region as well as for typical market centers: New England, via Boston to Lowell, Mass.; Middle Atlantic, via Philadelphia to Scranton, Pa.; East South, via Wilmington, N. C., to Spartanburg, S. C.; Central South, via Mobile to Lanett, Ala.; and West South, via Mobile to Corinth, Miss.

TABLE 12

INDUSTRY 22: TEXTILE MILL PRODUCTS*

Employment: 1947, 1951, 1952

Census Region	Employment			Per cent of Total		
	1952	1951	1947	1952	1951	1947
New England	201,977	225,184	262,561	19.0	20.8	22.7
Maine	23,103	22,888	25,810	2.2	2.1	2.2
Vermont	4,071	4,755	4,926	0.4	0.4	0.4
Massachusetts	92,496	112,278	130,274	8.7	10.4	11.3
Rhode Island	48,415	49,537	62,566	4.5	4.6	5.4
Connecticut	33,892	35,726	38,985	3.2	3.3	3.4
Middle Atlantic	255,562	275,005	292,939	24.0	25.4	25.4
New York	77,400	86,432	91,037	7.3	8.0	7.9
New Jersey	56,730	59,533	63,243	5.3	5.5	5.5
Pennsylvania	121,432	129,040	138,659	11.4	11.9	12.0
East North Central	26,444	24,754	28,466	2.3	2.3	2.5
Indiana	4,454	5,221	6,640	0.4	0.5	0.6
Illinois	10,740	9,657	10,716	1.0	0.9	0.9
Wisconsin	9,450	9,876	11,110	0.9	0.9	1.0
South Atlantic	492,915	467,762	471,325	46.2	43.3	40.9
Virginia	39,679	36,266	33,881	3.7	3.4	2.9
N. Carolina	218,993	203,829	210,350	20.5	18.8	18.2
S. Carolina	132,829	126,572	124,599	12.5	11.7	10.8
Georgia	101,414	101,095	102,535	9.5	9.4	8.9
East South Central	86,252	84,822	91,614	8.0	7.8	7.9
Kentucky	3,517	3,010	3,586	0.3	0.3	0.3
Tennessee	33,436	31,232	35,885	3.1	2.9	3.1
Alabama	49,299	50,580	52,143	4.6	4.7	4.5
West South Central						
Louisiana	2,135	2,219	2,347	0.2	0.2	0.2
Pacific States	3,385	2,087	3,639	0.3	0.2	0.3
Washington	585	—	573	0.1	—	0.1
Oregon	2,820	2,087	3,066	0.2	0.2	0.3
United States	1,066,870	1,081,833	1,152,891	100.0	100.0	100.0

* Source: *Annual Survey of Manufactures, 1952* (Washington: U. S. Government Printing Office, 1953), pp. 48–80.

Raw-Material Regions

The principal sources of hydrocarbons for organic chemical production are coal, petroleum, and natural gas. Wherever the necessary hydrocarbons exist in abundance as natural resource deposits organic chemical intermediates used in the making of synthetic fibers can be produced. After considering the distribution of hydro-carbon resources in the United States relative to the fiber-market regions, the Texas-Gulf Coast region and the West Virginia area were selected as the two major raw-material regions likely to be affected by the development of synthetic fibers.

The Texas-Gulf Coast

Chemical output in the Texas-Gulf region has shown remarkable growth in the post-World War II years because of the fabulous technology of petrochemical production. Two of the major hydro-carbon feedstocks for chemical manufacture are natural gas and the gases from cracking operations in the refining of petroleum. Other feedstocks can be used. Before natural gas is transported by pipeline the heavier, easily liquefiable hydrocarbons, or "natural" gasoline, are removed. In the process natural gasoline plants take off some of the lighter hydrocarbons for use as raw materials in chemical manufacture.[3]

The demand for high-octane motor fuel has led to the develop-ment of refining processes for upgrading gasoline. Reforming creates aromatic hydrocarbons for the manufacture of chemicals, such as benzene, toluene, and xylene. To a lesser extent, crude oil and distillate stocks (obtained in the initial step of the refining of crude oil) are used for chemical manufacture. Moreover, liquefied petroleum gas (LPG) is a chemical feedstock, since it contains raw materials, such as liquid propane and butane.

West Virginia

Chemical production is scattered all through the textile area of the United States, but the greatest concentration is in the Middle Atlantic region. For the location problem the area was broadened to include West Virginia, where chemical manufacture is based in the main on local raw materials, whereas the bulk of production in the rest of the Middle Atlantic region is dependent upon materials imported from other regions of the United States and abroad.[4]

[3] Walter Isard and Eugene W. Schooler, *Location Factors in the Petrochemi-cal Industry* (Washington, D. C.; Office of Technical Services, U. S. Depart-ment of Commerce, 1953), pp. 5-8; A. L. Burwell, "Raw Material Availability," *A Symposium on Resources of the Chemical Industry, Southwest, Industrial and Engineering Chemistry,* Vol. 43 (August, 1951), pp. 1712-1754.

[4] Borden R. Putman, Jr., and Richard F. Warren, "Production of Chemi-cals," *A Symposium on Resources for the Chemical Industry in the United States: Middle Atlantic, Industrial and Engineering Chemistry,* Vol. 45 (March 1953), pp. 524-528.

TABLE 13
CONSTANTS USED IN THE REGIONAL COST MODEL FOR THE LOCATION
ANALYSIS OF SYNTHETIC-FIBER PRODUCTION

Hypothetical Production Site	Cost Differences Relative to Texas			
	1000 Cu Ft Natural Gas (raw material in chemical manufacture)		Fuel Cost (per 1000 lb steam)	
	(1)		(2)	
	34-in. pipe	26- to 36-in. pipe	Low	High
Texas	$0.00	$0.00	$0.00	$0.00
Institute, W. Va.	0.1274	0.1666	0.00	0.00
Boston, Mass.	0.2080	0.2720	0.3120	0.4080
Wilmington, N. C.	0.1378	0.1802	0.2067	0.2703
Mobile, Ala.	0.0559	0.0731	0.0838	0.1126
Chattanooga, Tenn.	0.0910	0.1190	0.1365	0.1785
Birmingham, Ala.	0.0793	0.1037	0.1189	0.1555
Memphis, Tenn.	0.0624	0.0816	0.0936	0.1224
Puerto Rico	0.1378*	0.1775*	0.2067	0.2662

* Cost of oil-refinery waste gas relative to Houston, Texas, natural gas.

West Virginia has some natural gas and petroleum for petro-chemical manufacture, but the principal hydrocarbon resource is coal. As a raw-material region, it has the shortest supply lines to the major part of the textile area, and, in addition, many man-made fiber plants are already located there.

Puerto Rico

The other region in the analysis is Puerto Rico, regarded as an alternative to sites in the United States for any manufacturing operation which is labor intensive, such as fiber production. Most of the output of a fiber plant would have to be shipped to markets in the United States, since the demand on the island is insufficient to take the entire output of a large-scale plant.

Puerto Rico may also be a site for petrochemical production of some of the intermediates used in synthetic-fiber manufacture because of the existence there of oil-refining capacity.

TABLE 13 (*Continued*)

Hypothetical Production Site	Cost Differences Relative to Texas Power Cost (per kwhr)		Wage Rates per Hour	
			Chemical Manufacture	Synthetic-Fiber Manufacture
	Low (3)	High	(4)	(5)
Texas	$0.00	$0.00	$2.22	$1.95
Institute, W. Va.	0.00	0.00	2.10	1.79
Boston, Mass.	0.002184	0.002856	1.86	1.78
Wilmington, N. C.	0.001447	0.001892	1.82	1.78
Mobile, Ala.	0.000587	0.000768	1.82	1.78
Chattanooga, Tenn.	0.000955	0.001250	1.82	1.78
Birmingham, Ala.	0.000833	0.001089	1.82	1.78
Memphis, Tenn.	0.000655	0.000857	1.82	1.78
Puerto Rico	0.001447	0.001864	3.42	1.52
				1.31
				1.10

2. REGIONAL PARAMETERS FOR VARIABLE-COST COMPUTATIONS

With the exception of transportation outlays on raw materials other than natural gas and the shipment of intermediates to fiber plants, Table 13 contains the set of parameters to convert inputs per unit of output into variable costs at each hypothetical production site for both stages of the synthetic-fiber industry.

In location analysis the end result sought is cost differences between regions rather than the absolute magnitude of each cost. To compute regional variable-cost differences, the Texas-Gulf Coast was selected as the base region. The procedure for costing each input is described in the succeeding sections.

Transportation Costs

Chemical Intermediates and Raw Materials

In costing the alternatives of producing chemical intermediates

TABLE 13 (*Continued*)

Hypothetical Production Site	Weighted Average Cost of Transporting 100 Lb Synthetic Fibers to the National Market		
	Carload Rates	(6)	Less-than-Carload
Texas	$1.38		$2.17
Institute, W. Va.	0.98		1.51
Boston, Mass.	1.10		1.72
Wilmington, N. C.	0.96		1.34
Mobile, Ala.	1.16		1.63
Chattanooga, Tenn.	0.95		1.34
Birmingham, Ala.	0.94		1.34
Memphis, Tenn.	1.14		1.62
Puerto Rico	2.65†		2.89†

† Water—rail

in Puerto Rico, West Virginia, or the fiber-market regions, instead of the Texas-Gulf, transportation outlays on the assembly of raw materials or the shipment of intermediates to fiber plants were computed for both rail and water movements.

Rail Rates

The highest possible rail rates are class rates and the lowest are commodity rates established for bulk hauls. Both class rates and commodity rates (actual or estimated) were obtained for each raw material and each chemical intermediate. An example of the procedure is given in Table 14 for the shipment of nylon salt from Texas to the other hypothetical sites; a similar set of computations would be made for the alternative of assemblying the raw materials at the non-Texas sites.

Water Rates

The lowest possible transportation costs are for movements by water. Each hypothetical site was selected because it can be reached from tidewater locations on the Texas-Gulf by barge via the intercoastal system or the inland waterway system or by ocean-going chemical tanker. Moreover, by using water-transportation costs for sites in the United States Puerto Rico can be brought into the analysis on an equal basis.

A uniform procedure was followed in estimating the cost of water shipments for chemicals or chemical raw materials. Isard and Schooler have estimated that the following representative rates apply on chemicals for efficient barge operations over long distances:[5]

Type of Shipment	Mills per Ton-Mile
Noncorrosive chemicals using nonpressure tanks	3.0
Corrosive chemicals not requiring pressure tanks	3.5
Chemicals requiring pressure tanks	8.0

Estimated rates for water movements by ship have also been published in *Location Factors in the Petrochemical Industry* for both small and large tankers:[6]

Type of Shipment	Mills per Ton-Mile	
	5000-Ton Tanker	10,000–12,000-Ton Tanker
Noncorrosive chemicals using nonpressure tanks	4.5	3.5
Corrosive chemicals not requiring pressure tanks	5.0	4.0
Chemicals requiring pressure tanks	6.5	5.5

By use of these rates water-transport costs are tabulated in Table 15 by way of an example for the movement of 250 pounds of nylon salt, a noncorrosive, nonpressure chemical.

Natural Gas

One technological possibility for producing chemical intermediates in regions without local supplies of hydrocarbon raw materials is the use of natural gas. Whatever noncompetitive pricing practices may exist in the sale of natural gas, the only reasonable assumption in a location study is that in the long run the price at various sites will exceed the price at the source of the natural gas by at least the cost of transportation.

Isard and Schooler point out that the two most important variables which determine the cost of transporting natural gas by pipe-

[5] Isard and Schooler, *op. cit.,* p. 20.
[6] *Ibid.*

TABLE 14

RAIL SHIPMENT OF 250 POUNDS OF NYLON SALT IN SOLUTION FROM
ORANGE, TEXAS, TO HYPOTHETICAL PRODUCTION SITES*

Hypothetical Production Site	Rail Class Rates per 100 lb^a	Freight Charge 250 lb	Estimated Rail Commodity Rates per 100 lb^b	Freight Charge 250 lb
Boston, Mass	$2.42	$6.05	$1.91	$4.78
Institute, W. Va.	1.73	4.33	1.30^c	3.25
Wilmington, N. C.	1.80	4.50	1.35	3.38
Chattanooga, Tenn.	10.4^d	2.60	1.04	2.60
Birmingham, Ala.	1.21	3.03	0.90	2.25
Mobile, Ala.	0.97	2.43	0.75	1.88
Memphis, Tenn.	1.07	2.68	0.83^c	2.07

* Source: Except for the estimated commodity rates to Institute and Memphis, data are supplied by Mr. R. W. Marshall, Director, Traffic Department, E. I. du Pont de Nemours & Co., Wilmington, Del., by letter of May 28, 1954.

All rates have been computed to include the 15 per cent ex parte 175 increase and the 3 per cent Federal transportation tax.

^{a} Present class rail rates on hexamethylene diammonium adipate solution in tank cars, described as chemicals, NOIBN, are 40 per cent of first class, ICC Docket 28300 scale.

^{b} Estimated from existing commodity rates from Orange, Texas, to Chattanooga, Tenn., Martinsville, Va., Seaford, Del., and Washington, W. Va., based on 35 per cent of first class, ICC Docket 15879, Appendix E, scale for short-line distances.

^{c} Rates to Institute and Memphis were approximated. The existing commodity rate to Chattanooga was calculated as a percentage of first class, ICC 28300 scale. This percentage was then applied to first class, 28300, rates from Orange to Institute and Memphis.

^{d} At Chattanooga, Tenn., a commodity rate of $1.04 is already established.

line are the diameter of the pipe and the load factor in the operation.[7] For a 34-inch pipe with a 90 to 95 per cent load factor they estimate a transport cost of 1.3 cents per 1000 cubic feet per 100 miles; and for a smaller 26- to 30-inch pipe with a 60 to 65 per cent load factor, 1.7 cents per 1000 cubic feet per 100 miles.

To cost the natural gas at market sites in the United States, it is assumed that the gas is shipped hypothetically from Houston, Texas, a representative point of heavy chemical output in the Southwest. Straight-line distances are employed to estimate the cost differences at other regional sites over Houston: Boston, Mass., 1600 miles; Institute, W. Va., 980 miles; Wilmington, N. C., 1060

[7] *Ibid.*, pp. 18–19.

miles; Chattanooga, Tenn., 700 miles; Birmingham, Ala., 610 miles; Mobile, Ala., 430 miles; and Memphis, Tenn., 480 miles.

The transport-cost differences for each site relative to Texas per 1000 cubic feet of natural gas are given in column one of Table 13 and can be used to cost the natural-gas input for any production process based on its use.

It should be noted that West Virginia has local natural-gas supplies. For the location problem in question the natural-gas price in West Virginia for chemical manufacture is assumed to be the price in Texas, plus pipeline transport costs from Texas to Institute, even though Texas gas may not actually be used. Local supplies of natural gas will have in the long run an equivalent Btu price and, for obvious reasons, cannot have a higher Btu price. For the long run, therefore, the price difference between Texas and West Virginia natural gas can be approximated by the transport cost on natural gas hypothetically shipped from Houston to Institute.

Oil-Refinery Waste Gas in Puerto Rico

Puerto Rico, of course, has no natural gas, but it has oil-refining capacity. In all processes using natural gas as a raw material in the United States it is assumed that there is no technological barrier to the use of waste gas from cracking operations in Puerto Rican oil refineries. The problem is to determine theoretically what price will be put on oil-refinery gases in Puerto Rico.

TABLE 15

WATER SHIPMENT OF 250 POUNDS OF NYLON SALT IN SOLUTION FROM
ORANGE, TEXAS, TO HYPOTHETICAL PRODUCTION SITES

Hypothetical Production Site	Statute Miles from Orange, Texas[a]	Water-Transport Medium Barge (Mills)	Tanker	Water-Transport Cost
Boston, Mass.	2364		3.5/4.5	$1.03 to 1.33
Institute, W. Va.	1800	3.0		0.68
Wilmington, N. C.	1601		3.5/4.5	0.70 to 0.90
Chattanooga, Tenn.	1516	3.0		0.58
Birmingham, Ala.	910	3.0		0.33
Mobile, Ala.	414	3.0		0.15
Memphis, Tenn.	781	3.0		0.30
Puerto Rico	1871		3.5/4.5	0.83 to 1.05

[a] *Distances Between United States Ports.* U. S. Department of Commerce, Coast and Geodetic Survey, Serial No. 444. (Washington: U. S. Government Printing Office, 1938.)

Since waste gases can be used as fuel within the oil refinery, a price equivalent at least to alternative fuels on a Btu basis can be expected. Fuel oil is one of the principal refinery products in Puerto Rico. The source of the crude oil is Venezuela. Venezuelan crude- and fuel-oil prices are determined by the demand generated in the huge New York market; that is, crude- and fuel-oil prices in New York, *less* transport costs from Venezuela, yield fuel-oil and crude-oil prices in Venezuela. By a similar process of reasoning fuel- and crude-oil prices in Puerto Rico equal fuel- and crude-oil prices in Venezuela, *plus* transport costs. Since Puerto Rico is close to the straight line from Venezuela to New York, the price of fuel oil in Puerto Rico can be approximated by assuming that it is equal to the New York price *less* what it would theoretically cost to transport it from Puerto Rico to New York. If the price of fuel oil is determined in this way, so will the price of refinery gases on a Btu basis.

To compute the transport-cost differential which Houston, Texas, has over Puerto Rico for gas as a chemical raw material, the following must be done:

1. Calculate the transport cost on the required volume of natural gas to New York, where all fuel prices on a Btu basis must be equivalent, to obtain *Houston's advantage over New York*.
2. Compute the cost of transporting the Btu equivalent in fuel oil from Puerto Rico to New York to obtain *Puerto Rico's advantage over New York*.
3. The difference between Houston's advantage over New York and Puerto Rico's advantage over New York represents *Houston's advantage over Puerto Rico*.

The cost of transporting 1000 cubic feet of natural gas from Houston to New York (1420 straight-line miles) is 18.46 cents by 34-inch pipeline and 24.14 cents by 26- to 30-inch line. A cubic foot of natural gas contains on the average 1000 Btu, and the Btu equivalent in fuel oil (No. 6 or Bunker C) is 0.1587 barrel.[8] Published costs for transporting oil by tanker vary somewhat. For a 34-degree-gravity oil shipped by the large new tankers Emerson estimates the cost to be 1.5 to 1.8 cents per barrel per 100 statute

---

[8] A barrel of No. 6 fuel oil contains 6.3 million Btu. Since the Btu content of natural gas is approximately 1000 per cubic foot, 0.1587 barrel fuel oil equals 1000 cubic feet natural gas.

miles.[9]   Another report suggests 1.9 cents per barrel for crude oil and 2.2 cents for Bunker C fuel oil.[10]   Since the second figure on crude oil is close to Emerson's upper figure, it is assumed that 1.8 cents would be the cost of shipping fuel oil by large tanker. For a relatively small tanker it is believed that the cost would be a shade larger than the high estimate of 2.2 cents in the *Oil and Gas Journal* and is assumed to be 2.5 cents.

From the data above the cost disadvantage of oil-refinery gas in Puerto Rico with respect to natural gas at Houston can be obtained:

	34-in. pipe	26 to 30-in. pipe
(1) Houston's advantage over New York on 1000 cu ft natural gas	18.46 cents	24.14 cents
(2) Puerto Rico's advantage over New York on 0.1587 bbl No. 6 fuel oil (1611 miles)	(large tanker) 4.59 cents	(small tanker) 6.39 cents
(3) Houston's natural gas advantage over Puerto Rico's refinery gas per 1000 cu ft equals (1) − (2)	13.87 cents to 17.75 cents	

Thus the price of refinery gas at Puerto Rico is 13.87 to 17.75 cents per 1000 cubic feet *greater than* the price of natural gas at Houston, Texas, as shown in column one of Table 13.

Synthetic Fibers

The last column of Table 13 (which summarizes the parameters of the cost model) shows a weighted average cost of transporting 100 pounds of synthetic fibers to the total national market, obtained for each hypothetical production site by employing the regional market potentials developed earlier in this chapter: New England, 12 per cent; Middle Atlantic, 20 per cent; East South, 36 per cent; Central South, 22 per cent; and West South, 10 per cent.

[9] H. N. Emerson, "The Place of the Tanker in the Transportation of Energy," Paper presented before 32nd Annual Meeting, American Petroleum Institute, Chicago, November 11, 1952, p. 5.

[10] "How Transportation Costs Compare," *Oil and Gas Journal*, Vol. 52 (March 29, 1954), p. 132.

For hypothetical sites in the United States the transport medium is rail and both LCL and CL rates are employed. Rail rates are the same for all synthetic fibers. LCL rates are 50 per cent of first class, Uniform Freight Classification No. 1. For CL shipments within the Southern Territory rates are 31 per cent of ICC 13494 for 30,000 pounds minimum weight; and for all other movements, 32.5 per cent of ICC 28300.[11]

Combined water and rail costs were used to estimate the cost of transporting synthetic fibers from Puerto Rico to the fiber markets in the United States. The same rate applies on the shipment of fibers by water from Puerto Rico to any U. S. Atlantic or Gulf port. The cost figures were obtained by using a rate of $1.93 per 100 pounds (for a shipment of nylon yarn in boxes of 9 cubic feet weighing 121 pounds) from San Juan, Puerto Rico, to the U. S. ports for each fiber-market region. The figure of $1.93 per 100 pounds includes terminal charges at San Juan, but not marine insurance, and covers the movement of cargo from pier to pier only.[12] The charge was computed at rail rates from the ports of entry in the United States to consuming centers for synthetic fibers selected to represent the market regions.

Regional Differences in Fuel Costs

In chemical-intermediate manufacture a fuel input is given in each production function for process heat, and, in addition, a steam requirement in each case is listed separately. For synthetic-fiber manufacture the only fuel input is for steam production.

After long consideration it was concluded that differences in natural-gas costs (or oil-refinery gas at Puerto Rico) could also be used at all sites in the analysis to represent regional differences in fuel costs (except in the case of West Virginia). To cost the fuel input for process heat in chemical manufacture the transport-cost differences relative to Texas per 1000 cubic feet of natural gas, given in column one of Table 13, were used. For the steam requirement in both stages of manufacture the conversion factor utilized is an average Btu requirement of 1500 per pound of steam, and natural gas contains 1000 Btu per cubic foot. Column two of Table 13 shows fuel-cost differences relative to Texas per 1000 pounds of steam.

[11] Tariff East South 1008.
[12] Economic Development Administration, Commonwealth of Puerto Rico.

Why the use of natural gas can be assumed in obtaining regional differences in fuel costs—except for West Virginia—is explained below for each region.

New England

Boston represents New England, a region at a disadvantage with respect to all conventional fuels. Judging from the cost of alternative fuels used in the generation of electric power in Massachusetts in 1952, Btu prices were about the same for coal, fuel oil, and natural gas. The average cost per million Btu consumed reported by the Edison Electric Institute was $0.38 for coal, $0.351 for fuel oil, and $0.369 for natural gas.[13] Therefore it was concluded that the differences in natural-gas prices at Boston over Houston could represent New England's disadvantage for all fuels.

Middle Atlantic

Coal is used, of course, in West Virginia to generate heat and steam. The problem for economic theory is to determine how the Btu cost of coal in West Virginia compares with the Btu cost of natural gas in Texas, the base region for the calculation of cost differences.

In a market such as the greater New York-Philadelphia area all fuel costs on a Btu basis must be equated through time. Shipments of coal move to this area from West Virginia, as well as shipments of natural gas from Texas. The local price of coal at Institute (which is the hypothetical production site for West Virginia) should be lower than the price at New York, for example, by the cost of transportation to New York. Emerson has published costs on the movement of coal from West Virginia to the New York area:[14]

Transport Medium	Cost per 100 Miles per Long Ton	Btu Conversion Factor	Cost per Million Btu per Mile in Mills
Rail	$1.20 to $1.40	26 mil./ton	0.453 to 0.535
Coastwise collier	0.25 to 0.30	26 mil./ton	0.095 to 0.114

[13] *Analysis of Fuel for Electric Generation by the Electric Utility Industry.* Edison Electric Institute, Statistical Department. (New York: Edison Electric Institute, October, 1953.)

[14] Emerson, *op. cit.*, p. 8.

From these figures the cost of shipping coal from West Virginia by rail to Hampton Roads and collier to New York can be estimated:

	Lower Limit	Upper Limit
Coal by rail, 400 miles @ 0.458 to 0.535 mills per million Btu per mile	18.3 cents	21.4 cents
Coal by collier from Norfolk to New York, 340 statute miles @ 0.095 to 0.114 mills per million Btu per mile	3.2 cents	3.9 cents
Total	21.8 cents	25.3 cents

By comparison, the cost of transporting a million Btu of natural gas from Houston to New York (1420 straight-line miles) is 18.4 cents (34-inch pipe) to 24.1 cents (26- to 30-inch pipe). The comparative figures serve as the basis for assuming that in the long run the Btu price of fuel for steam and heat in West Virginia will be equated with the Btu price of natural gas in Texas. As shown in column two of Table 13, the two raw-material regions are equal in the advantage they possess over the other regions.

East South

For Wilmington, N. C., a comparison was made between the cost of delivering Btu equivalent amounts of coal from West Virginia and natural gas from Texas. To transport a million Btu of coal to Wilmington by rail-ocean collier, the cost is estimated to be 22.2 cents to 26.1 cents.[15] For the equivalent natural gas from Houston (1060 miles) the cost is 13.8 cents for 34-inch pipeline and 18 cents for 26- to 30-inch, which indicates that natural gas can be used to judge the relative position of the East South fiber-market region for fuel inputs.

Central South

Mobile, Ala., is very close to natural-gas fields, and it is believed that in the future natural gas will be the dominant fuel for industrial heat and steam. At Chattanooga coal deposits nearby in

---

[15] *Ibid.*   400 miles by rail, 18.3 to 21.4 cents; and 412 miles by collier, 3.9 to 4.7 cents.

upper Tennessee could make a difference. But in examining fuel
costs in Tennessee it appears that natural gas can be used to represent all fuel costs:[16]

Years	Average Cost per Million Btu Consumed in Cents		
	Coal	Fuel oil	Gas
1950	24.1	43.0	13.4
1951	20.7	44.0	13.5
1952	20.3	45.9	13.6

Birmingham, the other hypothetical site in the Central South,
also has coal resources but cannot be treated in the same manner
as West Virginia. The Birmingham area has no extensive surplus
of coal, and shipments are for short distances. In the long run, it
is believed that natural gas will have to augment coal for industrial steam and heat and that it can be used to obtain Birmingham's relative position for fuel costs.

West South, Puerto Rico, and Texas

Memphis, Tenn., which represents the West South fiber-market
region, is very close to the source of natural gas; this proximity
gives the fuel an advantage over all others.

Since refinery-gas prices in Puerto Rico are derived from the
pricing of fuel oil, the disadvantage relative to Houston's natural
gas can also measure the position of the island with respect to fuel
for heat and steam as well.

Because of the abundance of natural gas in the Texas-Gulf, the
region has an advantage in fuel costs for heat and steam over all
other regions in the problem except West Virginia.

Regional Differences in Power Costs

Once the method for dealing with differences in fuel costs was
evolved, it became clear that the same approach could be used to
generate power-cost differences for the sites in the problem. The
assumption underlying the treatment of power costs is that in the
long run increments in generating capacity will have to be supplied
by steam-electric plants, since the available hydroelectric capacity
at or near the sites in the analysis has been exhausted. An addi-

[16] *Analysis of Fuel for Electric Generation, op. cit.*

tional assumption made is that the chief differences in power costs at the sites will be attributable to differences in fuel costs.

A model steam-electric plant can be employed to estimate the fuel input necessary to generate a kilowatthour of electricity. Inasmuch as existing steam-electric plants vary considerably in thermal efficiency (Btu per kilowatthour) the model steam plant is based on the use of fuel in the steam-electric plants in 1952 which showed the highest efficiency. It is assumed that a new steam-electric plant based on natural gas would require the same input, 10,532 Btu per kilowatthour, as the W. L. Lee plant of the Duke Power Company.[17] Since natural gas contains approximately 1000 Btu per cubic foot, the output of one kilowatthour of electricity requires 10.5 cubic feet of natural gas.

Regional differences in power costs per kilowatthour, derived in the manner just described, are given on column three of Table 13 and are used to cost the power inputs in each production function.

Water Costs

The cost of water in synthetic-fiber manufacture does not enter into the regional cost model as a separate variable production cost. The cost of water is partially absorbed as a fixed cost through the outlay on the pumping installation and the necessary pipes; a part of the over-all power input is for the pumping station.

In Chapter 7 the general availability of water in each region is considered in summarizing the results of the study.

Regional Differences in Labor Costs

Chemical-Intermediate Manufacture

Straight-time average hourly earnings in industrial chemical plants for the United States by selected regions are given in Table 16 and are derived from studies made by the Bureau of Labor Statistics in 1946, 1949, and 1951. To provide a more realistic picture of the current wage level, the 1951 figures were adjusted upward to the January 1954 level but with no allowance for any intervening changes between regions.

---

[17] *Bituminous Coal Annual,* 1953 (Washington, D. C.: Bituminous Coal Institute, 1953), p. 101. It should be noted that if each chemical or fiber plant had its own power unit and if steam could be exhausted to process operations there would be a lower net Btu consumption of fuel per kilowatthour of electricity.

TABLE 16

STRAIGHT-TIME AVERAGE HOURLY EARNINGS IN INDUSTRIAL CHEMICAL ESTABLISHMENTS
FOR THE UNITED STATES AND SELECTED REGIONS*

Date of Study	U. S.[d]	New England	Middle Atlantic	Border States	Southeast	Great Lakes	Southwest	Pacific
January 1946[a]	$1.14	$1.03	$1.11	$1.20	$0.79	$1.16	$1.15	$1.22
April 1949[b]	1.51	1.35	1.46	1.61	1.20	1.54	1.62	1.55
November–December 1951[c]	1.76	1.53	1.77	1.80	1.48	1.72	1.94	1.78
January 1954, estimated[e]	2.04	1.81	2.05	2.08	1.76	2.00	2.22	2.06

* Sources:

[a] *Wage Structure, Industrial Chemicals, 1946.* Series 2, No. 25, p. 14, Table 4. U. S. Department of Labor, Bureau of Labor Statistics.

[b] *Wage Structure, Industrial Chemicals, 1949.* Series 2, No. 73, p. 4, Table 2.

[c] *Wage Structure, Industrial Chemicals, October–November 1951.* Series 2, No. 87; weighted averages were prepared from the data in Table 4, p. 7.

[d] Figures for the United States include data for regions not shown separately here.

[e] The hourly wage rate in industrial organic chemicals for January 1954 was $2.08 and for organic chemicals, $2.01. *Monthly Labor Review* (April 1954) Vol. 77, pp. 471–472. Since both industrial organic and inorganic chemicals are represented in the November–December 1951 study, an average of $0.28 per hour has been added to the United States and regional figures for 1951 to adjust them to the January 1954 level.

As far as one can judge from the 1951 data, the wage rates in the BLS study are for a set of high-wage-paying chemical operations in the Southwest and for a relatively low set of wage-paying industries in New England and the Southeast; therefore, it was necessary to adjust the wage differentials in row four of Table 16. For the complex chemical processes in this location study it is believed that relatively high-wage chemical occupations are involved. By using Texas (Southwest) as a bench mark the New England wage rate was increased by 5 cents per hour, the Southeast, by 6 cents, the Border States, by 2 cents, and the average for the United States, by 2 cents.

To give special consideration to the problem of obtaining the necessary production workers for a complex chemical operation in Puerto Rico, it is assumed that the direct labor cost would be at least one and two thirds of the average for the United States ($2.06), or $3.42 per hour.

The complete tabulation of hourly wage rates used to cost the labor input in chemical-intermediate manufacture is contained in column four of Table 13.

Synthetic Fiber Production

A special regional tabulation of gross average hourly earnings of production workers in the synthetic fibers industry (SIC 2825) was obtained from the Bureau of Labor Statistics for January 1954 but cannot be reproduced here because no tests were made for adequacy of sample and consistency of trend.[18] However, the results of the tabulation have been used to judge the direction of regional wage differentials. In column five of Table 13 hourly wage rates are given for each hypothetical site for costing the labor input in synthetic-fiber production.

The U. S. average hourly wage rate of $1.79 for January 1954 was used as a bench mark.[19] Judging from the present geographical concentration of synthetic-fiber capacity, it was decided that for Institute, W. Va., the average would be applicable. For New England and the South the BLS tabulation showed little reason for assuming a substantial wage difference at each hypothetical regional site, and the hourly wage used is $1.78.

To bring Texas into the analysis—to see if a raw-material region

---

[18] Letter of August 9, 1954, from Dudley E. Young, Assistant Chief, Division of Manpower and Employment Statistics, Bureau of Labor Statistics, U. S. Department of Labor. SIC 2825 includes the older man-made fibers, such as rayon and acetate, as well as the new synthetic fibers.

[19] *Monthly Labor Review,* Vol. 77 (June 1954), p. 706.

can attract fiber capacity—a wage rate was derived from prevailing wage rates in chemical manufacture. The Texas rate of $2.22 per hour in chemical output is 16 cents above the U. S. average; therefore, a wage rate of $1.95, 16 cents above the synthetic-fiber average, is used in the cost analysis.

Puerto Rico

In the case of Puerto Rico it was necessary to estimate wage rates separately for the polymer and spinning operation in synthetic-fiber production. In a "typical" fiber plant 15 per cent of the labor force is employed in the polymer and spinning area and the balance in the textile area and in administrative and general service occupations.[20] Because all the skills necessary for polymer and spinning occupations might not be available in the Puerto Rican labor force the supposition is made of an hourly wage rate of $3.09—one and one half times the U. S. average in chemical production—if any sizable number of workers has to be recruited from the United States. For the remaining 85 per cent of the labor force costs are calculated at alternative wage rates of $1.25, $1.00, and $0.75 per hour. The weighted average wage rates for costing the labor input in Puerto Rico, given in column five of Table 13, are $1.52 per hour, $1.31, and $1.10 for labor of equivalent efficiency to U. S. labor.

3. LARGE-SCALE PRODUCTION ECONOMIES IN CHEMICAL-INTERMEDIATE MANUFACTURE

In applying location theory to the synthetic-fiber industry it has been noted that agglomeration economies are very significant in determining the location of the chemical-intermediate stage but not in the fiber stage, except that fiber plants in Puerto Rico would have to be as large as those in the United States. Four types of agglomeration economy are important in the location of chemical-intermediate plants: (*a*) large-scale production economies; (*b*) integration economies; (*c*) localization economies; and (*d*) external economies.[21] Large-scale production economies can be estimated and utilized in the cost model to judge their significance in the location of chemical-intermediate plants. Qualitative weight alone is given to the other agglomeration economies.

---

[20] See p. 82.
[21] See pp. 54–56.

"Power" Rules

In chemical manufacture raw-material inputs and utility consumption tend to increase proportionately with the size of plant, but nonlinear average behavior is characteristic of cost categories associated with investment in plant and equipment and the labor input.

Chemical engineers use so-called "power" rules to relate annual plant capacity and (a) investment in plant and equipment and (b) labor hours per year. If the investment cost of a chemical plant with a given capacity is known, the cost of a plant with a different capacity can be estimated from the algebraic relationship $C_1/C_2 = (S_1/S_2)^n$ where C_1 is the capital cost of plant capacity S_1 and C_2, the capital cost of plant capacity S_2. The exponent n is often called the "plant" factor and is positive and less than 1. The plant factor varies from process to process. For a unit of production the plant factor can be used validly over a realistic capacity range only, since scale economies are not endless, and in each case there is a minimum initial capacity. Moreover, the investment behavior summarized in the plant factor applies to initial capacity only and not to capacity added later.[22]

The relationship between annual plant capacity and man-hours of labor per year can be expressed as $L_1/L_2 = (S_1/S_2)^n$ in which n is the so-called "labor" factor.[23]

Cost Behavior and Plant Size

By selecting a number of cost items which are related to plant investment and labor hours per year selected costs per 100 pounds of output can be computed to approximate the magnitude of scale economies along the lines of a procedure developed by Isard and Schooler.[24]

An example of the computation of scale economies per 100 pounds is given in Table 17 for nylon-salt plants of 60- and 90-million-pound annual capacity. The scale-economy factor gives the larger plant a cost advantage of $2.56 per 100 pounds over the smaller. How each cost component was estimated is described on p. 112:

[22] Cecil H. Chilton, " 'Six-Tenths' Factor Applies to Complete Plant Costs," *Chemical Engineering,* Vol. 57 (April 1950), pp. 112–114.

[23] Henry E. Wessel, "New Graph Correlates Operating Labor Data for Chemical Processes," *Chemical Engineering,* Vol. 59 (July 1952), pp. 209–210. For both power rules, if plant cost or man-hours of labor per year are plotted against annual plant capacity, the relationship will be a straight line on double logarithmic scale with a numerical slope equal to the plant or labor factor.

[24] Isard and Schooler, *op. cit.,* pp. 21–23.

TABLE 17

ESTIMATED SCALE ECONOMIES IN NYLON-SALT PRODUCTION

Plant Factor: 0.60^a	Labor Factor: 0.22^b	
Plant capacity (million lb per year)	60	90
Plant investment (in $ 000)^b	37,500	47,800
Labor man-hours per year^c	178,000	195,000
Selected Costs per Year in $ 000		
Operating labor	395	433
Supervision	40	43
Plant maintenance	1,500	1,912
Equipment and operating supplies	225	287
Payroll overhead	178	214
Indirect production cost	1,080	1,337
General office overhead	216	268
Depreciation	3,750	4,780
Taxes	375	478
Insurance	375	478
Interest	1,000	1,912
Total:	$9,634	$12,142
Selected Costs per 100 lb:	$16.05	$13.49

^{a} The plant factor is an average obtained for many different chemical process plants. Chilton, *op. cit.*, pp. 209–210.
^{b} The labor factor was derived by Wessel's procedure, *op. cit.*, pp. 209–210.
^{c} Labor man-hours per year were obtained by multiplying the labor coefficient for nylon salt per lb by 60 million lb per year.
^{d} The estimated plant and equipment cost of $37.5 million for a nylon-salt plant (starting from basic raw materials) with 60-million-lb annual capacity is the basis for estimating the investment cost of the plant with 90-million-lb capacity. The figure of $37.5 million was derived in the following way. When the nylon-salt plant at Orange, Texas, was built in 1945, the reported outlay was $20.0 million (*Oil and Gas Journal,* Vol. 44 (June 2, 1945), p. 54). In a Defense Production Administration release (DPA–434, September 3, 1952) it was reported that for January 1, 1951, the production capacity in the United States for adiponitrile and hexamethylene diamine, two nylon-salt intermediates, was 61 and 62 million lb, respectively; 0.53 of the former and 0.51 of the latter are required per lb of nylon salt so that nylon-salt capacity was about 120 million lb in 1951. Du Pont was the sole producer and had two nylon salt plants—at Orange, Texas, and Belle, W. Va. It was assumed that the capacity was split evenly. In this way the $20.0 million figure announced for Orange in 1945 was related to roughly 60-million-lb annual capacity. To bring the investment cost up to the 1954 price level, the Composite Construction Cost Index was used (U. S. Department of Commerce): 1945, 66.6; 1954, 122.0.

1. Operating labor: by multiplying labor man-hours per year by wage rates in chemical manufacture.

2. Supervisory labor: 10 per cent of operating labor.

3. Plant maintenance: 4 per cent of investment cost.

4. Equipment and operating supplies: 15 per cent of plant maintenance.

5. Payroll overhead: 15 per cent of direct labor and supervision, plus 7.5 per cent of plant maintenance.

6. Indirect production cost: 50 per cent of operating labor, supervision, plant maintenance, and equipment and operating supplies.

7. General office overhead: 10 per cent of the items in 6.

8. Depreciation: 10 per cent of total plant investment.

9. Taxes: One per cent of capital investment to cover property taxes, etc.

10. Insurance: One per cent of plant investment.

11. Interest: 4 per cent of plant investment.

4. THE COMPUTATION OF REGIONAL COST DIFFERENCES

In determining regional cost differences in the synthetic-fiber industry computations were first made of comparative outlays in the chemical intermediate stage of production alone. Below is a set of inputs for the manufacture of 100 pounds of the chemical intermediate for nylon 66 fiber from benzene via air oxidation of cyclohexane, first in the form of the original production function and then with adjustments for the cost computation:

Production Function for Nylon Salt*		Adjusted for Computing† Variable Costs
Raw Material Inputs		
Benzene	216 lb	216 lb
Ammonia	18 lb	18 lb
Natural gas	954 cu ft	954 cu ft
Utilities		
Steam	6,838 lb	10,257 cu ft natural gas
Electric power	85 kwhr	893 cu ft natural gas
Fuel gas	1,555 cu ft	1,555 cu ft natural gas
Labor		
Man-hours	0.205	0.205

* See p. 42, Table 4, column one.
† See pp. 94–95, 102–105. The fuel equivalent of 6838 lb of steam is 10,257 cu ft of natural gas; and of 85 kwhr, 893 cu ft of natural gas.

Illustrative Regional Cost Differences
in Chemical-Intermediate Manufacture

Table 18 shows the physical inputs converted into regional variable-cost differences per 100 pounds of nylon salt. To simplify the
matter, only four sites are used. The Texas-Gulf Coast raw-material region is the base for computing the cost differences, and
Orange, Texas, is the hypothetical production site for sample
costs; Boston represents the New England fiber-market region and
Mobile, the Central South; Puerto Rico is the fourth region in the
illustration.

For each 100 pounds of nylon 66 fiber 250 pounds of nylon salt
in solution must be transported from the chemical-intermediate
plant to the fiber plant.[25]   Column one of Table 18 shows the
transportation cost that would be incurred on shipping nylon salt
to the other points, if it were manufactured in Texas.   Columns
two, three, and four show the outlays on assembling the raw materials—natural gas, benzene, and ammonia—at the other sites to
test the alternative of producing at non-Texas points.   Column five
is obtained by subtracting the assembly costs from the cost of
transporting nylon salt from Texas to show the transport-cost advantage or disadvantage of the other sites relative to the raw-
material region.

Columns six, seven, and eight show the advantage or disadvantage relative to Texas in fuel, power, and labor costs; and the total
cost picture is summarized in column nine (by the summation of
columns five, six, seven, and eight).

By examining the total cost column of Table 18 the significance
of transportation costs in chemical-intermediate production is
made clear by the nylon-salt example.   For the United States
variable costs would be minimized by location in fiber-market
regions if the transportation medium is rail.   But for both the
United States and Puerto Rico variable costs are minimized by
producing in Texas if nylon salt is shipped to fiber plants by water.

In chemical-intermediate manufacture agglomeration economies
may be just as important a location factor as variable-cost minimization.   Table 17 shows selected production costs per 100 pounds
for nylon-salt plants with 60- and 90-million-pound annual capacity.
The scale-economy advantage of the larger plant over the smaller
is $2.56 per 100 pounds.[26]   If, for the sake of illustration, the
larger initial capacity were built in Texas but the smaller initial

[25] See p. 75.
[26] See p. 111.

TABLE 18

SELECTED VARIABLE COSTS PER 100 POUNDS OF NYLON SALT
TEXAS-GULF VS. PRODUCTION IN TEXTILE AREA OR PUERTO RICO

Hypothetical Plant Location		Transport Cost		Transport Cost from Nearest Large-Scale Producing Center	
		Nylon Salt from Orange, Texas	Natural Gas from Houston, Texas	Benzene[d]	Ammonia[e]
		(1)	(2)	(3)	(4)
Orange, Texas		$0.00	$0.00	$0.00	$0.00
Boston, Mass.	(1)[a]	6.05	0.20 to 0.26	1.38	0.14
	(2)[b]	4.78		0.71	0.14
	(3)[c]	1.03 to 1.33		0.20 to 0.26	0.03 to 0.06
Mobile, Ala.	(1)	2.43	0.05 to 0.07	1.10	0.13
	(2)	1.88		0.67	0.13
	(3)	0.15		0.15	0.06
Puerto Rico	(3)	0.83 to 1.05	0.13 to 0.17[f]	0.75 to 0.96	0.20 to 0.24

[a] Class rail rates.   [c] Water transport costs.
[b] Commodity rail rates.
[d] Benzene for Boston from Marcus Hook, Pa.; for Mobile, from Birmingham, Ala.; and for Puerto Rico, from Texas City, Texas.
[e] Ammonia for Boston from Philadelphia, Pa.; Mobile, rail from Vicksburg, Miss., and water from Lake Charles, La.; Puerto Rico, from Texas City, Texas.
[f] Cost disadvantage of oil refinery gas in Puerto Rico relative to Houston, Texas, natural gas.

TABLE 18 (*Continued*)

Hypothetical Plant Location		Cost Advantage (−) or Disadvantage (+) Relative to Texas-Gulf Production				
		Transport Costs (5)	Fuel Costs (6)	Power Costs (7)	Labor Costs (8)	Total Selected Costs (9)
Orange, Texas		$0.00	$0.00	$0.00	$0.00	$0.00
Boston, Mass.	(1)	−4.27 to −4.33	+2.45 to 3.20	+0.18 to 0.24	−0.07	−0.96 to −1.71
	(2)	−3.67 to −3.73				−0.36 to −1.11
	(3)	−0.43 to −0.48				+1.96 to +2.62
Mobile, Ala.	(1)	−1.13 to −1.15	+0.66 to 0.86	+0.05 to 0.07	−0.08	−0.29 to −0.50
	(2)	−1.01 to −1.03				−0.17 to −0.37
	(3)	+0.11 to +0.13				+0.82 to +1.00
Puerto Rico	(3)	+0.25 to +0.32	+1.63 to 2.10	+0.12 to 0.16	+0.25	+2.25 to +2.83

capacity in fiber-market regions or in Puerto Rico, then the raw-material region would have the scale-economy advantage. By comparing $2.56 with the total selected cost column of Table 18 it can be seen that in all cases the agglomeration saving of the raw-material region wipes out the variable-cost advantage—from rail transportation—of the fiber-market regions and increases the cost disadvantage of Puerto Rico. Thus, one could conclude from the illustration that nylon salt is raw-material oriented and could not be produced economically in the other regions. But, as Chapter 7 shows, there are cases in which the scale-economy consideration does not enter into the analysis and that nylon salt could also be produced advantageously outside raw-material regions.

**Illustrative Regional Cost Differences
in Synthetic-Fiber Manufacture**

Once the orientation of the chemical-intermediate stage is determined, it is possible to analyze the location of the synthetic-fiber stage. To continue the example, physical inputs are given below for the production of 100 pounds of nylon 66 staple fiber:

Production Function for Nylon 66 Staple Fiber*		Adjusted for Computing Variable Costs
Raw material inputs		
Nylon salt	250 lb	250 lb
Utilities		
Steam	5000 lb	7500 cu ft natural gas
Electric power	120 kwhr	1260 cu ft natural gas
Labor		
Man-hours	9.7	9.7

* See p. 73.

The physical inputs are converted into regional variable-cost differences in Table 19. In the illustration the assumption is made that nylon salt is manufactured in Texas for possible use there in fiber manufacture or for shipment to fiber plants located in fiber-market regions or in Puerto Rico. Transportation costs on nylon salt and the movement of fibers to the five regional markets are tabulated in columns one, two and three. Columns four and five show fuel- and power-cost differentials relative to Texas. Total labor costs are given in column six, and total selected costs for transportation, fuel, power, and labor, in column seven.

Plant location in the fiber stage is determined by regional differences in variable costs. Some general implications of the cost analysis—elaborated more fully in Chapter 7—can be gleaned from the sample in Table 19. Synthetic fibers are not likely to be produced in a raw-material region such as Texas because of high labor costs. New England is a high-cost region because of its disadvantage in transportation, fuel, and power costs. In the United States the southern portion of the textile area, as illustrated by Mobile in the example, is especially favored; and in spite of a cost disadvantage in transportation, fuel, and power the labor saving in Puerto Rico shows that the island can compete favorably with the United States.

TABLE 19

SELECTED VARIABLE COSTS PER 100 POUNDS OF NYLON 66 STAPLE FIBER

Hypothetical Plant Location	Transport Cost			
	Nylon Salt from Orange, Texas	Synthetic Fibers to National Market (weighted average)		Total Transport Cost
		Carload	LCL	
	(1)	(2)		(3)
Orange, Texas	$0.00	$1.38	$2.17	$1.38 to $2.17
Boston, Mass. (1)[a]	6.05	1.10	1.72	7.15 to 7.77
(2)[b]	4.78			5.88 to 6.50
(3)[c]	1.03 to 1.33			2.13 to 3.05
Mobile, Ala. (1)	2.43	1.16	1.63	3.59 to 4.06
(2)	1.88			3.04 to 3.51
(3)	0.15			1.31 to 1.78
Puerto Rico (3)	0.83 to 1.05	2.65	2.89	3.48 to 3.54

[a] Class rail rates.
[b] Commodity rail rates.
[c] Water, nylon salt; rail, fibers.

TABLE 19 (Continued)

Hypothetical Plant Location	Cost Differences Relative to Texas		Total Labor Cost	Total Selected Costs
	Fuel Costs	Power Costs		
	(4)	(5)	(6)	(7)
Orange, Texas	$0.00	$0.00	$18.92	$20.30 to $21.09
Boston, Mass. (1)	+1.56 to 2.04	+0.26 to 0.34	17.27	26.24 to 27.42
(2)				24.97 to 26.15
(3)				21.22 to 22.14
Mobile, Ala. (1)	+0.42 to 0.55	+0.07 to 0.09	17.27	21.35 to 21.97
(2)				20.80 to 21.42
(3)				19.07 to 19.69
Puerto Rico (3)	+1.03 to 1.33	+0.17 to 0.22	14.81^d	19.49 to 20.30
			12.74^d	17.42 to 18.23
			10.58^d	15.36 to 16.17

[d] $3.09 per hour for 15 per cent of labor force in polymer and spinning; and for 85 per cent in textile area and general service and administrative occupations, alternatively, $1.25, $1.00, and $0.75 per hour.   See pp. 106–109.

Chapter 7

The Location Pattern of
the Synthetic-Fiber Industry

The hypothesis which has guided this study began with the proposition that the general location factors of the synthetic-fiber industry could be deduced from production functions and analysis of agglomeration economies. Then a spatial framework made up of regions suitable for plant location in the light of the general location factors was established. General substitution analysis has been used to convert production functions into production and distribution cost differences at selected regional sites. Appendices A, B, and C contain the cost calculations in tabular form.[1]

Completion of the procedure now calls for the analysis of the cost results in order to point out basic regional advantages and disadvantages, to show for each stage of the synthetic-fiber industry the minimum-cost regions among all those tested, and to determine the basic type of location orientation of each stage. The results must also be compared with the existing geographical distribution of plants. A long-term forecast of the demand for synthetic fibers is to be used in conjunction with the location analysis to

[1] In the writer's thesis (*Location Factors in the Synthetic Fiber Industry*, 1957) on deposit in Widener Library at Harvard University the cost analysis of the chemical-intermediate stage consists of 44 tables with separate columns for regional differences in transport, fuel, power, labor, and total selected costs. To minimize publication costs, Appendix A has been reduced to four summary tables (A-1, -3, -4, and -5) of total selected variable costs *alone;* and one table (A-2) for which the complete analysis is retained.

complete the study by spelling out the future regional impact of plant location in terms of direct employment and capital investment.

Since there are two stages of manufacture in the industry, there are three location alternatives: (*a*) integrated output of both chemical intermediates and synthetic fibers in raw-material regions; (*b*) integrated output of both in market regions where synthetic fibers are sold; and (*c*) split production, i.e., output of chemicals in raw-material regions with shipment of intermediates to fiber plants located in fiber-market regions. In summarizing the results of the study Section 1 is concerned with the question whether the chemical-intermediate stage is raw-material oriented or market oriented. Once this aspect of the study is completed, the location analysis turns in Section 2 to the synthetic-fiber stage and in Section 3 to the market forecast and the estimate of the future regional impact.

1. REGIONAL ADVANTAGES IN THE PRODUCTION OF CHEMICAL INTERMEDIATES FOR SYNTHETIC FIBERS

In Chapter 4 exploration of chemical-intermediate technology, of variable-input production functions, and of agglomeration economies brought out the general location factors for the first stage of the industry: availability of hydrocarbon raw materials (as resource deposits, from oil refineries, from natural-gas pipelines, or from local chemical plants); transportation costs in the assembly of raw materials and shipment of the finished product; agglomeration economies; regional differences in fuel and power costs; the supply of water; and regional differences in labor costs. In addition, the assumption for the first stage is that the location problem can be solved by comparing regional differences in variable costs alone, if plants of the same predetermined size can be built in any region; and in cases in which this procedure is not realistic the analysis must include estimation of the effect of agglomeration economies on both fixed and variable costs.

Regions with basic hydrocarbon raw materials for chemical manufacture have an obvious attraction for plant location; yet fiber-market regions in the textile area could be minimum-cost sites and pull capacity away from raw-material regions. This can happen if transport costs of raw materials are substantially less than finished products, if the transport-cost saving is sufficient to outweigh the advantages of raw-material regions in fuel and power costs, and if agglomeration economies are equivalent to those in raw-material regions. Therefore, location in raw-material regions cannot be taken for granted a priori. The alternatives, including the possibility of production in Puerto Rico, are analyzed in separate subsections for each of the five fibers investigated.

Nylon 66

Nylon salt, the chemical intermediate for the production of nylon 66 fiber, can be manufactured from benzene or 85 per cent petroleum cyclohexane, from benzene or cyclohexane and butadiene, and from benzene or cyclohexane and furfural. Selected inputs per 100 pounds of output by alternative production processes are presented in Table 4 in Chapter 4. Sample regional variable-cost differences per 100 pounds of nylon salt, derived from the estimated production functions and the cost model of Chapter 6, are given in Tables A-1 and A-2 of Appendix A. Table B-1 of Appendix B contains estimated cost differences per 100 pounds for plants of different size, attributable to large-scale economies.

Regional Variable-Cost Differences

Under the assumption that nylon-salt plants of the same predetermined size can be built in any region, the initial analysis is that of determining minimum variable-cost regions. In this case is it cheaper to produce nylon salt in the Texas-Gulf Coast or the West Virginia raw-material regions and incur the cost of shipping it to fiber plants in the textile area of the United States or Puerto Rico; or is there a cost advantage in manufacturing the salt in the textile area or in Puerto Rico by substituting transport outlays on the raw materials and outlays on other inputs? Table A-1 of Appendix A is a summary of total selected variable costs per 100 pounds for the sample regional sites for the twelve nylon-salt production possibilities of Table 4, Part II.[2] In this case it has been assumed that benzene, 85 per cent petroleum cyclohexane, butadiene, and furfural are shipped to nylon-salt plants from existing production points and that the nylon-salt plants include units for the production of other chemicals, such as ammonia, chlorine, nitric acid, and

[2] See pp. 48–49.

sodium cyanide.[3] An examination of Table A-1 shows clearly that the region of variable-cost minimization depends on the transport medium employed in costing the substitution possibility. There are three alternatives: (a) rail shipment of nylon salt vs. rail and pipeline assembly of the raw materials; (b) water shipment of nylon salt vs. water shipment of the raw materials (except natural gas); and (c) water and natural-gas pipeline assembly of the raw materials vs. rail shipment of nylon salt. In computing the cost differences all other regions are compared with the Texas-Gulf, which was used as the base. The other raw-material region represented by a site in West Virginia is coextensive with the Middle Atlantic fiber-market region.

In the first case (for all three methods of producing nylon salt) variable costs are minimized by location at market sites in the textile area of the United States rather than in the Texas-Gulf Coast area. Since 250 pounds of nylon salt must be shipped for each 100 pounds of fiber, there is a considerable transport-cost advantage in avoiding the transportation of the intermediate by rail because of the weight loss. The manufacture of nylon salt at market sites from assembled raw materials involves a much lower transportation outlay, one which also overcomes the variable-cost disadvantages relative to the Texas-Gulf in fuel and power costs. In the second case (water vs. water) variable costs are minimized by location in the Texas-Gulf Coast area or in West Virginia, the raw-material regions in the analysis. In the third case, on the other hand, in

---

[3] The following summary from Appendix A shows for the three general routes in nylon-salt manufacture the points of origin used in costing the assembly of the main raw materials at the hypothetical sites:

Benzene from Baytown, Texas, Birmingham, Ala., Pittsburgh, Pa., or Marcus Hook, Pa.; petroleum cyclohexane from Baytown, Texas; butadiene from Texas City, Texas, or Institute, W. Va.; furfural from Cedar Rapids, Iowa, Omaha, Nebr., or Memphis, Tenn.; ammonia from natural gas assumed to be transported by pipeline from Houston, Texas; nitric acid from Houston natural gas via ammonia; local manufacture of chlorine; HCN from Houston natural gas via ammonia; sodium cyanide from HCN (via natural gas); and caustic soda manufactured jointly with chlorine.

In all cases in which any of the chemical inputs for nylon salt are now manufactured at the hypothetical sites a zero transportation cost was tabulated.

It should also be noted that the approach employed assumes that if raw materials are available at more than one source prices at the hypothetical production sites will differ in the main by the transportation cost; i.e., they are approximately equal at the shipping points on an F.O.B. basis.

which the assembly of the raw materials by water and gas pipeline is weighed against rail transportation of nylon salt, sites in the
textile area of the United States have a variable-cost advantage.

Regional Differences in Agglomeration Economies

In the case of nylon salt the basic agglomeration-economy consideration would seem to be the question whether individual company practices favor a production plant devoted to nylon-salt output alone or a nylon-salt unit integrated with units producing other
chemicals as well.

Nylon Salt Alone. For plants built to produce nylon salt alone
sites in the U. S. textile area or in Puerto Rico would not be at a
disadvantage with respect to large-scale production economies in
the salt unit.   Market potential would not vary from region to
region, since the principal use of nylon salt is in the manufacture
of nylon fiber.   The scale of the salt unit in this case would not depend on the region of location but the size of the fiber plant it
serves.   There is no reason to assume that fiber-plant size would
vary from region to region, since the output of a single plant is not
sold entirely in a specific region.[4]   However, the question of scale
economies must be considered for other plant units in nylon-salt
production, since it has been assumed in the variable-cost computations summarized in Table A–1 of Appendix A that many of the
chemical raw materials can be manufactured at the nylon-salt sites
to obtain the transport-cost saving.   Table 20, which follows, contains, for the twelve production possibilities examined, the estimated annual requirements (in millions of pounds) of the miscellaneous chemicals in question for a nylon-salt plant with an annual
capacity of 60 million pounds.[5]   Feasible ranges of annual capacity
for these miscellaneous chemical units, as well as relevant scale-
economy cost differences, are also listed in Table 20.   The extent
to which the variable cost results must be modified is summarized
below:

1. In each case the ammonia requirement per year is below the
minimum plant size for the production of this chemical from

---

[4] See p. 34.

[5] The largest initial capacity for a new synthetic-fiber plant detected in the
literature is 50 million pounds per year for a Chemstrand nylon plant at Pensacola, Fla.; 10 million pounds of additional capacity were added soon after
construction.

natural gas; therefore, nylon-salt plants can be expected to purchase their ammonia needs from large-scale producers.

2. The nitric-acid requirement of 119 million pounds per year for Plant Types II and IV could be manufactured at the hypothetical sites with no scale disadvantage relative to raw-material regions. In all other cases the annual input is 48 million pounds. As shown in Table 20, the cost difference (per 100 pounds of nylon salt) of a nitric-acid plant with 40-million-pound annual capacity relative to one with 100-million pounds is $0.60, an amount which equals or exceeds the transportation cost on the nitric acid.[6] There is some doubt, therefore, that for production possibilities VI, VIII, X, and XII the acid would be manufactured at the salt unit.

3. There is no need to consider the scale-economy question for the HCN requirement, since the chemical cannot be transported in large quantities and must be manufactured where it is used.

4. Chlorine plants range in size from 25 to 160 million pounds, and the requirement in nylon-salt production is approximately the minimum. Table 20 shows that the cost difference of a 25-million-pound chlorine plant relative to an 80-million-pound plant is $0.46 per 100 pounds of nylon salt. This exceeds the transport cost.[7] Moreover, the hypothetical sites in the regional analysis are not the lowest-cost power points for the electrolytic process of producing chlorine. The reasonable assumption seems to be that nylon-salt units would purchase chlorine.

5. The sodium cyanide input, 30 million pounds, is far short of the size of the most recent unit constructed, 100 million pounds.[8] The estimated cost difference, $0.76 per 100 pound of nylon salt, exceeds the transport cost, indicating that a nylon-salt unit in itself would not be sufficient to take all the sodium cyanide output of a large-scale plant.[9]

Since the agglomeration analysis with respect to production of the miscellaneous chemical inputs at nylon-salt plants is not conclusive, the twelve production possibilities of Table 4, Part I, were costed to obtain a new set of regional variable-cost differences on the assumption that *all* of the chemical requirements would have

---

[6] See for example "Nitric Acid" column of relevant tables in Airov, *op. cit.*

[7] See "Chlorine" column of relevant tables in Airov, *op. cit.*

[8] "New Plant and Facilities Underway in 1951," *Chemical Engineering*, Vol. 59 (February 1952), p. 185.

[9] See "Sodium Cyanide" column of relevant tables in Airov, *op. cit.*

TABLE 20

ANNUAL REQUIREMENTS (IN MILLIONS OF POUNDS) AND LARGE-
SCALE PRODUCTION ECONOMIES FOR MISCELLANEOUS
CHEMICALS IN NYLON-SALT PRODUCTION

Plant Types[a]	I	II	III	IV	V	VI	VII	VIII	IX	X	XI	XII
Nylon salt from benzene or petroleum cyclohexane:												
Ammonia	11	45	11	45								
Nitric acid		119		119								
Nylon salt from benzene or petroleum cyclohexane and butadiene:												
Ammonia					15	29	15	29				
Nitric acid						48		48				
HCN					17	17	17	17				
Chlorine					29	29	29	29				
Nylon salt from benzene or petroleum cyclohexane and furfural:												
Ammonia									14	28	14	28
Nitric acid										48		48
Sodium cyanide									30	30	30	30
Chlorine									28	28	28	28

[a] See Table 4, Chapter 4, p. 42.
[b] Capacity ranges and cost differences per 100 lb attributable to large-scale economies for ammonia and nitric acid are given in Isard and Schooler, *op. cit.*, p. B-11.
[c] Appendix Table B-2.
[d] Appendix Table B-3.

to be transported to the hypothetical market sites or to Puerto Rico.[10]   The results show that the conclusions about regions of minimum variable production costs drawn from Table A-1 still held, except in the case of process methods which require large amounts of nitric acid.   Since other methods can be used, the vari-able-cost findings are not modified at all by the consideration of

[10] See p. 161.   The following summary (from Appendix A) shows the points of origin for miscellaneous chemicals used to recompute the regional variable-cost differences: Ammonia—Belle, W. Va., Philadelphia, Pa., Vicksburg, Miss., Lake Charles, La., Hopewell, Va., and Texas City, Texas; nitric acid—Vicksburg, Miss., Hopewell, Va., and Texas City, Texas; chlorine—Syracuse, N. Y., Hopewell, Va., Baton Rouge, La., McIntosh, Ala., and Huntsville, Ala.; and sodium cyanide—Memphis, Tenn.

TABLE 20 (*Continued*)

Plant Types	Feasible Capacity	Scale Economy Cost Differences per 100 lb Nylon Salt
Nylon salt from benzene or petroleum cyclohexane:		
Ammonia	66 to 792	Below minimum size[b]
Nitric acid	10 to 100	No disadvantage[b]
Nylon salt from benzene or petroleum cyclohexane and butadiene:		
Ammonia	66 to 792	Below minimum size
Nitric acid	10 to 100	40 vs. 100: $0.60 per 100 lb
HCN		Not transportable
Chlorine	25 to 160	25 vs. 80: $0.46 per 100 lb[c]
Nylon salt from benzene or petroleum cyclohexane and furfural:		
Ammonia	66 to 792	Below minimum size
Nitric acid	10 to 100	40 vs. 100: $0.60 per 100 lb
Sodium cyanide	30 to 100	30 vs. 100: $0.76 per 100 lb[d]
Chlorine	25 to 160	25 vs. 80: $0.46 per 100 lb

agglomeration economies in the case of a production plant devoted to nylon-salt output alone.

Nylon Salt in Multiproduct Plants. If the production of nylon salt takes place in multiproduct chemical plants, how does this factor favor one type of region or another with respect to agglomeration economies? Since a multiproduct chemical plant requires a variety of raw materials, then raw-material regions would be favored. For a plant of this type to be located in the textile area or in Puerto Rico there would have to be a general market for the chemicals produced in addition to nylon salt.

No effort has been made to quantify the integration economies directly. Instead, it has been assumed that the principal capital outlay in the multiproduct case would be for the nylon-salt unit and that large-scale production economies in nylon-salt output is the best measure available of integration economies in the whole plant. Table B–1 of Appendix B contains estimated total selected costs per 100 pounds for nylon-salt units of 60- and 90-million-pounds-per-year capacity. The difference is $2.56 per 100 pounds, a disadvantage of location outside raw-material regions for the multiproduct plant that is sufficient to offset the variable-cost advantages of sites in the textile area or in Puerto Rico in all cases, no matter what medium of transportation is employed.

Orientation of Nylon-Salt Output. By combining the regional varible-cost and agglomeration-economy analysis some general conclusions can be drawn about the orientation of nylon-salt output.

Production in multiproduct chemical plants is raw-material oriented (in this particular case). Raw-material regions have marked advantages for multi-product petrochemical plants, such as variety of low-cost raw materials, agglomeration economies, and low-cost fuel and power. There is a definite transportation-cost disadvantage in shipping nylon salt by rail from plants in raw-material regions to fiber plants in the textile area, but it could be overcome by the use of water transportation.

Transportation orientation in fiber-market regions in the textile area is implied for plants devoted to nylon-salt alone, with the salt unit integrated with a nylon-fiber plant. This conclusion is based upon two findings: first, plants of this nature would have no disadvantage in agglomeration economies for producers who do not plan multiproduct chemical operations at such sites; and second, the most realistic transportation-cost alternative—assembly of raw materials by water and natural-gas pipeline vs. rail transportation of nylon salt from raw-material regions—makes the site in the textile area the minimum-cost site.

Present Geographical Distribution of Plants

The major raw materials for nylon-salt manufacture are benzene, petroleum, cyclohexane, butadiene, and furfural. In the cost analysis production sites for these chemicals were taken as given. Most benzene in the United States is obtained from coke-oven crude light oil. Geographically, output generally coincides with steel manufacture and is concentrated in Alabama, Indiana, New York, Ohio, Pennsylvania, and West Virginia. Benzene is also made by oil refineries with aromatic operations. Via this new route, output is centralized in Texas, with scattered manufacture in California, Illinois, Indiana, Louisiana, Michigan, Ohio, Oklahoma, and Pennsylvania.[11]

[11] *Mineral Market Report,* M.M.S. No. 2166 (July 1953), U. S. Department of Interior, Bureau of Mines; "Benzene, Toluene, and Xylene Plants in the United States," *Petroleum Processing,* Vol. 7 (April 1952), pp. 518–519; and "New Plants and Facilities Underway in 1953," *Chemical Engineering,* Vol. 61 (January 1954), pp. 170–208.

The main source of cyclohexane is petroleum, in particular the naphthenic crudes. In the refining of naphthenic oils cyclohexane is concentrated in the straight-run gasolines. West Coast stocks are particularly high in cyclohexane content, as are selected stocks in the Gulf Coast and mid-continent regions.[12] The major producers of petroleum cyclohexane are Humble Oil and Refining Co. at Baytown, Texas, Phillips Petroleum at Borger and Phillips, Texas, and Shell Oil Co. at Wilmington, Calif.

Butadiene is made from alcohol, from butylene recovered at oil refineries, from butane, and via the naphtha cracking process. Petrochemical routes dominate, and production is concentrated in the Texas and Louisiana Gulf Coast areas. Plants are also located in Arkansas, California, Kentucky, Ohio, Pennsylvania, and West Virginia.[13]

Furfural is manufactured by the Quaker Oats Co. from agricultural and cereal production wastes, such as oat hulls, corn cobs, and rice hulls. The three Quaker Oats furfural plants are located at Cedar Rapids, Iowa, Omaha, Nebr., and Memphis, Tenn.[14]

Nylon-Salt Plants

One Du Pont nylon-salt plant is located at Orange, Texas, and the raw materials are both petroleum cyclohexane and benzene. The plant was constructed in 1946 and has an adiponitrile-producing satellite at Victoria, Texas, where the intermediate is made from butadiene. A second unit for the production of nylon salt is at Belle, W. Va., and is part of an extensive and varied chemical operation. Here the first nylon chemical intermediates were produced back in 1939. Benzene is available from the company's own coke-oven operations at Belle and from the high concentration of steel-making facilities in the Pittsburgh area. The Belle salt plant is also served by an adiponitrile unit located elsewhere, in this case at Niagara Falls, N. Y., where the chemical is made from furfural. Other chemicals required are hydrogen chloride and sodium cyanide, both of which are manufactured at Niagara Falls, the latter

---

[12] M. D. Barnes, "Cyclohexane," *Encyclopedia of Chemical Technology,* ed. by R. E. Kirk and D. F. Othmer (New York: Interscience Publishing Co., 1949), Vol. 4, pp. 760–769.

[13] *Special Report of Office of Rubber Director on the Synthetic Rubber Program,* War Production Board, Washington, D. C., August 31, 1944.

[14] At Burnside, Ky., in a plant that produces charcoal briquettes, T. N. Peck and Associates are now recovering waste gases for conversion to furfural. "New Plants and Facilities," *Chemical Engineering,* Vol. 62 (Mid-October 1955), pp. 8–44.

from metallic sodium, a co-product with chlorine in the electrolysis of sodium chloride. A new Du Pont plant for the manufacture of sodium cyanide (from hydrogen cyanide by reaction with caustic soda) is at Memphis, Tenn.[15] The petrochemical route to HCN is via ammonia and natural gas.

Output of chemical intermediates for nylon by the Chemstrand Corp. is integrated with fiber production at a plant located at Pensacola, Fla. Either benzene or petroleum cyclohexane is the principal raw material and is obtained from the Texas-Gulf Coast via the Intercoastal canal and the Escambia River; the site is also on a natural-gas pipeline.[16]

Conclusions for Nylon Salt

The cost results explain the integrated output of nylon salt and nylon fiber at Pensacola, Fla. Costs are minimized in this case of transportation orientation by location in a fiber-market region, and there are no agglomeration-economy disadvantages, since it is not a multichemical operation.

In all other cases nylon salt is produced in multichemical plants located in raw-material regions and is shipped to fiber plants in the textile area.

It seems reasonable to estimate that about 60 per cent of future nylon-salt capacity will be placed in raw-material regions, among which two selective influences will be the petrochemical trend and close access to the heart of the textile area. Thus for raw-material regions 50 per cent for the Texas-Gulf and 10 per cent for West Virginia and neighboring states would seem to be a reasonable division. The Texas-Gulf has an overwhelming supply advantage in the petrochemical age, but West Virginia is much closer to the textile area and has a transport-cost advantage in the delivery of the intermediate to fiber plants.[17]

[15] "No Time for Juleps," *Chemical and Engineering News*, Vol. 32 (March 8, 1954), p. 914.

[16] "Integrated Nylon Plant Rising near Pensacola," *Chemical and Engineering*, Vol. 59 (September 1952), p. 250.

[17] Since the completion of this study, some additional plant locations have been made. Caprolactam, the chemical intermediate for nylon 6, is manufactured by Allied Chemical and Dye at Hopewell, Va., by Mathieson Chemical at Morgantown, W. Va., and by Spencer Chemical Co. at Henderson, Ky. Adipic acid manufacture has been announced by Monsanto Chemical Co. at Luling, La. *Textile Organon*, Vol. 28 (October 1957), p. 142, and (November 1957), p. 175; and "New Plants and Facilities," *Chemical Engineering*, Vol. 63 (Mid-September, 1956), pp. 8–43.

Plants for the sole production of nylon salt will be constructed in the textile area of the United States and integrated with nylon-fiber output. Which portion of the textile area obtains the remaining 40 per cent of nylon-salt production depends on regional advantages in synthetic-fiber output. As the findings of Section 2 will show, the South will get the lion's share of synthetic-fiber capacity; hence it will attract most of the nylon-salt capacity located outside raw-material regions; and in the textile South sites along the Gulf Coast have strong advantages for integrated nylon-salt, nylon-fiber manufacture.

In Puerto Rico there are cost disadvantages relative to U. S. raw-material regions or sites in the textile area for nylon salt for the production possibilities examined. At least in the short run, labor costs in chemical production would be higher because of the short supply of technicians. Higher fuel costs in steam and power also imply higher costs in the use of oil-refinery waste gas as a chemical raw material, since the waste gas would not be sold as a raw material for less than the value of the Btu equivalent in fuel.

The foregoing conclusion does not imply, however, that fiber plants cannot be located in Puerto Rico; again, the findings of Section 2 will show striking advantages for the island. Moreover, the bagasse generated in sugar refining in Puerto Rico can be used to produce furfural, one of the main chemicals used in nylon-salt manufacture. Without doubt, some future furfural capacity can be located in Puerto Rico.

Orlon and Acrilan

The principal chemical intermediate for the manufacture of Orlon and Acrilan fibers is acrylonitrile. Orlon is made from a 100 per cent acrylonitrile polymer, and Acrilan is a copolymer of 85 to 90 per cent acrylonitrile and 10 to 15 per cent vinyl acetate or vinyl pyridine. Since the specific content of Acrilan has not been published, the location analysis is restricted to acrylonitrile.

Acrylonitrile can be manufactured from HCN and acetylene or from HCN and ethylene oxide. All three chemicals can be produced from natural gas, so that the future possibility of producing acrylonitrile in the textile area of the United States hinges largely on the transportation substitution possibility of minimizing costs by transporting the natural-gas input rather than the finished acrylonitrile. For Puerto Rico acrylonitrile production depends on the substitution possibility of oil-refinery waste gas.

Table A–3 of Appendix A contains the sample regional variable-cost differences per 100 pounds of acrylonitrile based on the estimated production functions in Table 5 of Chapter 4.[18] In addition, the analysis requires some knowledge of large-scale production economies, and estimated costs per 100 pounds for acrylonitrile plants of different sizes are given in Table B–4, Appendix B.

Regional Variable Cost Differences

Six alternative production possibilities were explored in generating regional variable-cost differences in acrylonitrile output. Under the initial assumption of plants of the same predetermined size, the regions of cost minimization can be determined from the columns of Appendix Table A–3.

In all cases variable costs are minimized by a Texas-Gulf Coast location if acrylonitrile is shipped by water to synthetic-fiber plants at the selected hypothetical sites. For rail transportation of acrylonitrile the variable-cost results are summarized below:

Plant Type I. Via acetylene and HCN produced from natural gas. Variable costs are minimized by a Texas-Gulf Coast location.

Plant Type II. HCN from natural gas and acetylene from ethane stripped from natural gas. This production method reduces the natural-gas input, and when weighed against Texas-Gulf acrylonitrile shipped by rail the results show that variable costs would be minimized, except in the case of New England, by location in the textile area of the United States.

Plant Type III. Via HCN from natural gas and ethylene oxide from ethane stripped from natural gas. Except for New England, variable costs would be minimized at locations in the textile area.

Plant Type IV. Via ethylene oxide shipped to the hypothetical production sites from Texas City, Texas, or Institute, W. Va., and HCN made from natural gas. Variable costs are minimized by a Texas-Gulf Coast location.

Plant Type V. Via HCN from natural gas and ethylene oxide produced from ethane via the chlohydrin process, with chlorine shipped to the hypothetical sites. Variable costs are minimized by a Texas-Gulf Coast or West Virginia location.

Plant Type VI. Same as Plant Type V, except that the cost calculations provide for the local manufacture of chlorine. Variable costs would be minimized by location in the textile area.

[18] See p. 50.

Regional Differences in Agglomeration Economies

If acrylonitrile is produced in the textile area, the reasonable assumption to make about the size of the plant is that it would have the initial capacity necessary to supply a fiber plant with which it is integrated. So far, the initial capacity of Acrilan and Orlon fiber plants has been approximately 30 million pounds, so that the acrylonitrile unit might be of this size also. Table B–4 of Appendix B contains estimated cost differences attributable to scale economies for both the HCN—acetylene and the HCN—ethylene oxide routes and for plants of 30-, 60-, and 90-million-pounds annual capacity. The cost differences per 100 pounds are

	30 vs. 60	30 vs. 90
HCN—acetylene	$3.84	$5.92
HCN—ethylene oxide	2.88	4.44

Such scale-economy advantages would accrue to larger plants in raw-material regions.[19]

Orientation of Acrylonitrile. Of the six production possibilities, three show that variable costs would be minimized by plant location in the textile area if the alternative is to produce acrylonitrile in raw-material regions and ship it by rail. However, the agglomeration economies of raw-material regions surpass the variable-cost saving; hence the cost analysis leads to the conclusion that acrylonitrile is raw-material oriented.

Present Geographical Distribution of Plants

The newest method of manufacturing acrylonitrile is the petrochemical route from acetylene and HCN. The Monsanto Co. has an acrylonitrile plant at Texas City, Texas, which uses acetylene produced from methane (natural gas) via a modified Sachse process and hydrogen cyanide from the reaction of natural gas and ammonia. American Cyanamid has a plant at Avondale (New Orleans), La., which also utilizes the new acetylene—HCN route.

---

[19] In the foregoing analysis the demand for acrylonitrile in fiber-market regions or in Puerto Rico is considered solely from the standpoint of the synthetic fiber end use. If demands other than the fiber market exist, optimum-size plants could be built in market regions or in Puerto Rico. This observation also applies to the other chemical intermediates for synthetic-fiber production.

Goodrich Chemical Co. manufactures acrylonitrile at Calvert City, Ky., from HCN and acetylene, but the latter is generated from calcium carbide.

American Cyanamid has an older plant at Warners, N. J., where acrylonitrile is made via the dehydration of ethylene cyanohydrin, derived from ethylene oxide and HCN; and Union Carbide and Carbon at Institute, W. Va., also produces the chemical intermediate from ethylene oxide and HCN.[20]

Conclusions for Acrylonitrile

With the exception of the oldest plant at Warners, N. J., the cost analysis of the petrochemical route explains the raw-material orientation of acrylonitrile production. In addition the plant at Calvert City, Ky., is only partially a petrochemical operation, since acetylene is made from calcium carbide, so that low-cost power is an additional explanatory factor.

The major market for acrylonitrile is in the making of synthetic fibers, but there is an additional market in the manufacture of synthetic rubber. About 70 per cent of future acrylonitrile capacity is likely to be located in the Texas-Gulf Coast area because of the region's overwhelming cost advantage in natural gas. But production plants will be drawn more and more toward locations in states such as Louisiana and Mississippi, which also have natural-gas deposits and are geographically closer to the textile South, the most favored region for synthetic-fiber output.

Perhaps 10 per cent of future capacity will be located in West Virginia. Plants there have no agglomeration-economy disadvantage and are close to fiber plants in the textile area; however, the raw-material supply disadvantage relative to the Texas-Gulf is considerable.

A part of future acrylonitrile output will be destined for the manufacture of synthetic rubber. Perhaps the remaining 20 per cent of future capacity will be located in the Ohio Valley at the northern edge of the T.V.A. power area, where acetylene can be produced from calcium carbide and HCN from natural gas. Some of this acrylonitrile capacity may also be directed to synthetic-fiber plants.[21]

[20] "Latest nor Least," *Chemical Industries,* Vol. 67 (December 1950), pp. 875–876; and A. J. Weith, "New Process for Acrylonitrile," *Oil and Gas Journal,* Vol. 51 (August 3, 1953), pp. 78–82.

[21] One new acrylonitrile plant location has been announced since the completion of this study. Dow Chemical Co. plans to begin construction in 1958 of a plant at Freeport, Texas. *Textile Organon,* Vol. 28 (September 1957), p. 127.

Dynel

Dynel fiber is a copolymer of 40 per cent acrylonitrile and 60 per cent vinyl chloride. Although the analysis of the previous section shows that acrylonitrile production is raw-material oriented, nonetheless the possibility was tested of joint output of acrylonitrile and vinyl chloride in the textile area of the United States or Puerto Rico as an alternative to the manufacture of both in raw-material regions. Vinyl chloride can also be manufactured at sites on natural-gas pipelines via acetylene and ethylene dichloride with the use of chlorine. Production in Puerto Rico again rests on the assumed use of oil-refinery waste gas.

Regional Variable-Cost Advantages

To bring out regional variable-cost advantages in the joint output of acrylonitrile and vinyl chloride, Appendix Table A–4 was prepared from the production functions of Table 6 of Chapter 4.[22] Since the chlorine requirement per year represents a small chlorine unit and a scale-economy disadvantage, the variable-cost calculations assume that this chemical is shipped to the hypothetical sites.[23]

For all the production alternatives variable costs for water transportation are minimized by output in either raw-material area, the Texas-Gulf Coast or West Virginia. For rail transportation of acrylonitrile and vinyl chloride, as an alternative to the assembly of the raw materials at sites in the textile area, the results are not uniform. In each case West Virginia is a suitable alternative to the Texas-Gulf. For the other hypothetical regional sites the results are given below in summary form:

Plant Type I. Acrylonitrile via acetylene and HCN, both from natural gas; and vinyl chloride from acetylene via natural gas. The results are inconclusive, with an advantage at some market sites, a disadvantage at others.

Plant Type II. Same as Plant Type I, except that ethane stripped from natural gas is substituted for natural gas in the production of

---

[22] See p. 51.

[23] For a dynel plant with 30-million-pound annual capacity the chlorine input for the vinyl chloride would range from 12 to 16.5 million pounds (depending on the process) and for a 60-million-pound plant, from 24 to 33 million pounds per year. The chlorine transportation cost was calculated from Syracuse, N. Y., Hopewell, Va., Baton Rouge, La., McIntosh, Ala., Huntsville, Ala., or Texas City, Texas. Local production is assumed in the raw-material regions.

acetylene. Variable costs are minimized by plant location in the textile area.

Plant Type III. Acrylonitrile from ethylene oxide (via ethane) and HCN from natural gas; vinyl chloride from ethylene dichloride via ethane. Variable costs are minimized by location at market sites.

Plant Type IV. Acrylonitrile from ethylene oxide shipped to the hypothetical sites and HCN from natural gas; vinyl chloride manufactured at hypothetical sites from shipped-in ethylene dichloride.[24] Variable costs in this case are minimized by location in raw-material regions.

Plant Type V. Acrylonitrile from HCN via natural gas and ethylene oxide from ethane, chlorhydrin process; vinyl chloride from ethylene dichloride manufactured from ethane. The results are mixed but in general show raw-material orientation.

Plant Type VI. Acrylonitrile manufactured in raw material regions and shipped to the hypothetical sites; vinyl chloride produced at hypothetical sites via ethane acetylene. Raw-material orientation is indicated.

Plant Type VII. Vinyl chloride shipped to hypothetical sites from raw-material regions; acrylonitrile manufactured at hypothetical sites from ethane acetylene and natural gas HCN. The results are mixed but in general show market orientation.

Regional Scale-Economy Advantages

If there were joint output of acrylonitrile and vinyl chloride in the textile area of the U. S. or Puerto Rico, the size of the chemical-intermediate units would be determined by the capacity of the dynel unit. Since dynel fiber is not yet in large-scale production, the size of the plant could conceivably range from 30 million pounds per year (the initial size of the other acrylic fiber plants) to 60 million pounds per year (the size of the largest initial capacity built in nylon manufacture). For a 30-million-pound dynel plant the acrylonitrile input would be 12 million pounds and the vinyl chloride input, 18 million pounds; and for a 60-million-pound dynel plant the respective inputs would be 24 and 26 million pounds. Since the annual inputs are relatively small, the joint output of acrylonitrile and vinyl chloride for specific use at dynel plants in the textile area or Puerto Rico would be at a considerable scale-

[24] Transportation costs for both ethylene oxide and ethylene dichloride were calculated from Texas City, Texas, or Institute, W. Va.

economy disadvantage relative to larger units in raw-material regions.

For both the acetylene-HCN and the ethylene oxide-HCN routes to acrylonitrile scale-economy cost differences per 100 pounds are given in Table B–4 of Appendix B. Scale-economy cost differences per 100 pounds for vinyl chloride are published in *Location Factors in the Petrochemical Industry.*[25] By combining the scale economies in each case the total disadvantage of nonraw-material sites was obtained and the results are tabulated below:

	Acrylonitrile	Vinyl Chloride	Total
Plant Type	(12 and 24 million lb)	(18 and 36 million lb)	(30 and 60 million lb)
I	$3.84+	$0.74 to $1.16	$4.58 to $5.00+
II	Same as Plant Type I		4.58 to 5.00+
III	2.88+	0.92 to 1.48	3.80 to 4.36+
IV	No scale economy disadvantage		0.00
V	Same as plant Type III		3.80 to 4.36+
VI		0.74 to 1.16	0.74 to 1.16
VII	3.84+		3.84+

Orientation of Joint Output of Acrylonitrile and Vinyl Chloride

In combining the variable-cost results with the large-scale production economy estimates the scale-economy cost differences represent an advantage for raw-material regions where plant size need not depend on the initial size of a fiber plant. When this is done, the total cost advantage acrues to raw-material regions regardless of the process or the form of transportation for acrylonitrile and vinyl chloride. In short, production costs are minimized if dynel plants are furnished their acrylonitrile and vinyl chloride requirements from separate chemical-intermediate plants located in raw-material regions.

Present Regional Distribution of Plants

The geographical distribution of acrylonitrile plants was set forth in the preceding section.

---

[25] Walter Isard and Eugene W. Schooler, *Location Factors in the Petrochemical Industry* (Washington, D. C.: Office of Technical Services, U. S. Department of Commerce, 1955), p. B–7.

Petrochemical vinyl chloride plants are located, in the main, in the Texas-Gulf Coast area. Union Carbide and Carbon makes the chemical at South Charleston, W. Va., and Texas City, Texas, Dow Chemical, at Midland, Mich., and Freeport, Texas, Diamond-Alkali, at Pasadena, Texas, and Monsanto and American Petrochemical at Texas City, Texas, and Lake Charles, La., respectively.

Production plants which make acetylene for vinyl chloride from calcium carbide are those of the Goodrich Chemical Co. at Calvert City, Ky., and the Naugatuck Chemical Division, U. S. Rubber Co., at Painesville, Ohio.[26]

Conclusions for Dynel Copolymer

The analysis of acrylonitrile in the previous section suggests that 70 per cent of future capacity will be placed in the Texas-Gulf, 10 per cent in West Virginia, and 20 per cent in the Ohio Valley. This conclusion also applies to the acrylonitrile destined for dynel.

For vinyl chloride a plant location forecast must take into account the fact that only about 15 per cent of the total market is in synthetic fibers. However, to the extent that plant location is influenced by this demand, plants are likely to be located in the Texas-Gulf Coast and the West Virginia area in the ratio of 80 per cent to 20 per cent.[27]

Dacron

The final question in the location analysis of the chemical-intermediate stage of the synthetic-fiber industry concerns regional advantages in the output of chemicals for Dacron, a fiber which is made from ethylene glycol and dimethyl terephthalate.

To explore the possibility of producing ethylene glycol at sites in the textile area of the United States, it has been assumed that

[26] "U. S. Organic Petrochemical Plants," *Oil and Gas Journal,* Vol. 51 (October 26, 1953), pp. 90–95; "New Plants and Facilities Underway in 1953," *Chemical Engineering,* Vol. 61 (January 1954), pp. 120–208; "Construction—1953," *Industrial and Engineering Chemistry,* Vol. 46 (January 1954), pp. 41-A–57-A.

[27] New vinyl chloride plants announced since the completion of this study include Superior Coal and Chemical at Natchez, Miss., Allied Chemical and Dye at Moundsville, W. Va., and the Ethyl Corp. at Baton Rouge, La. *Chemical Engineering,* "New Plants and Facilities," Vol. 62 (Mid-October 1955), pp. 8–44; "New Plants and Facilities," Vol. 63 (Mid-September 1956), pp. 8–43; and "1957 Petrochemical Plant Directory," Vol. 64 (October 1957), pp. 263–278.

the chemical can be made from ethane, stripped from natural gas, via either the oxidation process or the chlorhydrin route. For Puerto Rico the ethane can be obtained from oil-refinery waste gas streams.

The principal raw material for the production of dimethyl terephthalate is paraxylene, an oil-refinery product. In the cost calculations the transport outlay on paraxylene was computed to all the hypothetical sites from two existing production points, Baytown, Texas, or Marcus Hook, Pa.; and two processes for producing dimethyl terephthalate were considered—the air and the nitric-acid oxidation routes.

Regional Variable Cost Differences

Table A–5 of Appendix A contains the variable-cost calculations necessary to explore the location alternative of producing ethylene glycol and dimethyl terephthalate in the Texas-Gulf Coast area or of manufacturing the two chemicals at sites in the textile area of the United States or Puerto Rico in conjunction with the output of Dacron fiber. The cost calculations stem from the production functions in Table 7 of Chapter 4.[28]

In setting up the cost analysis it was deduced that it would not be profitable to produce the minor chemical requirements at sites in the textile area or in Puerto Rico because the annual inputs are too small to permit economical production.[29] Instead, transport costs were included for the shipment of chlorine, methanol, and nitric acid from the nearest large-scale production centers.[30]

---

[28] See p. 55.

[29] Annual chlorine, methanol, and nitric-acid requirements were estimated by assuming the ethylene glycol and dimethyl terephthalate capacity needed for a 35-million-pound-per-year Dacron plant, the size of the Du Pont installation at Kinston, N. C. In developing scale economies in chlorine production (See Table B–2 of Appendix B) the capacity of a small unit was found to be 25 million pounds per year, and the input in this case is only 12.6 million pounds. For methanol the annual input of 2.5 million pounds is far below the 60-million-pound, minimum-size plant reported by Isard and Schooler, *op. cit.,* p. B–6. The nitric-acid input of 35.4 million pounds per year falls within the feasible range reported by Isard and Schooler, 10 to 100 million pounds per year; but in the nylon section it was shown (for a nitric-acid input of 48 million pounds) that the scale disadvantage relative to largest scale production is greater than the transport-cost saving.

[30] Chorine from Syracuse, N. Y., Hopewell, Va., Baton Rouge, La., McIntosh, Ala., or Huntsville, Ala.; nitric acid from Vicksburg, Miss., Hopewell, Va., and Texas City, Texas; and methanol from Institute, W. Va., or Texas City, Texas.

Seven alternative possibilities were considered for the production of chemical intermediates for Dacron. The regions of variable-cost minimization for rail and water transportation are given in the summary which follows:

Plant Types I and II. DMT via air-oxidation process; ethylene glycol alternatively via oxidation route (Plant Type I) and chlorhydrin route (Plant Type II). For both rail and water transportation variable costs are minimized by location in the textile area of the United States, but Puerto Rico would not be a point of variable-cost minimization. The rail cost case gives the market location in the textile area a substantial cost saving, and the water case, only a nominal one.

Plant Types III and IV. DMT via nitric-acid oxidation; ethylene glycol alternatively via oxidation route (Plant Type III) and chlorhydrin route (Plant Type IV). Raw-material orientation is indicated for water transportation. For rail transportation the results are not uniform but in general show raw-material orientation.

Plant Type V. DMT shipped to hypothetical sites from Texas City, Texas, or Institute, W. Va.; ethylene glycol manufactured at hypothetical sites via oxidation process. For both water and rail transportation variable costs would be minimized by production of ethylene glycol at sites in the textile area or in Puerto Rico.

Plant Type VI. Ethylene glycol is shipped to hypothetical sites from Texas City, Texas, or Institute, W. Va.; DMT is manufactured at the hypothetical sites via air-oxidation process. For rail transportation variable costs are minimized by market location in the textile area; this finding holds also for water transportation, except in the case of Puerto Rico.

Plant Type VII. Same as Plant Type VI, except that DMT is manufactured via nitric-acid route. The general finding in this case is that variable costs would be minimized by raw-material location.

Regional Differences in Agglomeration Economies

For a Dacron fiber plant with 35-million-pound annual capacity the dimethyl terephthalate requirement per year would be approximately 35 million pounds, the ethylene glycol, 11.2 million pounds. The alternative to be considered is that of producing the two chemicals in large-scale plants in raw-material regions against their production in smaller units built to the scale of a Dacron fiber plant. For dimethyl terephthalate cost differences per 100 pounds

lington, N. J., where the intermediate is made by Hercules Powder via the air-oxidation process.[32]

Ethylene glycol is manufactured in California at Long Beach and Torrence; in Texas, at Corpus Christi, Freeport, Orange, Port Neches, and Texas City; in Michigan, at Midland and Wyandotte; in West Virginia, at S. Charleston, Institute, and Belle; and at Lake Charles, La., Doe Run, Ky., Whiting, Ind., and Baltimore, Md.[33]

Conclusions for Chemical Intermediates for Dacron

Since the synthetic-fiber use is a small portion of the total market, no general findings can be made about the future location pattern of ethylene glycol from this study alone. Both the cost results and the existing distribution of plants show raw-material orientation, including manufacture at oil refineries, although, of course, many of these sites are in markets for ethylene glycol. If the Dacron market for ethylene glycol entered into location decisions, this would draw plants primarily to the Texas-Gulf Coast region and secondarily to the region represented by West Virginia. For the Dacron market an 80 per cent—20 per cent split seems reasonable.[34]

The cost analysis fails to explain the location of either dimethyl terephthalate plant. The two units were built at existing chemical plants. In addition, a portion of dimethyl terephthalate output goes into plastics production, and the Middle Atlantic region is a central location for serving both markets. In spite of this, a reasonable prediction for the future would seem to be 70 per cent of DMT production for the Texas-Gulf Coast area and 30 per cent for the Middle Atlantic region.[35]

[32] "The Chementator," *Chemical Engineering,* Vol. 58 (April 1951), p. 76; and "Hercules Will Make Basic Material for ICI Terylene," *Chemical and Engineering News,* Vol. 32 (January 11, 1954), p. 128. The output of the Burlington, N. J., plant is principally for Canadian manufacture of Terylene.

[33] "Petrochemical Plants in the United States," *Petroleum Processing,* Vol. 7 (April 1952), pp. 509–520; and *The Shell Process for Manufacturing Ethylene Oxide and Ethylene Glycol,* The Lummus Co., New York, 1953.

[34] Two new ethylene glycol plants are located at Geismar, La., and at Seadrift, Texas. "1957 Petrochemical Plant Directory," *Chemical Engineering,* Vol. 64 (October 1957), pp. 263–278.

[35] New plants announced since the completion of the study are at Joliet, Ill., where Amoco Chemicals will manufacture terephthalic acid and dimethyl terephthalate; and the plans of Du Pont for a new Dacron plant at Old Hickory, Tenn., include a unit for the production of dimethyl terephthalate. *Textile Organon.,* Vol. 28 (July 1957), p. 93; and "1957 Petrochemical Plant Directory," *Chemical Engineering,* Vol. 64 (October 1957), pp. 263–278.

2. REGIONAL ADVANTAGES IN SYNTHETIC-FIBER PRODUCTION

Since the basic considerations in the location analysis of synthetic-fiber production are less complex than those in the chemical-intermediate stage, a different approach is employed in summarizing the results.

As indicated in Chapter 3, there is no reason to assume that the size of a synthetic-fiber plant depends on the region in which it is located, except that plants in Puerto Rico must be equal in size to those in the United States, for most of the output of a fiber plant on the island would have to be marketed on the mainland.[36]

In the regional variable-cost model for the location analysis of synthetic-fiber output the only cost item that is a function of the particular fiber produced is the transportation cost on the shipment of chemical intermediates and solvents from raw-material regions to fiber plants or, in the case of nylon 66, on the shipment of raw materials to integrated chemical-intermediate-fiber plants in the textile area of the United States. For this reason a fiber-by-fiber cost comparison is unnecessary, and, instead, a region-by-region comparison is employed to bring out general advantages and disadvantages in synthetic-fiber manufacture as revealed by the five selected fibers.

Since agglomeration economies are uniform from region to region, the future location pattern of synthetic-fiber plants depends on regional differences in variable production costs. A uniform set of utility and labor inputs has been used for all staple fibers and another set for all continuous filament yarns. In the realm of transportation costs rail rates on the shipment of fibers from plant sites to the U. S. markets are the same regardless of the kind of fiber and so is the water cost from Puerto Rico to the United States.

The cost analysis for determining regional advantages in synthetic-fiber production is encompassed in the tables of Appendix C. The particular set of inputs in each case was determined by the results of the location analysis of the chemical-intermediate stage. Thus Tables C–1 and C–2 are for nylon 66 staple fiber and nylon 66 continuous filament yarn and represent the case in which nylon salt is manufactured either in Texas or West Virginia and shipped to synthetic-fiber plants in the textile area or in Puerto Rico. Alternatively, Table C–3 represents the integrated production of

[36] See pp. 33–34.

nylon salt and nylon 66 fiber at hypothetical sites in the textile region of the United States from assembled chemical raw materials. In this connection only one method of producing nylon salt was tested: from benzene via the air-oxidation route to adipic acid.

In all other cases chemical-intermediate and solvent shipments from plants located in raw-material regions are assumed. Table C–4 contains some of the cost analysis for Orlon and can also be used for Acrilan, since the chemical-intermediate requirement is almost the same. For dynel and Dacron some of the cost tabulations are in Tables C–5 and C–6 of Appendix C.

Orientation of Synthetic-Fiber Production

Chapter 5 showed that the general location factors in synthetic-fiber production are

1. Regional differences in labor, fuel, and power costs.
2. Transportation costs on the shipment of the major chemical inputs or, alternatively, the raw materials for their manufacture.
3. Transportation costs on the delivery of the fibers to markets.
4. The regional availability of an abundant supply of water.

For the United States the cost analysis in Appendix C shows clearly that synthetic-fiber production is market oriented in the textile area. However, among fiber-market regions in the textile area the strongest selective influence is labor costs. Fiber-market regions which also have the basic hydrocarbon raw materials for chemical-intermediate manufacture are also favored for plant location. In addition, the cost results for Puerto Rico show the merit of plant location at a nonmarket site with a decided labor-cost advantage. It would seem best, therefore, to say that the location pattern of synthetic-fiber plants implied in the cost model is combined labor and market orientation.

The detailed analysis which follows brings out specifically the minimum-cost regions for synthetic-fiber production.

Synthetic-Fiber Production in the
Texas-Gulf Coast Area

If synthetic-fiber plants were to be located in the Texas-Gulf Coast region, fuel and power costs would be the lowest of any other region in the analytical framework, except that West Virginia possesses an equal advantage. In addition, no transportation costs would be incurred on the movement of chemical inputs.   On the shipment of fibers to the national textile market, sites in the Texas-Gulf Coast would have high transportation costs, exceeded only by the cost of serving the national market from Puerto Rico. There is also substantial pressure on the use of water in the region, so that the water-supply requirement could be met more satisfactorily in other regions, especially in the textile South.

Since the synthetic-fiber industry is strongly labor oriented in the fiber stage, the principal Texas-Gulf Coast cost disadvantage is in labor costs.   No other region (suitable for synthetic-fiber output) has hourly wage rates as high as those that can be expected to prevail in the region, for the wage structure would be affected by the very high wage rates that already exist in the region's chemical industry.

No synthetic-fiber plants have yet been located in the region, and on the basis of the cost analysis none is likely to be located in the Texas-Gulf Coast area in the future.

The New England Market Region

None of the plants for the production of the synthetics examined in this study is located in New England, the first of the five geographical areas which make up the market for fibers in the United States; and the cost analysis in Appendix C points to the conclusion that new synthetic-fiber capacity is unlikely to be located there.[37]

The most striking disadvantage for New England sites is in fuel and power costs, for the region has the greatest disadvantage relative to the Texas-Gulf or the West Virginia areas.   In addition, the region has a transport-cost disadvantage.   On the shipment of chemical intermediates from West Virginia, New England would be at no particular cost disadvantage; however, most future capacity will be located in the Texas-Gulf.   Even if chemical intermediates were shipped by water, the cost would be greater from Texas to New England than to other regions in the textile area.   Since the center of textile production has shifted to the South and the movement still continues, New England sites would be at a cost disadvantage in the delivery of fibers to other textile markets.   Although

---

[37] Pilot-plant production of American Cyanamid's new acrylic fiber **Creslan** has been taking place at Stamford, Conn., but a full-scale plant is being constructed at Pensacola, Fla.

New England has the water resources for synthetic-fiber output, sites are not so abundant as they are in the South.

For the important labor input the regional wage-rate data available for synthetic-fiber production does not disclose any existing labor-cost disadvantage for New England.[38]

The Middle Atlantic Raw-Material– Fiber-Market Region

The only portion of the textile area which is also a raw-material region for chemical manufacture is the Middle Atlantic region, represented in the cost framework by a site in West Virginia. Production of synthetics at sites in a chemical raw-material region with close access to the center of the textile market has marked advantages.   West Virginia coal can provide fuel and power at costs as low as those obtainable from the use of natural gas in the Texas-Gulf Coast area, hence lower than costs which prevail at the other hypothetical sites in the textile area.   In addition, chemical intermediates can be produced in West Virginia, and transportation costs on the movement of raw materials to fiber plants there can be minimized.   The cost of serving the national fiber market as measured by rail rates for carload and less-than-carload movements would be the lowest, except for sites in the very heart of the textile area.   Water resources in the region are adequate.

A raw-material supply area close to the textile area could draw synthetic-fiber plants or influence their location in contiguous areas.   The first synthetic-fiber plant constructed in the United States is located in the Middle Atlantic region at Seaford, Del.; however, new synthetic-fiber capacity is not likely to be located in New York, Pennsylvania, New Jersey, or even Delaware because of the labor orientation factor.[39]   Therefore, the implications of the analysis of the raw-material supply area in question suggest that synthetic-fiber plants would be drawn to West Virginia or that their location in Virginia, the nearest part of the textile South and a state which also has a sizable chemical industry, would be enhanced.

A Du Pont nylon plant is located at Martinsville, Va., and dynel is produced at Charleston, W. Va.   The attraction of West Virginia in the future may be limited by the course of hourly wage rates

---

[38] See Table 13, p. 108.
[39] Poliafil, Inc., now produces nylon 66 at Scranton, Pa.

relative to the South. All factors taken into consideration, perhaps 20 per cent of future synthetic-fiber capacity will be drawn to the states of West Virginia and Virginia.[40]

The Textile South

For the purpose of preparing regional cost comparisons the South was divided into three fiber-market regions: the East South region—Virginia, North Carolina, and South Carolina; the Central South—Georgia and the eastern portions of Alabama, Tennessee, and Kentucky; and the West South—the western portions of Alabama, Kentucky, and Tennessee and Mississippi and Louisiana. However, in summarizing the location results the best approach is to consider the textile South as a whole.

From the standpoint of all the general locational factors in synthetic-fiber production sites in the textile area of the South have at least average and, in most cases, outstanding advantages. Of the regions in which synthetic-fiber production is possible, only the West Virginia area has lower fuel and power costs. The most important factor is the new availability of natural gas to augment the coal of Alabama, Tennessee, and Kentucky. Within the South the western and central portions of the textile area can expect to benefit more from the use of natural gas for steam and power production than the East South. Closer proximity to the source of natural gas means that prices will be lower because of lower transportation costs.

The South offers the possibility of minimum expenditure in transporting chemical intermediates from raw-material regions to sites where synthetic fibers can be manufactured. The region is unique in that it can be served cheaply from either chemical-producing area—West Virginia or the Texas-Gulf. In the future the South's water connections with the Texas-Gulf Coast will be a most important advantage, since most chemical intermediates for synthetic fibers will be produced there. Barge transportation makes possible the cheapest of hauls from tidewater sites in the Texas-Gulf to coastal sites in the South or even to locations on the highly developed inland waterway system. With respect to water

[40] New synthetic-fiber plant locations for Virginia since the completion of this study are Allied Chemical and Dye (Caprolan, nylon 6), Chesterfield, Va.; Dow Chemical (Zefran, acrylic), Lee-Hall, Va.; Du Pont (Teflon, tetrafuluoroethylene), Richmond, Va., (nylon 66), Richmond, Va., and (Orlon), Waynesboro, Va.; and Industrial Rayon (IRC, nylon 6), Covington, Va.

connections with the Texas-Gulf, the West South and the Central South have advantages over the East South, since the haul around Florida has to be made by chemical tanker at higher water rates.

Now that the center of the geographical concentration of the textile industry (the market for synthetic fibers) is in the South, the region has an advantage in transportation costs on the delivery of fibers. In this respect transport costs are minimized by North Carolina, South Carolina, or Virginia locations.

The South has an abundant supply of water, and the lag in industrialization means that firms such as synthetic-fiber producers have a wide choice of excellent sites on rivers, lakes, and at coastal points.

Data on regional hourly wage rates in the synthetic-fiber industry show that the South at present has a very small advantage in labor costs. For new plants, however, an important requirement is labor availability, and the South's rural reserve is a major attraction to industry.

Nylon 66 plants are located at Chattanooga, Tenn., Martinsville, Va., and Pensacola, Fla.; Orlon is produced at Camden, S. C.; Acrilan is manufactured at Decatur, Ala., and Dacron at Kinston, N. C. Probably 80 per cent of the U. S. synthetic-fiber industry will be located in the East South, the Central South, and the West South regions of the textile-fiber market. To date the East South has been favored, but in the future more plants will undoubtedly be located in the central and western portions of the South.[41]

Puerto Rico

Of all the hypothetical sites examined for synthetic-fiber production, the region of lowest total variable production costs is Puerto Rico. The basic advantage, of course, is in labor costs, and the saving is sufficient to offset higher costs with respect to the other location factors. Fuel and power costs are higher than at most sites in the United States, and a higher transportation outlay is necessary, since the chemical intermediates would be shipped from the United States and the fibers, in turn, would have to be

[41] New synthetic-fiber plant locations for the textile South other than Virginia since the completion of this study are American Cyanamid (Creslan, acrylic), Pensacola, Fla.; American Enka (Enka and Nylenka, nylon 6), Enka, N. C.; Du Pont (Dacron), Old Hickory, Tenn.; and Tennessee Eastman (Verel, acrylic), Kingsport, Tenn. In addition, North American Rayon is producing nylon 6 and 66 in a pilot plant at Elizabethton, Tenn.

transported by water and then by rail or truck to the mainland fiber markets.

Clearly, considerations other than cost advantages must be taken into account in judging the future attraction of Puerto Rico for synthetic-fiber production. In the United States some fiber producers are still experiencing short-run technical production problems. In addition, the market potentialities are not fully known, since all of the possible end uses for synthetic fibers have not yet been explored. These factors suggest that when the U. S. synthetic-fiber industry has achieved greater stability then Puerto Rico will be looked upon favorably as a production site. By 1965 the labor attraction in Puerto Rico should induce the location of at least one fiber plant, and location of additional capacity will depend on the success of the first.

3. THE 1975 MARKET FOR SYNTHETIC FIBERS

A forecast of the future demand for synthetic fibers must necessarily cope with problems peculiar to a new industry. Sales data have not been released for individual fibers, nor have all the possible end uses been established. Moreover, the discovery of new synthetics will change the market positions of those already in commercial production. For the natural fibers, such as cotton and wool, which are being displaced in many uses by man-made fibers, there is the possibility through technological research of acquiring the desirable properties of the new fibers so that markets which are now being lost may be regained in the future.

In view of the degree of uncertainty the best analytical approach is a simple forecast employing data on fiber consumption per capita and a population projection. So that the procedure will be clear, the basic assumptions behind the forecast are listed below:

1. The most important textile fibers are cotton, wool, rayon and acetate, and the new synthetics. The long-term logarithmic trend of total fiber consumption per capita of these four types of fiber can be used as a control figure to set an upper limit for 1975 on the total demand.

2. A logarithmic trend projection of combined cotton and wool consumption per capita will establish the portion of the 1975 market that will *not* go to the man-made fibers, rayon and acetate and the new synthetics.

3. The difference between total per capita consumption and per

capita consumption of cotton and wool is the best estimate of the 1975 market for man-made fibers. In turn, by relying on expert opinion the expected shares of the 1975 market for man-made fibers that will go to rayon and acetate and to the new synthetics can be determined.

This indirect procedure is necessary because nonsensical results are obtained from a logarithmic projection of man-made fiber consumption alone, and there is insufficient data to fit other types of growth curves.

Per Capita Fiber Consumption

Current figures on per capita consumption of textile fibers are published in *Textile Organon,* beginning with 1920. Similar data were made available by Barkley Meadows for the period 1892–1948.[42]

Trend Projections of Per Capita Fiber Consumption

Logarithmic trends of total per capita fiber consumption were fitted to both series.[43] For the longer series (1892–1948) the average annual rate of increase is 0.87 per cent and for the shorter series (1920–1954), 1.29 per cent. The projected total per capita consumption figures for 1975 obtained from the longer series is 46.9 pounds per capita; and for the shorter series, 47 pounds per capita. Although the growth rates differ, the projected trends cross in 1975. Because the impact of man-made fibers on the textile market was strongest after 1920 the shorter series was used in all subsequent computations.

The projected value for 1975 of total cotton and wool consumption per capita based on the 1920–1954 series is 30.2 pounds, and the growth rate is only 0.42 per cent per year.[44] The difference between total per capita consumption of 47 pounds and 30.2 pounds

[42] Barkley Meadows, *Trends in the Consumption of Fibers in the United States, 1892-1948.* Statistical Bulletin No. 89, U. S. Department of Agriculture (Washington: U. S. Government Printing Office, December 1950).

[43] The equation for the 1892–1948 series is $\log y = 1.35625 + 0.00375\ (x)$ or, in natural numbers, $y = 22.710\ (1.0087)^x$. The equation for the 1920–1954 series is $\log y = 1.36035 + 0.00557(x)$ or $y = 22.930\ (1.0129)^x$.

[44] The equation is $\log y = 1.37678 + 0.00183(x)$ or $y = 23.810\ (1.0042)^x$.

for cotton and wool yields an estimated per capita consumption for man-made fibers of 16.8 pounds in 1975. Table 21 summarizes all the computed trend values. In the last two columns the computed trend values for man-made fibers are compared with the actual man-made per capita consumption figures.

TABLE 21

COMPUTED TREND VALUES OF FIBER CONSUMPTION, 1920-1975

(pounds per capita)

Year	Total	Cotton and Wool	Computed Man-Made	Actual Man-Made
1920	23.2	23.9	−0.7	0.1
1921	23.5	24.0	−0.5	0.2
1922	23.8	24.1	−0.3	0.2
1923	24.1	24.2	−0.1	0.3
1924	24.5	24.3	0.2	0.4
1925	24.8	24.4	0.4	0.6
1926	25.1	24.5	0.6	0.6
1927	25.4	24.6	0.8	0.9
1928	25.7	24.7	1.0	0.9
1929	26.1	24.8	1.3	1.1
1930	26.4	24.9	1.5	1.0
1931	26.7	25.0	1.7	1.3
1932	27.1	25.2	1.9	1.3
1933	27.4	25.3	2.1	1.8
1934	27.8	25.4	2.4	1.6
1935	28.2	25.5	2.7	2.1
1936	28.5	25.6	2.9	2.6
1937	28.9	25.7	3.2	2.5
1938	29.3	25.8	3.5	3.5
1939	29.6	25.9	3.7	3.6
1940	30.0	26.0	4.0	3.6
1941	30.4	26.1	4.3	4.3
1942	30.8	26.2	4.6	4.5
1943	31.2	26.4	4.8	4.4
1944	31.6	26.5	5.1	4.5
1945	32.0	26.6	5.4	4.7
1946	32.4	26.7	5.7	6.1
1947	32.8	26.8	6.0	6.1
1948	33.2	26.9	6.3	7.4
1949	33.7	27.0	6.7	6.3

TABLE 21 (*Continued*)

COMPUTED TREND VALUES OF FIBER CONSUMPTION, 1920–1975

(pounds per capita)

Year	Total	Cotton and Wool	Computed Man-Made	Actual Man-Made
1950	34.1	27.1	7.0	9.2
1951	34.6	27.3	7.3	8.5
1952	35.0	27.4	7.6	8.5
1953	35.5	27.5	8.0	8.6
1954	35.9	27.6	8.3	8.2
Projected				
1955	36.4	27.7	8.7	
1960	38.8	28.3	10.5	
1965	41.3	28.9	12.4	
1970	44.1	29.5	14.6	
1975	47.0	30.2	16.8	

Population Growth

In *Illustrative Projections of the Population of the United States* the Bureau of the Census has provided population projections for 1960, 1965, 1970, and 1975.[45] Four projections were made and the high and low series were selected for the fiber forecast.[46] Table 22 contains the projected per capita fiber-consumption figures, the population projections, and the resulting demand estimates.

The Forecast

For 1975 the estimated demand for man-made fibers is 3.3 to 3.7 billion pounds. In Section 4 the final demand for synthetic fibers in 1975 is translated into capital investment and employment figures for the regions of impact disclosed by the location analysis and into the demand for chemical inputs created by the develop-

[45] *Illustrative Projections of the Population of the United States, by Age and Sex: 1955 to 1975.* U. S. Department of Commerce, Bureau of the Census, Series P–25, No. 78, August 21, 1953.

[46] The high series involves the assumption that present age-specific fertility rates will continue to 1975; and the low series, that present age-specific rates will decline linearly from the present to roughly the 1940 level by 1960 and then continue at that level to 1975.

TABLE 22

PROJECTED DEMAND FOR TEXTILE FIBERS, 1960–1975

Fiber Consumption (lb per capita)	Projected Population (millions)		Estimated Fiber Demand (billion lb)
	Low	High	
1954[a]			
Total	32.6		6012.2
Cotton and wool	24.4		4515.6
Man-made	8.2		1887.6
Projected[b]			
1960			
Total	38.8	173.8	177.4	6.7 to 6.9
Cotton and wool	28.3		4.9 to 5.0
Man-made	10.5		1.8 to 1.9
1965			
Total	41.3	180.9	189.9	7.5 to 7.8
Cotton and wool	28.9		5.2 to 5.5
Man-made	12.4		2.2 to 2.4
1970			
Total	44.1	189.1	204.2	8.3 to 9.0
Cotton and wool	29.5		5.6 to 6.0
Man-made	14.6		2.8 to 3.0
1975			
Total	47.0	198.6	221.0	9.3 to 10.4
Cotton and wool	30.2		6.0 to 6.7
Man-made	16.8		3.3 to 3.7

[a] *Textile Organon,* Vol. 27 (August 1956), p. 116.

[b] A number of other fiber consumption forecasts have been made. In J. Frederic Dewhurst and Associates, *America's Needs and Resources, A New Survey* (New York: Twentieth Century Fund, 1956), p. 778, per capita consumption estimates for 1960 are given for cotton (32 lb), man-made fibers (14 lb) and wool, silk, and flax (2 lb). The per capita consumption forecasts were made by plotting trends through selected full-employment years of a per capita fiber consumption series from 1913 to 1952.

Robert C. Shook in "You Can Expect Big Future Gains for Man-made Fibers," *Modern Textiles Magazine,* Vol. 36 (April 1955), pp. 39–40, 54, forecasts that the total demand for the four principal textile fibers in 1965 will be 7.7 billion lb, for cotton and wool, 5.4 billion lb, and for man-made fibers, 2.3 billion lb.

J. Paul Sanderson, "The Synthetic Fibers Industry," *The Technology Behind Investment* (Papers presented by members of A. D. Little, Inc., Investment Banking Seminar, University of Pennsylvania, June 23–27, 1952), p. 11,

ment of the synthetics. Before this can be done the share of the 1975 man-made fiber market which will go to the new synthetics and then the shares for individual fibers must be estimated.

Wheeler has estimated that the new synthetic fibers will make up 50 per cent of the man-made fiber market in 1975.[47]   This would mean a 1975 market for the new synthetics of 1.65 to 1.85 million pounds, based on the trend projections.

The most difficult part of the forecast is the determination of the shares of the 1975 market for the five fibers examined in this study.   The estimated demand for all synthetic fibers in 1975, as indicated above, is 1.65 to 1.85 billion pounds.   The initial assumption made is that 85 per cent of this total will be held by the three general classes of synthetics examined in this study: polyamides, acrylics, and polyesters.   It is assumed that 15 per cent of the 1975 market will be taken up by other miscellaneous fibers.   For the three classes in question it is estimated that 35 per cent will go to polyamides, 40 per cent to acrylics, and 25 per cent to polyesters. Nylon is the oldest synthetic fiber, and the nylon 66 type considered in this study will probably retain as much as 90 per cent of the polyamide market in 1975.   On the other hand, the acrylic field is still wide open to new fibers, and the three in commercial pro-

---

[47] "70 Per Cent Growth in Textile Industry by 1975 Indicated," *America's Textile Reporter,* Vol. 68 (February 18, 1954), pp. 75–78.

---

estimates that the total demand in 1970 will be from 7.1 to 7.6 billion lb; for cotton and wool, 4.4 billion; and for man-made fibers, 2.7 to 3.2 billion lb.

Two forecasts project the demand to 1975.   "70 Per Cent Growth in Textile Industry by 1975 Indicated," *America's Textile Reporter,* Vol. 68 (February 18, 1954), pp. 75–78, is a review of a study made by Willard C. Wheeler of Anderson and Cairns, Inc., New York, presented before the Textile Seminar of Columbia University.   The total demand for 1975 was estimated to be 11 billion lb, with cotton comprising 50 per cent, rayon and acetate, 20 per cent, other man-made fibers, 19 per cent, wool, 10 per cent, and silk, 1 per cent. Translated in terms of four fibers only, the total 1975 market is 10.9 billion lb, for cotton and wool, 6.6 billion lb, and for man-made fibers, 4.3 billion lb.   In *Resources for Freedom,* Volume II: *The Outlook for Key Commodities* (A Report to the President by the President's Materials Policy Commission, Washington: U. S. Government Printing Office, June 1952), pp. 105–106, an estimate of 7.5 billion lb for total fiber demand is given for 1975, for cotton and wool, 4.3 billion lb, and for man-made fibers, 3.2 billion lb.   The population figure used is 193.4 million, and the per capita figures are 39 (total), 2.2 (wool), 20.2 (cotton), and 16.6 (rayon and synthetics).

duction at present—Acrilan, Orlon, and dynel—can be expected to retain no more than 65 per cent of the 1975 market, divided about equally. In the polyester field Dacron is well entrenched, even though new, and a 70 per cent share for 1975 seems reasonable. From the foregoing analysis the following individual (rounded) estimates were obtained for the 1975 markets of the five fibers examined; the 1954 estimated capacity is also given.

	Millions of Pounds	
Fiber	Estimated 1954 Capacity*	Projected 1975 Market
Nylon 66	250	450 to 500
Orlon	30	120 to 135
Acrilan	30	120 to 135
Dynel	5	120 to 135
Dacron	35	250 to 275

* See Table 3, p. 25.

4. 1975 REGIONAL IMPACT OF NEW SYNTHETIC FIBERS

Given present technology and dollar investment costs and the demand projections above, the regional impact of the 1975 market for nylon 66, Orlon, Acrilan, dynel, and Dacron can be translated into investment and employment figures.

Estimated Total Investment

Table 23 contains for both chemical intermediates and fiber plants the estimated total investment required by 1975 (in 1954 dollars) in new plants and equipment, a figure ranging from $1,327,537,000 to $1,612,689,000.[48] The estimate was made by multiplying new capacity in each case by the relevant capital coefficient, as described in footnotes (a) and (b) of Table 23.

---

[48] The estimates in both Tables 23 and 24 take into account direct investment and employment in chemical intermediate and fiber plants only, and do not include indirect investment and employment created through the secondary demand for chemical inputs.

TABLE 23

ESTIMATED NEW INVESTMENT IN PLANT AND FACILITIES REQUIRED
BY 1975 FOR NYLON 66, ORLON, ACRILAN, DYNEL, AND DACRON*

Chemical Intermediates[a]

Nylon salt (nylon 66)	$125,000,000 to $156,250,000
Acrylonitrile (Orlon, Acrilan, dynel)	66,750,000 to 84,550,000
Vinyl chloride (dynel)	10,557,000 to 11,934,000
Dimethyl terephthalate (Dacron)	27,680,000 to 32,005,000
Ethylene glycol (Dacron)	8,050,000 to 9,200,000
Total:	$238,037,000 to $293,929,000

Fiber Plants[b]

Nylon 66	$ 425,000,000 to $ 530,000,000
Orlon	99,500,000 to 150,000,000
Acrilan	112,500,000 to 131,250,000
Dynel	143,750,000 to 162,500,000
Dacron	308,750,000 to 345,000,000
Total:	$1,089,500,000 to $1,318,750,000

* In 1954 dollars.

[a] For chemical-intermediate facilities the estimates were made as follows:
Nylon salt. Capacity in 1954 is estimated to be 250 million lb, and the new
capacity for 1975 is 200 to 250 million lb. The capital investment was derived
from the estimate of $0.625 per lb for a 60-million-lb plant given in Appendix
Table B-1. *Acrylonitrile.* The HCN—acetylene process is assumed, and the
investment cost per pound is $0.445 (from Appendix Table B-4). A. J. Weith,
"New Process for Acrylonitrile," *Oil and Gas Journal,* Vol. 52 (August 3, 1953),
pp. 78–82, estimates that the 1955 capacity for acrylonitrile is 200 million lb,
with 60 per cent for synthetic fibers (Orlon, Acrilan, and dynel), or 120 million lb. The added capacity required for 1975 for these three fibers is estimated to be 150 to 190 million lb, and the per pound investment cost of $0.445
yields the estimated investment figure. *Vinyl chloride.* The additional 1975
capacity for dynel is estimated to be 69 to 78 million lb, and the acetylene route
is assumed. Isard and Schooler, *op. cit.,* p. B-8, estimate that the cost per
pound for a 70-million-lb plant is $0.153. *Dimethyl terephthalate.* Present
capacity is estimated to be 60 million lb, and the additional capacity required
by 1975 is 160 to 185 million lb. The capital coefficient used is $0.173 per lb,
derived from Appendix Table B-5 for a 60-million-lb plant. *Ethylene glycol.*
The oxidation process is assumed. The additional capacity for 1975 for
Dacron is estimated to be 70 to 80 million lb. The capital coefficient of $0.115
per lb is from Isard and Schooler, *op. cit.,* p. 21, for a 60-million-lb plant.

[b] J. Paul Sanderson, *op. cit.,* p. 15, estimates that the capital investment per
annual pound of synthetic fibers in staple form is $1.00 to $1.50 and in continuous-filament form, $2.50. A coefficient of $1.25 was used for staple fiber.
For each fiber the estimates were made as follows: *Nylon 66.* New capacity
required for the 1975 market of 200 to 250 million lb was assumed to be 70

Estimated New Employment

The estimated new employment, 31,595 to 37,330 jobs, created by the 1975 markets for the five fibers is given in Table 24. Footnotes (*a*) and (*b*) of the table explain how the job estimates were obtained by multiplying new capacity by the individual labor coefficients.

The Regional Impact

In accordance with the findings of the location analysis summarized in Sections 1 and 2, the investment and employment figures have been allocated in Table 25 to the regions which will be affected by the development of synthetic fibers.

For the Texas-Gulf Coast region the new investment in chemical-intermediate facilities is estimated to be $155,156,850 to $191,416,950; and the new employment, 632 to 752 jobs.

For West Virginia and Virginia the estimated investment in chemical-intermediate plants is $32,869,150 to $40,022,050; and in fiber plants, $217,900,000 to $263,750,000. Added employment in chemical-intermediate plants is estimated to be 148 to 173 and in fiber plants, 6131 to 7245.

The balance of the allocation is to the textile South, other than Virginia and Puerto Rico. Investment in chemical-intermediate facilities for the textile South is estimated to be $50,000,000 to $62,500,000 and employment, 160 to 180 jobs. The combined investment in fiber plants in the South and in Puerto Rico is $871,600,000 to $1,055,000,000, and the new employment estimate is 24,524 to 28,980 jobs.

There is no basis for making a separate estimate of the extent to which Puerto Rico will share in the development of synthetic fibers. It can be noted, however, that a typical 60-million-pound continuous-filament fiber plant would call for an investment of $150,000,000 and create approximately 4285 jobs; and a staple plant of the same capacity, an investment of $75,000,000 and 1000 jobs.

---

per cent continuous filament and 30 per cent staple. *Orlon.* Additional 1975 capacity of 90 to 105 million lb assumed to be all staple. *Acrilan.* New capacity for 1975 of 90 to 105 million lb assumed to be all staple. *Dynel.* New capacity of 115 to 130 million lb assumed to be all staple. *Dacron.* Estimated new 1975 capacity of 215 to 240 million lb assumed to be 85 per cent staple and 15 per cent continuous filament.

TABLE 24
ESTIMATED NEW EMPLOYMENT BY 1975 FOR
NYLON 66, ORLON, ACRILAN, DYNEL, AND DACRON*

Chemical Intermediates^a			
Nylon salt (nylon 66)	400	to	450
Acrylonitrile (Orlon, Acrilan, dynel)	270	to	345
Vinyl chloride (dynel)	30	to	35
Dimethyl terephthalate (Dacron)	200	to	230
Ethylene glycol	40	to	45
Total	940	to	1,150

Fiber Plants^b			
Nylon 66	12,000	to	15,000
Orlon	3,485	to	4,070
Acrilan	2,990	to	3,490
Dynel	3,820	to	4,320
Dacron	8,360	to	9,345
Total	30,655	to	36,225

* Direct labor only is included in chemical-intermediate manufacture; both direct and indirect for synthetic-fiber production.

^{a} A 40-hour, 50-week year was assumed, and the employment figures were derived from the additional capacity estimates for 1975 by employing labor coefficients as follows: *Nylon salt.* It was assumed that ⅓ would be produced by each general route, 50/50 from benzene and petroleum cyclohexane and 50/50 via air oxidation or nitric-acid oxidation. The labor coefficients are given in Table 4, pp. 42–43. *Acrylonitrile.* For the acetylene route (together with HCN) the labor coefficient of 0.36 man-hours per 100 lb is given in Table 5, p. 50. *Vinyl chloride.* The labor coefficient employed is 0.14 man-hours per 100 lb, from Table 6, p. 51. *Ethylene glycol.* For the oxidation route a labor coefficient of 0.11 man-hours per 100 lb is given in Isard and Schooler, *op. cit.,* p. 21. *Dimethyl terephthalate.* It was assumed that 50 per cent would be produced via the air-oxidation route and 50 per cent via the nitric-acid oxidation process. The labor coefficients are given in Table 7, p. 55.

^{b} A 365-day-per-year plant operation is assumed. A labor coefficient of 9.7 man-hours per 100 lb was used for staple fiber (see Table 9, p. 73) and for continuous filament, 20.8 man-hours per 100 lb (see Table 10, p. 74). The assumed breakdown between staple and continuous filament for each fiber is given in footnote (*b*), Table 23.

TABLE 25

ESTIMATED NEW INVESTMENT AND EMPLOYMENT BY REGIONS, 1975*

Region	Investment		Employment	
	Chemical Intermediates	Fiber Plants	Chemical Intermediates	Fiber Plants
Texas-Gulf Coast	$155,167,850 to 191,416,950		632 to 752	
West Virginia and Virginia	$ 32,869,150 to 40,022,050	$ 217,900,000 to 263,750,000	148 to 173	6,131 to 7,245
Textile South and Puerto Rico[a]	$ 50,000,000 to 62,500,000	$ 871,600,000 to 1,055,000,000	160 to 180	24,524 to 28,980

* Obtained by multiplying the totals of Tables 23 and 24 by the regional distribution forecast in the summary: *Nylon salt*—50 per cent Texas-Gulf Coast, 10 per cent West Virginia and neighboring states, 40 per cent in South. *Acrylonitrile* (for synthetic fibers). 87.5 per cent Texas-Gulf Coast, 12.5 per cent West Virginia. *Vinyl chloride.* 80 per cent Texas-Gulf, 20 per cent West Virginia. *Dimethyl terephthalate.* 70 per cent Texas-Gulf Coast, 30 per cent West Virginia-Middle Atlantic. *Ethylene glycol.* 80 per cent Texas-Gulf, 20 per cent West Virginia. For synthetic fibers, 20 per cent West Virginia-Virginia and 80 per cent textile South. No separate estimate was made for Puerto Rico but combined with textile South.

[a] For Puerto Rico the investment and employment figures are for fiber plants.

Regional Variable-Cost
Differences in
Chemical-Intermediate Manufacture

Appendix A contains the tabular presentation of regional variable-cost differences in chemical intermediate manufacture. Except for the details on transportation costs, the procedure for calculating the selected outlays is described in Chapter 6. The data sources on transport outlays, shipping points, etc., are described below for each chemical intermediate.

In all cases rail rates for tank-car shipments of chemicals were obtained and increased by 15 per cent to take into account the general increase under ex parte 175-B and by 3 per cent for the transportation tax. In each instance rail class rates were obtained from the classification of the chemical in Uniform Freight Classification No. 1.

With few exceptions the chemicals used in the manufacture of intermediates for synthetic fibers are already manufactured in the two raw-material regions, the Texas-Gulf Coast and West Virginia, so that zero transportation costs are incurred. The exceptions are noted, and, in addition, zero transportation costs are also incurred on some chemicals manufactured locally at other hypothetical sites.

Transportation Costs in Nylon-Salt Manufacture

Ammonia

Rates for ammonia—both class and commodity—are 35 per cent of first class, ICC 28300 scale. Some specific rates were furnished by the Du Pont company, and in addition some rates were estimated from the scale referred to above.[1]   For water movements pressure chemical rates were applied.   The shipping points used in the cost calculations are

To	From
Boston, Mass.	Rail and water: Philadelphia, Pa.
Memphis, Tenn.	Rail and water: Vicksburg, Miss.
Mobile, Ala.	Rail: Vicksburg, Miss.; water: Lake Charles, La.
Wilmington, N. C.	Rail: Belle, W. Va.; water: Hopewell, Va.
Chattanooga, Tenn.	Rail and water: Vicksburg, Miss.
Birmingham, Ala.	Rail and water: Vicksburg, Miss.
Puerto Rico	Water: Texas City, Texas.

Benzene

Class and commodity rates on benzene were furnished by several companies.[2]   Some additional rates were estimated from this information.   In calculating water rates benzene was treated as an ordinary chemical.   The shipping points employed are summarized below:

To	From
Institute, W. Va.	Rail and water: Pittsburgh, Pa.
Boston, Mass.	Rail and water: Marcus Hook, Pa.
Memphis, Tenn.	Rail and water: Baytown, Texas.
Mobile, Ala.	Rail: Birmingham, Ala.; water: Baytown, Texas.
Wilmington, N. C.	Rail: Birmingham, Ala.; water: Marcus Hook, Pa.
Chattanooga, Tenn.	Rail: Birmingham, Ala.; water: Baytown, Texas.
Birmingham, Ala.	Local
Puerto Rico	Water: Baytown, Texas.

Butadiene

Several railroads furnished the information that rail class rates on butadiene are 35 per cent of first class.   Commodity rates were estimated from a group of rates in a study of chemical transportation costs furnished the Center for Urban and Regional Studies,

[1] Mr. R. W. Marshall, General Traffic Manager, E. I. du Pont de Nemours & Co., Wilmington, Del.

[2] Mr. E. W. Gerloff, Traffic Manager, Humble Oil and Refining Co., Houston, Texas; Mr. R. M. Reid, Traffic Manager, Tennessee Coal and Iron Division, U. S. Steel Corp., Birmingham, Ala.; and Mr. R. C. Harvey, Assistant Traffic Manager, Sun Oil Co., Philadelphia, Pa.

Massachusetts Institute of Technology, by the Department of Commerce. For water movements ordinary chemical rates were used, and the shipping points for both rail and water are

To	From
Boston, Mass.	Rail: Institute, W. Va.; water: Texas City, Texas.
Memphis, Tenn.	Rail and water: Texas City, Texas.
Mobile, Ala.	Rail and water: Texas City, Texas.
Wilmington, N. C.	Rail: Institute, W. Va.; water; Texas City, Texas.
Chattanooga, Tenn.	Rail: Institute, W. Va.; water; Texas City, Texas.
Birmingham, Ala.	Rail and water: Texas City, Texas.
Puerto Rico	Water: Texas City, Texas.

Chlorine

Forty-five per cent of first class for both class and commodity rates was the basis for costing chlorine movements. Sample rates were furnished by several companies.[3] Pressure chemical rates were used in water movements. Specific shipping points are listed below:

To	From
Boston, Mass.	Rail: Syracuse, N. Y.; water: Hopewell, Va.
Memphis, Tenn.	Rail and water: Baton Rouge, La.
Mobile, Ala.	Rail: McIntosh, Ala.; water: Baton Rouge.
Wilmington, N. C.	Rail and water: Hopewell, Va.
Chattanooga, Tenn.	Rail only: Huntsville, Ala.
Birmingham, Ala.	Rail: Huntsville, Ala.; water: Baton Rouge, La.
Puerto Rico	Water: Texas City, Texas.

Petroleum Cyclohexane

A sample of both class and commodity rates was obtained from Mr. E. W. Gerloff, Traffic Manager, Humble Oil and Refining Co., Houston, Texas, and others were estimated on the basis of existing commodity rates on benzene. Ordinary chemical rates were used in costing water movements. All shipments were costed for both rail and water from Baytown, Texas.

---

[3] Mr. John H. Wilharm, Director of Traffic, Diamond Alkali Co., Cleveland, Ohio; and Mr. Carl P. Greeley, Director of Traffic, National Petro-Chemicals Corp., New York, N. Y.

Furfural

Class and commodity rail rates on the movement of furfural were supplied by Mr. A. J. Carr, Assistant Manager, Traffic Department, Quaker Oats Co., Chicago, Ill. For water movements furfural was treated as an ordinary chemical, requiring no special equipment. Rates to each hypothetical producing point were calculated from the points shown below:

To	From
Orange, Texas	Rail and water: Memphis, Tenn.
Institute, W. Va.	Rail and water: Memphis, Tenn.
Boston, Mass.	Rail: Omaha, Nebr.; water: Memphis, Tenn.
Memphis, Tenn.	Local
Mobile, Ala.	Rail and water: Memphis, Tenn.
Wilmington, N. C.	Rail and water: Memphis, Tenn.
Chattanooga, Tenn.	Rail and water: Memphis, Tenn.
Birmingham, Ala.	Rail and water: Memphis, Tenn.
Puerto Rico	Water: Memphis, Tenn., by barge to New Orleans and tanker.

Nitric Acid

Both class and commodity rates on nitric acid were calculated as 35 per cent of first class on the advice of several railroads. For water movements rates on corrosive chemicals were utilized. Some rates were furnished by Mr. F. W. Brown, General Traffic Manager, Nitrogen Division, Allied Chemical and Dye Corp., New York, N. Y., and others were estimated from the ICC 28300 scale. The shipping points for nitric acid are

To	From
Boston, Mass.	Rail and water: Hopewell, Va.
Memphis, Tenn.	Rail and water: Vicksburg, Miss.
Mobile, Ala.	Rail and water: Vicksburg, Miss.
Wilmington, N. C.	Rail and water: Hopewell, Va.
Chattanooga, Tenn.	Rail and water: Vicksburg, Miss.
Birmingham, Ala.	Rail and water: Vicksburg, Miss.
Puerto Rico	Water: Texas City, Texas.

Nylon Salt

Mr. R. W. Marshall, Director, Traffic Department, E. I. du Pont de Nemours & Co., Wilmington, Del., supplied rates on nylon salt for both class and commodity movements. Rates to all hypothetical sites were computed from Orange, Texas; and for water movements nylon salt was treated as an ordinary chemical.

Sodium Cyanide. Mr. Marshall of Du Pont also supplied class and rail rates on sodium cyanide, and some additional rates were estimated from the sample by application of the ICC 28300 scale. For Boston rates were computed from Niagara Falls, N. Y.; Memphis has local production; the shipping point for Puerto Rico was assumed to be Texas City, Texas; and for both rail and water movements to all other points the city of origin is Memphis, Tenn.

Acrylonitrile Transport Costs

Acrylonitrile

Class rail rates were computed as 31 per cent of ICC 28300 scale on the basis of information furnished by Mr. E. R. Rista, Assistant Manager, Freight Traffic Department, Union Carbide and Carbon Corp., New York, N. Y. For commodity movements a rate of 21.2 per cent of first class, ICC 28300, was used, derived from the rate on acrylonitrile from Texas City, Texas, to Decatur, Ala., which was furnished by Mr. H. F. Klocker, General Traffic Manager, Monsanto Chemical Co.

Acrylonitrile was treated as an ordinary chemical in applying barge and tanker rates; and all movements were costed from Texas City, Texas.

Ethylene Oxide

Class rail rates for tank-car movements are 35 per cent of first class for ethylene oxide. Commodity rates were estimated from the Department of Commerce study referred to in the section on butadiene. In general, a figure of 25 per cent of first class was used.

For water movements pressure chemical rates were employed; and for all the hypothetical sites the costs were calculated for both rail and water from Texas City, Texas, or Institute, W. Va.

Chlorine is required in some of the production functions; the rates used are given under nylon-salt transportation costs.

Transport Costs for Dynel Copolymer

In addition to acrylonitrile, chlorine, and ethylene oxide, dynel copolymer requires vinyl chloride and ethylene dichloride.

Vinyl Chloride

The rail class rate for movements of vinyl chloride in tank cars is 50 per cent, but, instead of utilizing class rates, two groups of commodity rates were estimated. One is approximately 40 to 42 per cent of first-class ICC 28300 scale and was supplied by the Monsanto Chemical Co. A second set of commodity rates was estimated from the rate in Tariff SWL 20U (ICC 3967) on the movement of vinyl chloride from Texas City, Texas, to Midland, Mich., which, on the basis of ICC 28300, is about 28 per cent of the first-class rate. For water movements pressure chemical rates were used; and Texas City, Texas, and Institute, W. Va., are the shipping points for all rail and water movements.

Ethylene Dichloride

Class rates for ethylene dichloride, as supplied by Monsanto Chemical Co., are 30 per cent of first-class ICC 28300. Some commodity rates of approximately 24 per cent of first class were estimated on the basis of SWL 20U ICC 3967. For water movements ordinary chemical rates were utilized. Two shipping points were used in the cost calculations, Texas City, Texas, and Institute, W. Va.

Transportation Costs for Dacron

In the cost analysis production of dimethyl terephthalate is assumed to take place hypothetically at Texas City, Texas, and Institute, W. Va. Class and commodity rates from these points to the other hypothetical sites were estimated from information furnished by the Du Pont traffic department. Class rates are 40 per cent of first-class ICC 28300. On an existing commodity movement from New Jersey to Graingers, N. C., the rate applicable is 35 per cent of first-class ICC 15879, Appendix E scale. Since this scale was not available, the commodity-rate basis was found to be approximately 31 per cent of ICC 28300. For water movements, dimethyl terephthalate is an ordinary chemical.

Ethylene Glycol

For both class and commodity rail rates movements of ethylene glycol were costed from rates which are 27.5 per cent of ICC 28300, as furnished by the Monsanto Chemical Co. Water movements treat ethylene glycol as an ordinary chemical. All shipments were costed from Texas City, Texas, or Institute, W. Va.

Methanol

Transport rates by rail and water for methanol are identical with those for ethylene glycol.

Paraxylene

Class and commodity rates on movements of paraxylene were obtained from several sources.[4] For water movements the chemical would move under ordinary chemical rates. The specific shipping points assumed are

To	From
Institute, W. Va.	Rail: Marcus Hook, Pa., water: Baytown, Texas.
Boston, Mass.	Rail and water: Marcus Hook, Pa.
Memphis, Tenn.	Rail and water: Baytown, Texas.
Mobile, Ala.	Rail and water: Baytown, Texas.
Wilmington, N. C.	Rail and water: Marcus Hook, Pa.
Chattanooga, Tenn.	Rail and water: Baytown, Texas.
Puerto Rico	Water: Baytown, Texas.

Chlorine and nitric acid are also used in the manufacture of chemical intermediates for Dacron; the rate bases were given in the nylon-salt section.

[4] Mr. Richard M. Leader, Manager, Special Products Division, Phillips Petroleum Co.; Mr. E. W. Gerloff, Traffic Manager, Humble Oil and Refining Co.; Mr. W. D. Ohle, General Traffic Manager, Sinclair Refining Co.; and Department of Commerce study.

TABLE A-1

REGIONAL VARIABLE-COST DIFFERENCES PER 100 POUNDS: NYLON SALT

Summary of Total Selected Costs for Table 4(II), Plant Types I-XII*

Hypothetical Plant Site		Cost Advantage (−) or Disadvantage (+) Relative to Texas-Gulf Production					
		Plant Type I	Plant Type II	Plant Type III	Plant Type IV	Plant Type V	Plant Type VI
Orange, Texas		$0.00	$0.00	$0.00	$0.00	$0.00	$0.00
Institute, W. Va.	(1)	−2.73 to −2.78	−2.98 to −3.06	−1.44 to −1.46	−2.04 to −2.10	−3.26 to −3.34	−3.36 to −3.45
	(2)	−2.36 to −2.41	−2.42 to −2.50	−1.34 to −1.36	−1.68 to −1.74	−2.59 to −2.67	−2.61 to −2.70
	(3)	−0.37 to −0.42	−0.28 to −0.36	+0.13 to +0.15	+0.03 to +0.09	−0.35 to −0.43	−0.29 to −0.40
Boston, Mass.	(1)	−0.98 to −1.73	−1.53 to −2.26	−0.68 to −1.05	−1.15 to −1.78	−1.96 to −2.49	−2.08 to −2.52
	(2)	−0.38 to −1.13	−0.75 to −1.38	−0.50 to −0.87	−0.68 to −1.31	−1.24 to −1.77	−1.29 to −1.73
	(3)	+2.03 to +2.70	+1.86 to +2.49	+1.48 to +1.95	+1.34 to +2.10	+1.53 to +2.05	+1.56 to +2.06
Memphis, Tenn.	(1)	−0.34 to −0.56	−0.79 to −0.96	−0.88 to −0.99	−1.24 to −1.34	−0.84 to −0.98	−0.96 to −1.22
	(2)	−0.08 to −0.30	−0.44 to −0.61	−0.27 to −0.38	−0.63 to −0.72	−0.53 to −0.67	−0.61 to −0.77
	(3)	+0.78 to +1.04	+0.63 to +0.88	+0.40 to +0.53	+0.30 to +0.45	+0.52 to +0.74	+0.49 to +0.73
Mobile, Ala.	(1)	−0.40 to −0.60	−0.79 to −0.95	−0.06 to −0.15	−0.58 to −0.63	−0.81 to −0.95	−0.94 to −1.06
	(2)	−0.28 to −0.48	−0.56 to −0.72	−0.35 to −0.44	−0.63 to −0.71	−0.59 to −0.73	−0.67 to −0.79
	(3)	+0.71 to +0.95	+0.58 to +0.82	+0.35 to +0.46	+0.28 to +0.41	+0.47 to +0.67	+0.45 to +0.65
Wilmington, N. C.	(1)	−0.28 to −0.76	−0.92 to −1.32	−0.34 to −0.61	−1.05 to −1.27	−1.30 to −1.62	−1.60 to −1.90
	(2)	−0.05 to −0.43	−0.38 to −0.78	−0.31 to −0.59	−0.73 to −0.95	−0.76 to −1.08	−0.85 to −1.15
	(3)	+1.40 to +1.87	+1.22 to +1.65	+0.96 to +1.29	+0.84 to +1.14	+0.99 to +1.34	+0.99 to +1.25
Chattanooga, Tenn.	(1)	−0.27 to +0.06	−0.34 to −0.61	+0.72 to +0.91	+0.06 to +0.20	−0.50 to −0.70	−0.61 to −0.81
	(2)	−0.91 to −1.19	−0.78 to −1.05	−0.36 to −0.51	−0.72 to −0.86	−0.94 to −1.14	−0.99 to −1.19
	(3)	+1.14 to +1.53	+0.91 to +1.30	+0.62 to +0.81	+0.47 to +0.68	+0.82 to +1.14	+0.77 to +1.09
Birmingham, Ala.	(1)	−1.69 to −1.97	−1.79 to −2.03	−0.14 to −0.28	−0.69 to −0.81	−1.67 to −1.85	−1.66 to −1.85
	(2)	−0.91 to −1.19	−1.01 to −1.25	−0.30 to −0.44	−0.62 to −0.74	−1.03 to −1.21	−1.02 to −1.21
	(3)	+0.73 to +1.01	+0.67 to +0.91	+0.49 to +0.65	+0.43 to +0.63	+0.60 to +0.78	+0.54 to +0.83
Puerto Rico	(3)	+2.12 to +2.68	+2.08 to +2.57	+1.29 to +1.61	+1.38 to +1.68	+1.89 to +2.28	+1.96 to +2.33

* See pp. 48–49.   (1) Rail class rates.   (2) Rail commodity rates.   (3) Water transportation.

TABLE A-1 *(Continued)*

Hypothetical Plant Site		Cost Advantage (−) or Disadvantage (+) Relative to Texas-Gulf Production					
		Plant Type VII	Plant Type VIII	Plant Type IX	Plant Type X	Plant Type XI	Plant Type XII
Orange, Texas		$0.00	$0.00	$0.00	$0.00	$0.00	$0.00
Institute, W. Va.	(1)	−2.38 to −2.44	−2.78 to −2.86	−3.24 to −3.31	−3.35 to −3.43	−2.36 to −2.41	−2.75 to −2.82
	(2)	−1.91 to −1.97	−2.15 to −2.23	−2.59 to −2.66	−2.62 to −2.70	−1.91 to −1.96	−2.14 to −2.21
	(3)	−0.01 to −0.07	−0.08 to −0.16	−0.37 to −0.44	−0.34 to −0.42	−0.03 to −0.08	−0.09 to −0.16
Boston, Mass.	(1)	−1.50 to −1.80	−2.05 to −2.32	−1.82 to −2.32	−1.95 to −2.44	−1.43 to −1.74	−1.94 to −2.23
	(2)	−1.08 to −1.38	−1.46 to −1.73	−1.13 to −1.63	−1.19 to −1.68	−1.04 to −1.35	−1.38 to −1.67
	(3)	+1.35 to +1.79	+1.20 to +1.59	+1.60 to +2.20	+1.58 to +2.20	+1.35 to +1.87	+1.23 to +1.71
Memphis, Tenn.	(1)	−1.04 to −1.13	−1.25 to −1.36	−2.07 to −2.21	−2.24 to −2.38	−2.31 to −2.39	−2.51 to −2.59
	(2)	−0.53 to −0.62	−0.74 to −0.85	−1.35 to −1.49	−1.48 to −1.62	−1.39 to −1.47	−1.59 to −1.67
	(3)	+0.34 to +0.59	+0.28 to +0.43	+0.25 to +0.47	+0.19 to +0.42	+0.05 to +0.19	0.00 to +0.14
Mobile, Ala.	(1)	−0.49 to −0.58	−0.81 to −0.89	−1.36 to −1.50	−1.51 to −1.64	−1.06 to −1.15	−1.37 to −1.45
	(2)	−0.54 to −0.63	−0.71 to −0.78	−1.00 to −1.14	−1.10 to −1.23	−0.97 to −1.06	−1.15 to −1.23
	(3)	+0.29 to +0.42	+0.25 to +0.39	+0.35 to +0.55	+0.30 to +0.51	+0.15 to +0.18	+0.12 to +0.26
Wilmington, N. C.	(1)	−1.11 to −1.31	−1.60 to −1.77	−1.81 to −2.16	−1.67 to −2.00	−1.33 to −1.55	−1.78 to −2.01
	(2)	−0.81 to −1.01	−1.04 to −1.21	−0.87 to −1.22	−1.00 to −1.33	−0.97 to −1.19	−1.25 to −1.46
	(3)	+0.85 to +1.17	+0.72 to +0.98	+1.00 to +1.41	+0.96 to +1.38	+0.80 to +1.14	+0.75 to +1.03
Chattanooga, Tenn.	(1)	+0.03 to +0.16	−0.29 to −0.41	−1.00 to −1.24	−1.14 to −1.36	−0.40 to −0.54	−0.82 to −0.96
	(2)	−0.73 to −0.86	−0.98 to −1.10	−1.20 to −1.44	−1.28 to −1.50	−1.05 to −1.19	−1.27 to −1.41
	(3)	+0.58 to +0.74	+0.46 to +0.69	+0.53 to +0.87	+0.45 to +0.80	+0.25 to +0.47	+0.17 to +0.39
Birmingham, Ala.	(1)	−0.62 to −0.73	−1.00 to −1.08	−2.35 to −2.54	−2.37 to −2.55	−1.69 to −1.72	−1.68 to −1.79
	(2)	−0.57 to −0.68	−0.80 to −0.88	−1.48 to −1.67	−1.50 to −1.74	−1.42 to −1.45	−1.25 to −1.36
	(3)	+0.48 to +0.67	+0.42 to +0.60	+0.30 to +0.50	+0.38 to +0.68	+0.07 to +0.10	+0.27 to +0.46
Puerto Rico	(3)	+1.51 to +1.79	+1.47 to +1.73	+2.19 to +2.62	+2.20 to +2.60	+1.76 to +2.08	+1.73 to +2.04

(1) Rail class rates.   (2) Rail commodity rates.   (3) Water transportation.

TABLE A-2
REGIONAL VARIABLE-COST DIFFERENCES PER 100 POUNDS: NYLON SALT
Table 4(II), Plant Type VII*

Hypothetical Plant Site		Transport Cost		Transport Cost from Nearest Large-Scale Producing Center	
		Nylon Salt from Orange, Texas $0.00	Natural Gas from Houston, Texas $0.00	Petroleum Cyclohexane $0.00	Butadiene $0.00
Institute, W. Va.	(1)	4.33		1.76	0.00
	(2)	3.25		1.15	
	(3)	0.68	0.18 to 0.24	0.48	
Boston, Mass.	(1)	6.05		2.25	0.51
	(2)	4.78		1.57	0.34
	(3)	1.03 to 1.33	0.29 to 0.38	0.72 to 0.93	0.26 to 0.31
Memphis, Tenn.	(1)	2.68		0.83	0.40
	(2)	2.07		0.83	0.30
	(3)	0.30	0.09 to 0.12	0.21	0.14
Mobile, Ala.	(1)	2.43		1.22	0.37
	(2)	1.88		0.70	0.29
	(3)	0.15	0.08 to 0.10	0.12	0.08
Wilmington, N. C.	(1)	4.50		1.88	0.39
	(2)	3.38		1.19	0.26
	(3)	0.70 to 0.90	0.19 to 0.25	0.51 to 0.64	0.18 to 0.21
Chattanooga, Tenn.	(1)	2.60		1.72	0.36
	(2)	2.60		0.94	0.25
	(3)	0.58	0.13 to 0.17	0.40	0.25
Birmingham, Ala.	(1)	3.03		1.43	0.41
	(2)	2.25		0.84	0.27
	(3)	0.33	0.11 to 0.15	0.24	0.15
Puerto Rico	(3)	0.83 to 1.05	0.19 to 0.25	0.58 to 0.75	0.21 to 0.25

* See p. 49.   (1) Rail class rates.   (2) Rail commodity rates.   (3) Water transportation.

TABLE A-2 *(Continued)*

Hypothetical Plant Site		Cost Advantage (−) or Disadvantage (+) Relative to Texas-Gulf Production				
		Transport Costs	Fuel Costs	Power Costs	Labor Costs	Total Selected Costs
Orange, Texas		$0.00	$0.00	$0.00	$0.00	$0.00
Institute, W. Va.	(1)	−2.33 to −2.39	0.00	0.00	−0.05	−2.38 to −2.44
	(2)	−1.86 to −1.92				−1.91 to −1.97
	(3)	−0.02 to +0.04				−0.01 to −0.07
Boston, Mass.	(1)	−2.91 to −3.00	+0.99 to +1.29	+0.27 to +0.36	−0.15	−1.50 to −1.80
	(2)	−2.49 to −2.58				−1.08 to −1.38
	(3)	+0.24 to +0.29				+1.35 to +1.79
Memphis, Tenn.	(1)	−1.33 to −1.36	+0.29 to +0.38	+0.08 to +0.11	−0.17	−1.04 to −1.13
	(2)	−0.82 to −0.85				−0.53 to −0.62
	(3)	+0.14 to +0.17				+0.34 to +0.59
Mobile, Ala.	(1)	−0.74 to −0.76	+0.26 to +0.35	+0.07 to +0.09	−0.17	−0.49 to −0.58
	(2)	−0.79 to −0.81				−0.54 to −0.63
	(3)	+0.13 to +0.15				+0.29 to +0.42
Wilmington, N. C.	(1)	−1.98 to −2.04	+0.66 to +0.86	+0.18 to +0.24	−0.17	−1.11 to −1.31
	(2)	−1.68 to −1.74				−0.81 to −1.01
	(3)	+0.18 to +0.24				+0.85 to +1.17
Chattanooga, Tenn.	(1)	−0.35 to −0.39	+0.43 to +0.56	+0.12 to +0.16	−0.17	+0.03 to +0.16
	(2)	−1.24 to −1.28				−0.73 to −0.86
	(3)	+0.20 to +0.24				+0.58 to +0.74
Birmingham, Ala.	(1)	−1.04 to −1.08	+0.38 to +0.49	+0.10 to +0.14	−0.17	−0.62 to −0.73
	(2)	−0.99 to −1.03				−0.57 to −0.68
	(3)	+0.16 to +0.21				+0.48 to +0.67
Puerto Rico	(3)	+0.15 to +0.20	+0.66 to +0.84	+0.18 to +0.23	+0.52	+1.51 to +1.79

(1) Rail class rate. (2) Rail commodity rates. (3) Water transportation.

TABLE A-3

REGIONAL VARIABLE-COST DIFFERENCES PER 100 POUNDS: ACRYLONITRILE

Summary of Total Selected Costs for Table 5, Plant Types I-VI*

Hypothetical Plant Site		Cost Advantage (−) or Disadvantage (+) Relative to Texas-Gulf Production		
		Plant Type I	Plant Type II	Plant Type III
Texas City, Texas		$0.00	$0.00	$0.00
Institute, W. Va.	(1)	−0.43 to −0.67	−0.80 to −0.95	−0.77 to −0.93
	(2)	−0.23 to +0.01	−0.36 to −0.51	−0.37 to −0.51
	(3)	+0.46 to +0.74	+0.18 to +0.32	+0.20 to +0.36
Boston, Mass.	(1)	+0.68 to +1.50	+0.26 to +0.29	+0.07 to +0.13
	(2)	+1.29 to +2.11	+0.87 to +1.00	+0.68 to +0.74
	(3)	+2.18 to +2.88	+1.47 to +1.96	+1.30 to +1.78
Memphis, Tenn.	(1)	−0.06 to −0.14	−0.33 to −0.35	−0.42 to −0.43
	(2)	+0.06 to +0.30	−0.05 to −0.07	−0.14 to −0.15
	(3)	+0.55 to +0.79	+0.33 to +0.53	+0.26 to +0.43
Mobile, Ala.	(1)	−0.11 to −0.17	−0.39 to −0.40	−0.44 to −0.46
	(2)	+0.03 to +0.25	−0.11 to −0.12	−0.16 to −0.18
	(3)	+0.52 to +0.74	+0.30 to +0.45	+0.24 to +0.40
Wilmington, N. C.	(1)	+0.20 to +0.75	−0.05 to −0.08	−0.18 to −0.22
	(2)	+0.67 to +1.22	−0.39 to −0.42	−0.25 to −0.29
	(3)	+1.37 to +1.84	+0.90 to +1.23	+0.77 to +1.09
Chattanooga, Tenn.	(1)	−0.13 to +0.02	−0.26 to −0.29	−0.38 to −0.40
	(2)	+0.26 to +0.63	−0.08 to −0.11	−0.01 to −0.03
	(3)	+0.81 to +1.18	+0.50 to +0.79	+0.41 to +0.65
Puerto Rico	(3)	+1.91 to +2.32	+1.42 to +1.72	+1.44 to +1.72

* See p. 50.

(1) Rail class rates.   (2) Rail commodity rates.   (3) Water transportation.

TABLE A-3 (*Continued*)

Hypothetical Plant Site		Cost Advantage (−) or Disadvantage (+) Relative to Texas-Gulf Production		
		Plant Type IV	Plant Type V	Plant Type VI
Texas City, Texas		$0.00	$0.00	$0.00
Institute, W. Va.	(1)	−1.09 to −1.17	−0.89 to −1.02	−0.93 to −1.06
	(2)	−0.65 to −0.73	−0.45 to −0.58	−0.49 to −0.62
	(3)	−0.04 to +0.04	+0.11 to +0.24	+0.07 to +0.20
Boston, Mass.	(1)	+1.18 to +1.50	+0.78 to +1.27	+0.28 to +0.54
	(2)	+1.20 to +1.52	+1.39 to +1.88	+0.89 to +1.15
	(3)	+1.15 to +1.47	+1.34 to +1.77	+1.56 to +2.14
Memphis, Tenn.	(1)	+0.33 to +0.41	+0.40 to +0.55	−0.37 to −0.44
	(2)	+0.32 to +0.40	+0.68 to +0.88	−0.09 to −0.16
	(3)	+0.41 to +0.49	+0.59 to +0.74	+0.26 to +0.47
Mobile, Ala.	(1)	+0.27 to +0.37	−0.09 to −0.10	−0.40 to −0.47
	(2)	+0.27 to +0.37	+0.12 to +0.25	−0.12 to −0.19
	(3)	+0.26 to +0.36	+0.51 to +0.64	+0.24 to +0.43
Wilmington, N. C.	(1)	+0.77 to +0.97	+0.62 to +0.93	−0.11 to +0.05
	(2)	+0.77 to +0.97	+1.09 to +1.40	+0.36 to +0.52
	(3)	−0.72 to +0.93	+0.87 to +1.10	+0.91 to +1.29
Chattanooga, Tenn.	(1)	+0.50 to +0.64	0.00 to −0.02	−0.25 to −0.35
	(2)	+0.50 to +0.64	+0.75 to +0.97	+0.02 to +0.12
	(3)	+0.73 to +0.90	+0.80 to +1.02	+0.47 to +0.77
Puerto Rico	(3)	+1.24 to +1.44	+2.09 to +2.46	+1.98 to +2.32

(1) Rail class rates. (2) Rail commodity rates. (3) Water transportation.

TABLE A-4

REGIONAL VARIABLE-COST DIFFERENCES PER 100 POUNDS: DYNEL COPOLYMER

Summary of Total Selected Costs for Table 6, Plant Types I–VII*

Hypothetical Plant Site		Cost Advantage (−) or Disadvantage (+) Relative to Texas-Gulf Production		
		Plant Type I	Plant Type II	Plant Type III
Texas City, Texas		$0.00	$0.00	$0.00
Institute, W. Va.	(1)	−1.03 to −1.18	−1.33 to −1.41	−1.35 to −1.43
	(2)	−0.54 to −0.69	−0.84 to −0.92	−0.86 to −0.94
	(3)	−0.09 to +0.06	−0.24 to −0.32	−0.26 to −0.34
Boston, Mass.	(1)	−0.01 to −0.19	−0.71 to −0.74	−0.97 to −0.99
	(2)	+0.23 to +0.85	−0.06 to +0.03	−0.29 to −0.31
	(3)	+1.11 to +1.51	+0.56 to +0.77	+0.31 to +0.45
Memphis, Tenn.	(1)	−0.33 to −0.36	−0.52 to −0.53	−0.59 to −0.60
	(2)	−0.01 to +0.16	−0.11 to −0.12	−0.19 to −0.20
	(3)	+0.23 to +0.40	+0.07 to +0.18	+0.02 to +0.03
Mobile, Ala.	(1)	−0.43 to −0.48	−0.63 to −0.65	−0.71 to −0.73
	(2)	−0.12 to −0.17	−0.32 to −0.34	−0.40 to −0.42
	(3)	+0.32 to +0.47	+0.17 to +0.25	+0.08 to −0.16
Wilmington, N. C.	(1)	−0.19 to −0.32	−0.67 to −0.69	−0.85 to −0.86
	(2)	−0.11 to +0.46	−0.13 to −0.15	−0.31 to −0.32
	(3)	+0.78 to +1.05	+0.41 to +0.57	+0.25 to +0.34
Chattanooga, Tenn.	(1)	−0.44 to −0.50	−0.74 to −0.75	−0.87 to −0.88
	(2)	−0.02 to −0.10	−0.34 to −0.35	−0.47 to −0.48
	(3)	+0.29 to +0.53	+0.12 to +0.13	−0.01 to 0.00
Puerto Rico	(3)	+1.12 to +1.40	+0.75 to +0.91	+0.70 to +0.82

* See p. 51.

(1) Rail class rates.　(2) Rail commodity rates.　(3) Water transportation.

TABLE A-4 (*Continued*)

Hypothetical Plant Site		Cost Advantage (−) or Disadvantage (+) Relative to Texas-Gulf Production			
		Plant Type IV	Plant Type V	Plant Type VI	Plant Type VII
Texas City, Texas		$0.00	$0.00	$0.00	$0.00
Institute, W. Va.	(1)	−1.53 to −1.56	−1.44 to −1.47	−0.97 to −1.00	−0.28 to −0.35
	(2)	−1.04 to −1.07	−0.95 to −0.98	−0.65 to −0.68	−0.11 to −0.18
	(3)	−0.44 to −0.47	−0.35 to −0.38	−0.33 to −0.36	+0.10 to +0.17
Boston, Mass.	(1)	+0.19 to +0.36	−0.59 to −0.62	−0.83 to −0.83	+0.11 to +0.14
	(2)	+0.39 to +0.56	+0.06 to +0.09	−0.39 to −0.39	+0.35 to +0.38
	(3)	+0.34 to +0.53	+0.31 to +0.44	+0.03 to +0.03	+0.60 to +0.80
Memphis, Tenn.	(1)	−0.01 to −0.02	−0.25 to −0.26	−0.36 to −0.37	−0.13 to −0.14
	(2)	+0.15 to +0.18	+0.12 to +0.20	−0.06 to −0.07	−0.02 to −0.03
	(3)	+0.02 to +0.05	+0.08 to +0.17	+0.16 to +0.19	+0.14 to +0.23
Mobile, Ala.	(1)	−0.01 to −0.01	−0.57 to −0.57	−0.47 to −0.48	−0.14 to −0.15
	(2)	+0.06 to +0.09	−0.26 to −0.26	−0.26 to −0.27	−0.03 to −0.04
	(3)	+0.05 to +0.09	+0.13 to +0.19	+0.06 to +0.09	+0.13 to +0.20
Wilmington, N. C.	(1)	+0.11 to +0.11	−0.46 to −0.46	−0.63 to −0.64	−0.02 to −0.02
	(2)	+0.24 to +0.32	+0.08 to +0.08	−0.30 to −0.31	+0.17 to +0.17
	(3)	+0.24 to +0.35	+0.36 to +0.42	+0.07 to +0.09	+0.37 to +0.50
Chattanooga, Tenn.	(1)	+0.04 to +0.04	−0.72 to −0.73	−0.61 to −0.62	−0.11 to −0.11
	(2)	+0.11 to +0.05	−0.32 to −0.33	−0.35 to −0.36	−0.09 to −0.09
	(3)	+0.05 to +0.09	+0.07 to +0.18	−0.10 to −0.11	+0.19 to +0.31
Puerto Rico	(3)	+0.49 to +0.59	+0.98 to +1.11	+0.20 to +0.25	+0.58 to +0.70

(1) Rail class rates.   (2) Rail commodity rates.   (3) Water transportation.

TABLE A-5
REGIONAL VARIABLE-COST DIFFERENCES PER 100 POUNDS: DACRON POLYMER
Summary of Total Selected Costs for Table 7, Plant Types I-VII*

Hypothetical Plant Site		Cost Advantage (−) or Disadvantage (+) Relative to Texas-Gulf Production		
		Plant Type I	Plant Type II	Plant Type III
Texas City, Texas		$0.00	$0.00	$0.00
Institute, W. Va.	(1)	−1.53 to −1.54	−1.55 to −1.56	−1.74 to −1.75
	(2)	−1.38 to −1.39	−1.40 to −1.41	−1.43 to −1.44
	(3)	−0.10 to −0.11	−0.12 to −0.13	−0.14 to −0.15
Boston, Mass.	(1)	−2.22 to −2.26	−1.89 to −1.93	−0.70 to −0.82
	(2)	−1.85 to −1.89	−1.52 to −1.56	−0.24 to −0.36
	(3)	−0.37 to −0.45	−0.25 to −0.37	+0.09 to +0.13
Memphis, Tenn.	(1)	−0.85 to −0.87	−0.59 to −0.60	0.00 to −0.04
	(2)	−0.68 to −0.70	−0.43 to −0.44	+0.13 to +0.19
	(3)	−0.07 to −0.09	−0.01 to +0.02	+0.08 to +0.12
Mobile, Ala.	(1)	−0.57 to −0.60	−0.46 to −0.47	+0.29 to +0.31
	(2)	−0.65 to −0.69	−0.54 to −0.55	+0.25 to +0.27
	(3)	−0.03 to −0.06	+0.06 to +0.07	+0.17 to +0.19
Wilmington, N. C.	(1)	−1.51 to −1.58	−1.21 to −1.24	−0.69 to −0.77
	(2)	−1.30 to −1.32	−1.00 to −1.02	−0.29 to −0.37
	(3)	−0.26 to −0.27	−0.13 to −0.15	0.00 to +0.06
Chattanooga, Tenn.	(1)	−0.98 to −1.00	−0.84 to −0.86	+0.05 to +0.11
	(2)	−0.89 to −0.91	−0.75 to −0.77	+0.23 to +0.31
	(3)	−0.15 to −0.17	−0.01 to −0.03	+0.14 to +0.20
Puerto Rico	(3)	+0.12 to +0.13	+0.35 to +0.35	+0.75 to +0.89

* See p. 55.
(1) Rail class rates.   (2) Rail commodity rates.   (3) Water transportation.

TABLE A-5 (*Continued*)

Hypothetical Plant Site		Cost Advantage (−) or Disadvantage (+) Relative to Texas-Gulf Production			
		Plant Type IV	Plant Type V	Plant Type VI	Plant Type VII
Texas City, Texas		$0.00	$0.00	$0.00	$0.00
Institute, W. Va.	(1)	−1.74 to −1.77	−0.45 to −0.46	−1.85	−1.41
	(2)	−1.45 to −1.46	−0.33 to −0.34	−1.04	−1.10
	(3)	−0.16 to −0.17	−0.11 to −0.12	+0.02	−0.03
Boston, Mass.	(1)	−0.36 to −0.47	−0.52 to −0.52	−1.85 to −1.88	−0.39 to −0.50
	(2)	−0.01 to +0.10	−0.34 to −0.34	−1.51 to −1.48	−0.04 to +0.07
	(3)	+0.14 to +0.20	−0.10 to −0.12	−0.23 to −0.30	−0.17 to +0.22
Memphis, Tenn.	(1)	−1.21 to −1.24	−0.21 to −0.21	−0.63 to −0.64	+0.17 to +0.21
	(2)	+0.39 to +0.44	−0.21 to −0.21	−0.45 to −0.46	+0.35 to +0.39
	(3)	+0.17 to +0.22	−0.03 to −0.03	−0.04 to −0.05	+0.11 to +0.15
Mobile, Ala.	(1)	+0.39 to +0.44	−0.20 to −0.20	−0.37 to −0.38	+0.47 to +0.51
	(2)	+0.35 to +0.40	−0.20 to −0.20	−0.45 to −0.46	+0.43 to +0.47
	(3)	+0.26 to +0.31	0.00 to 0.00	−0.03 to −0.04	+0.15 to +0.19
Wilmington, N. C.	(1)	−0.40 to −0.47	−0.29 to −0.29	−1.20 to −1.22	−0.42 to −0.49
	(2)	0.00 to −0.07	−0.29 to −0.29	−0.99 to −1.01	−0.02 to −0.09
	(3)	+0.13 to +0.18	−0.07 to −0.09	−0.16 to −0.17	+0.08 to +0.11
Chattanooga, Tenn.	(1)	+0.19 to +0.26	−0.25 to −0.25	−0.71 to −0.73	+0.29 to +0.35
	(2)	+0.38 to +0.45	−0.25 to −0.25	−0.62 to −0.63	+0.48 to +0.54
	(3)	+0.28 to +0.35	−0.08 to −0.08	−0.04 to −0.06	+0.22 to +0.28
Puerto Rico	(3)	+0.98 to +1.16	−0.01 to −0.03	+0.19 to +0.20	+0.78 to +0.94

(1) Rail class rates.   (2) Rail commodity rates.   (3) Water transportation.

Appendix B

Estimated Scale Economies
in Chemical-Intermediate Production

TABLE B-1

ESTIMATED SCALE ECONOMIES IN NYLON-SALT PRODUCTION

Plant Factor: 0.60	Labor Factor: 0.22	
Plant capacity (million lb per year)	60	90
Plant investment (in $ 000)	37,500	47,800
Labor man-hours per year	178,000	195,000
Selected costs per year in $ 000		
Operating labor	395	433
Supervision	40	43
Plant maintenance	1,500	1,912
Equipment and operating supplies	225	287
Payroll overhead	178	214
Indirect production cost	1,080	1,337
General office overhead	216	268
Depreciation	3,750	4,780
Taxes	375	478
Insurance	375	478
Interest	1,000	1,912
Total:	$9,634	$12,142
Selected costs per 100 lb:	$16.05	$13.49

Plant Factor. C. H. Chilton, " 'Six-Tenths' Factor Applies to Complete Plant Costs," *Chemical Engineering,* Vol. 57 (April 1950), pp. 112–114.

Labor Factor. Derived by the procedure described in H. E. Wessel, "New Graph Correlates Operating Labor Data for Chemical Processes," *Chemical Engineering,* Vol. 59 (July 1952), pp. 209–210.

Plant Investment. See Table 17, p. 111.

Labor Man-Hours. Labor coefficient for Plant Type I, Table 4(I), p. 42.

178

TABLE B-2

ESTIMATED SCALE ECONOMIES IN CHLORINE PRODUCTION

Plant Factor: 0.80		Labor Factor: 0.22	
Plant capacity (million lb per year)	25	80	160
Plant investment (in $ 000)	2,720	8,700	15,400
Labor man-hours per year	96,000	124,000	143,000
Selected costs per year in $ 000			
Operating labor	213	275	317
Supervision	21	28	32
Plant maintenance	109	348	616
Equipment and operating supplies	16	52	92
Payroll overhead	43	71	98
Indirect production cost	180	352	529
General office overhead	18	35	106
Depreciation	272	870	1,540
Taxes	27	87	154
Insurance	27	87	154
Interest	109	348	616
Total:	$1,035	$2,553	$4,254
Selected costs per 100 lb:	$4.14	$3.19	$2.66

Plant Factor. Derived from outlays on a number of chlorine plants given in "New Plants and Facilities Underway in 1951," *Chemical Engineering,* Vol. 59 (February 1952), pp. 175–176.

Labor Factor. Wessel, *op. cit.*

Plant Investment. An outlay of $8,700,000 for a chlorine plant with annual capacity of 80 million lb is reported in "New Plants and Facilities Underway in 1951," *op. cit.*

Labor Man-Hours. A labor coefficient of 0.18 per 100 lb of chlorine for a 66-million-lb plant is given by Isard and Schooler, *op. cit.*, p. 26.

TABLE B-3

ESTIMATED SCALE ECONOMIES IN SODIUM CYANIDE PRODUCTION

Plant Factor: 0.60		Labor Factor: 0.22	
Plant capacity (million lb per year)	30	50	100
Plant investment (in $ 000)	3,640	4,945	7,500
Labor man-hours per year	54,500	60,800	71,170
Selected costs per year in $ 000			
Operating labor	121	135	158
Supervision	12	14	16
Plant maintenance	146	198	300
Equipment and operating supplies	22	30	75
Payroll overhead	31	37	49
Indirect production cost	150	189	275
General office overhead	30	38	55
Depreciation	364	495	750
Taxes	36	50	75
Insurance	36	50	75
Interest	146	198	300
Total:	$1,094	$1,434	$2,128
Selected costs per 100 lb:	$3.64	$2.87	$2.13

Plant Factor.   Chilton, *op. cit.*
Labor Factor.   Wessel, *op. cit.*
Plant Investment.   A figure of $7.5 million for a plant with an annual capacity of 100 million lb is given in "New Plants and Facilities Underway in 1951," *op. cit.,* p. 185.
Labor Man-Hours.   Derived from an input of 0.122 per 100 lb for a 50-million-lb plant.

TABLE B-4
ESTIMATED SCALE ECONOMIES IN ACRYLONITRILE PRODUCTION

Plant Factor: 0.60 (Via HCN and Acetylene)		Labor Factor: 0.22	
Plant capacity (million lb per year)	30	60	90
Plant investment (in $ 000)	17,300	26,800	33,400
Labor man-hours per year	128,000	149,000	163,000
Selected costs per year in $ 000			
Operating labor	284	331	362
Supervision	28	33	36
Plant maintenance	692	1,072	1,336
Equipment and operating supplies	104	161	200
Payroll overhead	99	135	160
Indirect production cost	554	798	967
General office overhead	111	160	193
Depreciation	1,730	2,680	3,340
Taxes	173	268	334
Insurance	173	268	334
Interest	692	1,072	1,336
Total:	$4,640	$6,978	$8,598
Selected costs per 100 lb:	$15.47	$11.63	$9.55

(Via Ethylene Oxide and HCN)

Selected Costs per 100 lb:*	$11.60	$8.72	$7.16

Plant Factor. Chilton, *op. cit.*
Labor Factor. Wessel, *op. cit.*
Plant Investment. For an acrylonitrile plant with a capacity of 75 million lb an investment cost of $30 million is given in "Latest Nor Least," *Chemical Industries,* Vol. 67 (December 1950), pp. 875–876.
Labor Man-Hours. Labor coefficient for Plant Type I, Table 5, p. 50.
* Selected costs per 100 lb of acrylonitrile via the ethylene oxide route were obtained by taking 75 per cent of the figures in the acetylene route. R. W. Messing and R. L. James, "Acrylonitrile," *Chemical Industries Week,* Vol. 68 (January 27, 1951), pp. 19-24, report that the investment outlay via the acetylene route is 25 per cent greater than the ethylene oxide route.

TABLE B-5

ESTIMATED SCALE ECONOMIES IN DIMETHYL TEREPHTHALATE
PRODUCTION

Plant Factor: 0.60		Labor Factor: 0.22	
Plant capacity (million lb per year)	12	35	60
Plant investment (in $ 000)	4,000	7,600	10,500
Labor man-hours per year	21,620	45,550	51,350
Selected costs per year in $ 000			
Operating labor	48	101	114
Supervision	5	10	11
Plant maintenance	160	304	420
Equipment and operating supplies	24	46	63
Payroll overhead	20	40	51
Indirect production cost	119	231	304
General office overhead	24	46	61
Depreciation	400	760	1,050
Taxes	40	76	105
Insurance	40	76	105
Interest	160	304	420
Total:	$1,040	$1,994	$2,704
Selected costs per 100 lb:	$8.67	$5.70	$4.51

Plant Factor. Chilton, *op. cit.*
Labor Factor. Wessel, *op. cit.*
Plant Investment. An investment figure of $4.0 million for a plant with a
capacity of 12 million lb is given in "Hercules Will Make Basic Materials for
ICI Terylene," *Chemical and Engineering News,* Vol. 32 (January 11, 1954),
p. 22.
Labor Man-Hours. Plant Type I, Table 7, p. 55.

Appendix C

Regional Cost Differences
in the Production of Synthetic Fibers

The computation of regional cost differences in synthetic-fiber production is based on the findings in each case with respect to the orientation of chemical-intermediate production.

Nylon 66 Fiber

Analysis of the production of nylon salt indicated that production could take place in raw-material regions or in the textile area of the United States.[1]

Tables C–1 and C–2 assume that nylon salt is manufactured in the raw-material regions—the Texas-Gulf and West Virginia—and shipped to fiber plants in the textile area of the United States or Puerto Rico. The specific raw-material region that would supply each hypothetical site was determined by selecting the lowest transportation cost.

Table C–1 also contains the complete and detailed calculation of the weighted average transport cost of shipping fibers to the five regional markets from each hypothetical site. Since the transport cost is the same for all fibers, the detailed computation is not repeated in the other tables, which include only a column designated "Weighted Average Transport Cost of Synthetic Fibers to the National Market."

Table C–3 shows regional cost differences for the integrated output of nylon salt and nylon 66 fiber. The points of origin for the assembly of benzene and ammonia were given in Appendix A.[2]

[1] See pp. 130–131.
[2] See pp. 161–162.

The Other Fibers

For the other fibers the analysis of the chemical-intermediate stage shows raw-material orientation. Transportation costs are included for both raw-material regions so that the lowest could be selected.

Transportation costs for the rail shipment of dimethyl formamide (the solvent for acrylonitrile in the manufacture of Orlon) in Table C–4 were derived from data furnished by the Traffic Department of the Du Pont company. For water costs ordinary chemical rates were used.

For acetone (see Table C–5) rail-transportation costs are 27.5 per cent of ICC 28300, and information to this effect was supplied by the Monsanto Chemical Co. Ordinary chemical rates apply on water shipments.

TABLE C-1
REGIONAL VARIABLE-COST DIFFERENCES PER 100 POUNDS: NYLON 66 STAPLE FIBER
Table 9, Column 1*

Hypothetical Plant Site		Transport Cost of Nylon Salt in Solution		Transport Cost of Synthetic Fibers to New England Market		
		From Orange, Texas	From Institute, W. Va.	To	Carload	Less-than-Carload
Orange, Texas		$0.00		Boston	$1.96	$3.02
Institute, W. Va.	(1)	6.05	$0.00 + 0.29 = $0.29[a]	Boston	1.22	1.87
	(2)	4.78		Lowell	0.34	0.51
	(3)	1.03 to 1.33				
Boston, Mass.	(1)	2.68	3.73 + 0.29 = 4.02			
	(2)	2.07	3.10 + 0.29 = 3.39			
	(3)	0.30				
Memphis, Tenn.	(1)	2.43	3.14 + 0.29 = 3.43	Boston	1.62	2.49
	(2)	1.88	2.45 + 0.29 = 2.74			
	(3)	0.15	0.45 + 0.29 = 0.74			
Mobile, Ala.	(1)	4.50	3.73 + 0.29 = 4.02	Boston	1.67	2.58
	(2)	3.38	2.90 + 0.29 = 3.19			
	(3)	0.70 to 0.90				
Wilmington, N. C.	(1)	2.60	2.84 + 0.29 = 3.13	Boston	1.20	1.83
	(2)	2.60	2.25 + 0.29 = 2.54			
	(3)	0.58				
Chattanooga, Tenn.	(1)	3.03	2.05 + 0.29 = 2.34	Boston	1.38	2.13
	(2)	2.25	2.05 + 0.29 = 2.34			
	(3)	0.33	0.46 + 0.29 = 0.75			
Birmingham, Ala.	(1)		3.02 + 0.29 = 3.31	Boston	1.50	2.31
	(2)		2.37 + 0.29 = 2.66			
Puerto Rico	(4)	0.83 to 1.05		Lowell via Boston	2.27	2.44

* See p. 73.

[a] Excess cost of process natural gas at Institute over Texas ($0.16) and benzene by water ($0.13) makes up the $0.29 per 100-lb cost disadvantage relative to Orange.

(1) Rail class rates.   (2) Rail commodity rates.   (3) Water transportation.   (4) Water and rail.

TABLE C-1 (*Continued*)

		Transport Cost of Synthetic Fibers to:					
		Middle Atlantic Market			East South Market		
Hypothetical Plant Site		To	Carload	Less-than-Carload	To	Carload	Less-than-Carload
Orange, Texas	(1)	Philadelphia	$1.76	$2.88	Spartanburg	$1.29	$1.99
Institute, W. Va.	(1)	Philadelphia	0.91	1.48	Spartanburg	0.89	1.37
Boston, Mass.	(1)	Philadelphia	0.73	1.13	Spartanburg	1.27	1.95
Memphis, Tenn.	(1)	Philadelphia	1.39	2.13	Spartanburg	1.15	1.52
Mobile, Ala.	(1)	Philadelphia	1.42	2.19	Spartanburg	1.09	1.43
Wilmington, N. C.	(1)	Philadelphia	0.89	1.37	Spartanburg	0.78	1.03
Chattanooga, Tenn.	(1)	Philadelphia	1.14	1.75	Spartanburg	0.82	1.10
Birmingham, Ala.	(1)	Philadelphia	1.26	1.93	Spartanburg	0.88	1.16
Puerto Rico	(4)	Scranton, Pa., via Philadelphia	2.45	2.74	Spartanburg via Wilmington	2.71	2.96

(1) Rail class rates. (4) Water and rail.

TABLE C-1 (*Continued*)

Hypothetical Plant Site		Transport Cost of Synthetic Fibers					Weighted Average Transport Cost of Synthetic Fibers to National Market	
	Central South Market			West South Market				
	To	Carload	Less-than-Carload	To	Carload	Less-than-Carload	Carload	Less-than-Carload
Orange, Texas (1)	Lanett, Ala.	$1.08	$1.66	Corinth, Miss.	$0.95	$1.46	$1.38	$2.17
Institute, W. Va. (1)	Lanett	1.01	1.54	Corinth	1.04	1.60	0.98	1.51
Boston, Mass. (1)	Lanett	1.47	2.25	Corinth	1.56	2.40	1.10	1.72
Memphis, Tenn. (1)	Lanett	0.96	1.26	Corinth	0.46	0.66	1.14	1.62
Mobile, Ala. (1)	Lanett	0.79	1.03	Corinth	1.07	1.43	1.16	1.63
Wilmington, N. C. (1)	Lanett	1.05	1.37	Corinth	1.29	1.75	0.96	1.34
Chattanooga, Tenn. (1)	Lanett	0.86	1.13	Corinth	0.71	0.95	0.95	1.34
Birmingham, Ala. (1)	Lanett	0.60	0.83	Corinth	0.60	0.81	0.94	1.34
Puerto Rico (4)	Lanett via Mobile	2.72	2.96	Corinth via Mobile	3.10	3.36	2.65	2.89

(1) Rail class rates.   (4) Water and rail.

TABLE C-1 (*Continued*)

Hypothetical Plant Site		Total Transport Cost	Cost Differences Relative to Texas		Total Labor Cost	Total Selected Costs
			Fuel Costs	Power Costs		
Orange, Texas	(1)	$1.38 to 2.17	$0.00	$0.00	$18.92	$20.30 to 21.09
Institute, W. Va.	(1)	1.27 to 1.80	0.00	0.00	17.36	18.63 to 19.16
Boston, Mass.	(1)	5.12 to 5.74	+1.56/2.04	+0.26/0.34	17.27	24.21 to 25.39
	(2)	4.49 to 5.11				23.58 to 24.76
	(3)	2.13 to 3.05				21.22 to 22.70
Memphis, Tenn.	(1)	3.82 to 4.30	+0.47/0.61	+0.08/0.10	17.27	21.64 to 22.28
	(2)	3.21 to 3.69				21.03 to 21.67
	(3)	1.44 to 1.92				19.26 to 19.90
Mobile, Ala.	(1)	3.59 to 4.06	+0.42/0.55	+0.07/0.09	17.27	21.35 to 21.97
	(2)	3.04 to 3.51				20.80 to 21.42
	(3)	1.31 to 1.78				19.07 to 19.69
Wilmington, N. C.	(1)	4.09 to 4.47	+1.03/1.35	+0.17/0.23	17.27	22.56 to 23.32
	(2)	3.50 to 3.88				21.97 to 22.73
	(3)	1.66 to 2.24				20.13 to 21.09
Chattanooga, Tenn.	(1)	3.29 to 3.68	+0.68/0.89	+0.11/0.15	17.27	21.35 to 21.99
	(2)	3.29 to 3.68				21.35 to 21.99
	(3)	1.53 to 1.92				19.59 to 20.23
Birmingham, Ala.	(1)	3.97 to 4.37	+0.59/0.78	+0.10/0.14	17.27	21.93 to 22.56
	(2)	3.19 to 3.59				21.15 to 21.78
	(3)	1.27 to 1.67				19.23 to 19.86
Puerto Rico	(4)	3.48 to 3.94	+1.03/1.33	+0.17/0.22	14.81[b]	19.49 to 20.30
					12.74	17.42 to 18.23
					10.68	15.36 to 16.17

(1) Rail class rates. (2) Rail commodity rates. (3) Water transportation. (4) Water and rail.
[b] See p. 109. Alternatively at weighted average hourly wage rates of $1.52, $1.31, and $1.10.

TABLE C-2

REGIONAL VARIABLE-COST DIFFERENCES PER 100 POUNDS: NYLON 66 CONTINUOUS-FILAMENT YARN

Table 10, Column 1*

Hypothetical Plant Site		Total Transport Cost	Cost Differences Relative to Texas		Total Labor Cost	Total Selected Costs
			Fuel Costs	Power Costs		
Orange, Texas	(1)	$1.38 to 2.17	$0.00	$0.00	$40.56	$41.94 to 42.73
Institute, W. Va.	(1)	1.27 to 1.80	0.00	0.00	37.23	38.50 to 39.02
Boston, Mass.	(1)	5.12 to 5.74	+1.72/2.24	+0.33/0.43	37.02	44.19 to 45.43
	(2)	4.49 to 5.11				43.56 to 44.80
	(3)	2.13 to 3.05				41.20 to 42.74
Memphis, Tenn.	(1)	3.82 to 4.30	+0.51/0.67	+0.10/0.13	37.02	41.45 to 42.12
	(2)	3.21 to 3.69				40.84 to 41.51
	(3)	1.44 to 1.92				39.07 to 39.24
Mobile, Ala.	(1)	3.59 to 4.06	+0.46/0.60	+0.09/0.11	37.02	41.16 to 41.79
	(2)	3.04 to 3.51				40.61 to 41.24
	(3)	1.31 to 1.78				38.83 to 39.51
Wilmington, N. C.	(1)	4.09 to 4.47	+1.14/1.49	+0.22/0.28	37.02	42.47 to 43.26
	(2)	3.50 to 3.88				41.88 to 42.67
	(3)	1.66 to 2.24				40.04 to 41.03
Chattanooga, Tenn.	(1)	3.29 to 3.68	+0.74/0.98	+0.14/0.09	37.02	41.20 to 41.87
	(2)	3.29 to 3.68				41.20 to 41.87
	(3)	1.53 to 1.92				39.44 to 40.11
Birmingham, Ala.	(1)	3.97 to 4.37	+0.65/0.86	+0.12/0.16	37.02	41.76 to 42.41
	(2)	3.19 to 3.59				40.98 to 41.63
	(3)	1.27 to 1.67				39.06 to 39.71
Puerto Rico	(3)	3.48 to 3.94	+1.14/1.46	+0.22/0.28	31.61[a]	36.45 to 37.29
					27.24	32.08 to 32.92
					22.88	27.72 to 28.56

* See p. 74.   (1) Rail class rates.   (2) Rail commodity rates.   (3) Water transportation.
[a] See p. 109.   Alternatively at weighted average hourly wage rates of $1.52, $1.31, $1.10.

TABLE C-3

REGIONAL VARIABLE-COST DIFFERENCES PER 100 POUNDS:
INTEGRATED OUTPUT OF NYLON SALT AND NYLON 66 STAPLE FIBER
Table 4(I), Plant Type I, and Table 9, Column 1*

Hypothetical Plant Site		Transport Cost from Nearest Large-Scale Producing Center		Natural Gas from Houston, Texas	Weighted Average Transport Cost of Synthetic Fibers to the National Market	
		Benzene	Ammonia		Carload	LCL
Texas City, Texas	(1)	$0.00	$0.00	$0.00	$1.38	$2.17
Institute, W. Va.	(1)	1.42	0.00	0.12/0.16	0.98	1.51
	(2)	0.71				
	(3)	0.13				
Boston, Mass.	(1)	1.38	0.14	0.20/0.26	1.10	1.72
	(2)	0.71	0.14			
	(3)	0.20/0.26	0.03/0.06			
Memphis, Tenn.	(1)	1.30	0.12	0.06/0.08	1.14	1.62
	(2)	0.95	0.12			
	(3)	0.28	0.05			
Mobile, Ala.	(1)	1.10	0.13	0.05/0.07	1.16	1.63
	(2)	0.67	0.13			
	(3)	0.15	0.06			
Wilmington, N. C.	(1)	1.81	0.18	0.13/0.17	0.96	1.34
	(2)	1.02	0.18			
	(3)	0.23/0.30	0.04			
Chattanooga, Tenn.	(1)	1.10	0.16	0.08/0.11	0.95	1.34
	(2)	0.52	0.16			
	(3)	0.52	0.11			
Birmingham, Ala.	(1)	0.00	0.13	0.08/0.10	0.94	1.34
	(2)		0.13			
	(3)		0.10			
Puerto Rico	(3)	0.75/0.96	0.20/0.24	0.13/0.17	2.65	2.89

* See pp. 42 and 73.
(1) Rail class rates.   (2) Rail commodity rates.   (3) Water transportation.

TABLE C-3 (*Continued*)

Hypothetical Plant Site		Total Transport Cost	Cost Differences Relative to Texas		Total Labor Cost	Total Selected Costs
			Fuel Costs	Power Costs		
Texas City, Texas	(1)	$1.38 to 2.17	$0.00	$0.00	$19.38	$20.76 to 21.55
Institute, W. Va.	(1)	2.52 to 3.09	0.00	0.00	17.79	20.31 to 20.88
	(2)	1.81 to 2.38				19.60 to 19.59
	(3)	1.23 to 1.80				19.02 to 19.59
Boston, Mass.	(1)	2.82 to 3.50	+4.01/5.24	+0.44/0.58	17.65	24.92 to 26.97
	(2)	2.15 to 2.83				24.25 to 26.30
	(3)	1.53 to 2.30				23.63 to 25.77
Memphis, Tenn.	(1)	2.62 to 3.12	+1.21/1.47	+0.14/0.17	17.64	21.61 to 22.40
	(2)	2.27 to 2.77				21.26 to 22.05
	(3)	1.53 to 2.03				20.52 to 21.31
Mobile, Ala.	(1)	2.44 to 2.93	+1.08/1.41	+0.12/0.16	17.64	21.28 to 22.14
	(2)	2.01 to 2.50				20.85 to 21.71
	(3)	1.42 to 1.91				20.26 to 21.12
Wilmington, N. C.	(1)	3.08 to 3.50	+2.65/3.48	+0.29/0.39	17.64	23.66 to 25.01
	(2)	2.29 to 2.71				22.87 to 24.22
	(3)	1.36 to 1.85				21.94 to 23.36
Chattanooga, Tenn.	(1)	2.32 to 2.71	+1.76/2.30	+0.19/0.26	17.64	21.91 to 22.91
	(2)	1.71 to 2.13				21.30 to 22.33
	(3)	1.66 to 2.08				21.29 to 22.28
Birmingham, Ala.	(1)	1.15 to 1.57	+1.40/1.78	+0.17/0.23	17.64	20.36 to 21.22
	(2)	1.15 to 1.57				20.36 to 21.22
	(3)	1.12 to 1.55				20.33 to 21.20
Puerto Rico	(3)	3.73 to 4.26	+2.66/3.43	+0.29/0.38	15.51[a]	22.19 to 23.58
					13.44	20.12 to 21.51
					11.38	18.06 to 19.45

(1) Rail class rates. (2) Rail commodity rates. (3) Water transportation.
[a] See p. 109. Alternatively at weighted average hourly wage rates of $1.52, $1.31, $1.10.

TABLE C-4

REGIONAL VARIABLE-COST DIFFERENCES PER 100 POUNDS: ORLON STAPLE FIBER

Table 9, Column 2*

Hypothetical Plant Site		Transport Cost of Acrylonitrile		Transport Cost of Dimethyl Formamide from La Porte	Weighted Average Transport Cost of Synthetic Fibers to the National Market	
		From Texas City	From Institute		Carload	LCL
Texas City, Texas	(1)	$0.00	$0.00 + 0.50 = 0.50^a	$0.00	$1.38	$2.17
Institute, W. Va.	(1)			0.24 to 0.28	0.98	1.51
Boston, Mass.	(1)	1.93	1.16 + 0.50 = 1.66	0.33 to 0.65	1.10	1.72
	(2)	1.32	0.79 + 0.50 = 1.29	0.33 to 0.65		
	(3)	0.43/0.55		0.12 to 0.32		
Memphis, Tenn.	(1)	0.90	0.97 + 0.50 = 1.47	0.15 to 0.31	1.14	1.62
	(2)	0.62	0.66 + 0.50 = 1.16	0.15 to 0.31		
	(3)	0.13	0.15 + 0.50 = 0.65	0.04 to 0.08		
Mobile, Ala.	(1)	0.85	1.16 + 0.50 = 1.66	0.14 to 0.29	1.16	1.63
	(2)	0.57	0.79 + 0.50 = 1.29	0.14 to 0.29		
	(3)	0.08		0.02 to 0.04		
Wilmington, N. C.	(1)	1.47	0.89 + 0.50 = 1.39	0.25 to 0.50	0.96	1.34
	(2)	1.00	0.61 + 0.50 = 1.11	0.25 to 0.50		
	(3)	0.30/0.38		0.08 to 0.24		
Chattanooga, Tenn.	(1)	1.16	0.81 + 0.50 = 1.31	0.20 to 0.39	0.95	1.34
	(2)	0.79	0.55 + 0.50 = 1.05	0.20 to 0.39		
	(3)	0.24	0.18 + 0.50 = 0.68	0.08 to 0.16		
Puerto Rico	(3)	0.35/0.44		0.10 to 0.28	2.65	2.89

* See p. 73.

^{a} Excess cost of Institute, W. Va., natural gas over Houston, Texas, natural gas.

(1) Rail class rates. (2) Rail commodity rates. (3) Water transportation.

TABLE C-4 (Continued)

Hypothetical Plant Site		Total Transport Cost	Cost Differences Relative to Texas		Total Labor Cost	Total Selected Costs
			Fuel Costs	Power Costs		
Texas City, Texas	(1)	$1.38 to 2.17	$0.00	$0.00	$18.92	$20.30 to 21.19
Institute, W. Va.	(1)	1.72 to 2.49	0.00	0.00	17.36	19.08 to 19.85
Boston, Mass.	(1)	3.09 to 4.03	+1.56/2.04	+0.26/0.34	17.27	22.18 to 23.68
	(2)	2.72 to 3.66				21.81 to 23.31
	(3)	1.65 to 2.59				20.74 to 22.24
Memphis, Tenn.	(1)	2.19 to 2.83	+0.47/0.61	+0.08/0.10	17.27	20.01 to 20.81
	(2)	1.91 to 2.55				19.73 to 20.53
	(3)	1.31 to 1.83				19.13 to 19.81
Mobile, Ala.	(1)	2.15 to 2.77	+0.42/0.55	+0.07/0.09	17.27	19.91 to 20.68
	(2)	1.87 to 2.49				19.63 to 20.40
	(3)	1.26 to 1.75				19.02 to 19.66
Wilmington, N. C.	(1)	2.60 to 3.23	+1.03/1.35	+0.17/0.23	17.27	21.07 to 22.08
	(2)	2.32 to 2.95				20.79 to 21.80
	(3)	1.34 to 1.96				19.81 to 20.71
Chattanooga, Tenn.	(1)	2.31 to 2.89	+0.68/0.89	+0.11/0.15	17.27	20.37 to 21.20
	(2)	1.94 to 2.52				20.00 to 20.83
	(3)	1.27 to 1.74				19.33 to 20.05
Puerto Rico	(3)	3.10 to 3.61	+1.03/1.33	+0.17/0.22	14.81[b]	19.11 to 19.97
					12.74	17.04 to 17.90
					10.68	14.98 to 15.84

(1) Rail class rates. (2) Rail commodity rates. (3) Water transportation.
[b] See p. 109. Alternatively at weighted average hourly wage rates of $1.52, $1.31, $1.10.

TABLE C-5
REGIONAL VARIABLE-COST DIFFERENCES PER 100 POUNDS: DYNEL STAPLE FIBER
Table 9, Column 3*

Hypothetical Plant Site		Transport Cost of Acrylonitrile		Transport Cost of Vinyl Chloride	
		From Texas City	From Institute	From Texas City	From Institute
Texas City, Texas	(1)	$0.00		$0.00	
Institute, W. Va.	(1)		$0.00 + 0.20 = 0.20^a		$0.00 + 0.09 = 0.09^a
Boston, Mass.	(1)	0.77	0.46 + 0.20 = 0.66	1.49	0.89 + 0.09 = 0.98
	(2)	0.53	0.32 + 0.20 = 0.52	1.05	0.63 + 0.09 = 0.72
	(3)	0.17/0.22		0.40/0.48	
Memphis, Tenn.	(1)	0.36	0.39 + 0.20 = 0.59	0.70	0.76 + 0.09 = 0.85
	(2)	0.25	0.26 + 0.20 = 0.46	0.40	0.53 + 0.09 = 0.62
	(3)	0.05	0.06 + 0.20 = 0.26	0.21	0.25 + 0.09 = 0.34
Mobile, Ala.	(1)	0.34	0.46 + 0.20 = 0.66	0.66	0.89 + 0.09 = 0.98
	(2)	0.23	0.32 + 0.20 = 0.52	0.46	0.63 + 0.09 = 0.72
	(3)	0.03		0.11	
Wilmington, N. C.	(1)	0.59	0.36 + 0.20 = 0.56	1.15	0.68 + 0.09 = 0.77
	(2)	0.40	0.24 + 0.20 = 0.44	0.80	0.49 + 0.09 = 0.58
	(3)	0.12/0.15		0.24/0.29	
Chattanooga, Tenn.	(1)	0.46	0.32 + 0.20 = 0.52	0.89	0.63 + 0.09 = 0.72
	(2)	0.32	0.22 + 0.20 = 0.42	0.63	0.44 + 0.09 = 0.53
	(3)	0.10	0.07 + 0.20 = 0.27	0.38	0.29 + 0.09 = 0.38
Puerto Rico	(3)	0.14/0.18		0.33/0.38	

* See p. 73.

^{a} Excess cost of Institute natural gas over Texas natural gas.

(1) Rail class rates.   (2) Rail commodity rates.   (3) Water transportation.

TABLE C-5 (Continued)

Hypothetical Plant Site		Transport Cost of Acetone		Weighted Average Transport Cost of Synthetic Fibers to the National Market	
		From Texas City	From Institute	Carload	LCL
Texas City, Texas	(1)	$0.00		$1.38	$2.17
Institute, W. Va.	(1)		$0.00	0.98	1.51
Boston, Mass.	(1)	0.34/0.68	0.21/0.42	1.10	1.72
	(2)	0.34/0.68	0.21/0.42		
	(3)	0.18/0.36	---		
Memphis, Tenn.	(1)	0.16/0.32	0.18/0.36	1.14	1.62
	(2)	0.16/0.32	0.18/0.36		
	(3)	0.05/0.10	---		
Mobile, Ala.	(1)	0.15/0.30	0.21/0.42	1.16	1.63
	(2)	0.15/0.30	0.21/0.42		
	(3)	0.03/0.06	---		
Wilmington, N. C.	(1)	0.26/0.52	0.16/0.32	0.96	1.34
	(2)	0.26/0.52	0.16/0.32		
	(3)	0.13/0.26	---		
Chattanooga, Tenn.	(1)	0.21/0.42	0.14/0.28	0.95	1.34
	(2)	0.21/0.42	0.14/0.28		
	(3)	0.21/0.42	0.08/0.16		
Puerto Rico	(3)	0.18/0.36	---	2.65	2.89

(1) Rail class rates. (2) Rail commodity rates. (3) Water transportation.

TABLE C-5 (Continued)

Hypothetical Plant Site		Total Transport Cost	Cost Differences Relative to Texas		Total Labor Cost	Total Selected Costs
			Fuel Costs	Power Costs		
Texas City, Texas	(1)	$1.38 to 2.17	$0.00	$0.00	$18.92	$20.30 to 21.09
Institute, W. Va.	(1)	1.27 to 1.80	0.00	0.00	17.36	18.63 to 19.16
Boston, Mass.	(1)	2.95 to 3.78	+1.56/2.04	+0.26/0.34	17.27	22.04 to 23.43
	(2)	2.55 to 3.38				21.64 to 23.03
	(3)	1.85 to 2.78				20.94 to 22.43
Memphis, Tenn.	(1)	2.36 to 3.00	+0.46/0.61	+0.08/0.10	17.27	20.17 to 20.98
	(2)	1.95 to 2.59				19.76 to 20.57
	(3)	1.45 to 1.98				19.26 to 19.96
Mobile, Ala.	(1)	2.31 to 2.93	+0.43/0.55	+0.07/0.09	17.27	20.08 to 20.84
	(2)	2.00 to 2.62				19.77 to 20.53
	(3)	1.33 to 1.83				19.10 to 19.74
Wilmington, N. C.	(1)	2.45 to 2.99	+1.03/1.35	+0.17/0.23	17.27	20.92 to 21.84
	(2)	2.14 to 2.69				20.61 to 21.54
	(3)	1.45 to 2.04				19.92 to 20.89
Chattanooga, Tenn.	(1)	2.27 to 2.80	+0.68/0.89	+0.11/0.15	17.27	20.33 to 21.11
	(2)	1.94 to 2.47				20.00 to 20.78
	(3)	1.51 to 1.98				19.57 to 20.29
Puerto Rico	(3)	3.30 to 3.81	+1.03/1.33	+0.17/0.22	14.81[b]	19.31 to 20.17
					12.74	17.24 to 18.10
					10.68	15.18 to 16.04

(1) Rail class rates.   (2) Rail commodity rates.   (3) Water transportation.
[b] See p. 109. Alternatively at weighted average hourly wage rates of $1.52, $1.31, $1.10.

TABLE C-6
REGIONAL VARIABLE-COST DIFFERENCES PER 100 POUNDS: DACRON STAPLE FIBER
Table 9, Column 5*

Hypothetical Plant Site		Transport Cost of Dimethyl Terephthalate		Transport Cost of Ethylene Glycol		Weighted Average Transport Cost of Synthetic Fibers to National Market	
		From Texas City	From Institute	From Texas City	From Institute	Carload	LCL
Texas City, Texas	(1)	$0.00	$0.00 + 0.11 = 0.11^a	$0.00	$0.00 + 0.07 = 0.07^a	$1.32	$2.17
Institute, W. Va.	(1)					0.98	1.51
Boston, Mass.	(1)	2.51	1.50 + 0.11 = 1.61	0.55	0.33 + 0.07 = 0.40	1.10	1.72
	(2)	1.95	1.17 + 0.11 = 1.28	0.55	0.33 + 0.07 = 0.40		
	(3)	0.43/0.56		0.28/0.36			
Memphis, Tenn.	(1)	1.17	1.26 + 0.11 = 1.37	0.26	0.28 + 0.07 = 0.35	1.14	1.62
	(2)	0.91	0.98 + 0.11 = 1.09	0.26	0.28 + 0.07 = 0.35		
	(3)	0.13	0.15 + 0.11 = 0.26	0.08	0.10 + 0.07 = 0.17		
Mobile, Ala.	(1)	1.10	1.50 + 0.11 = 1.61	0.24	0.33 + 0.07 = 0.40	1.16	1.63
	(2)	0.86	1.17 + 0.11 = 1.28	0.24	0.33 + 0.07 = 0.40		
	(3)	0.08		0.24			
Wilmington, N. C.	(1)	2.00	1.15 + 0.11 = 1.26	0.42	0.25 + 0.07 = 0.32	0.96	1.34
	(2)	1.48	0.89 + 0.11 = 1.00	0.42	0.25 + 0.07 = 0.32		
	(3)	0.30/0.38		0.20/0.22			
Chattanooga, Tenn.	(1)	1.50	1.06 + 0.11 = 1.17	0.33	0.23 + 0.07 = 0.30	0.95	1.34
	(2)	1.17	0.82 + 0.11 = 0.93	0.33	0.23 + 0.07 = 0.30		
	(3)	0.24	0.18 + 0.11 = 0.29	0.33	0.12 + 0.07 = 0.19		
Puerto Rico	(3)	0.35/0.45		0.22/0.28		2.65	2.89

* See p. 73.

^{a} Excess cost of Institute natural gas over Texas natural gas.

(1) Rail class rates.   (2) Rail commodity rates.   (3) Water transportation.

TABLE C-6 (*Continued*)

Hypothetical Plant Site		Total Transport Cost	Cost Differences Relative to Texas		Total Labor Cost	Total Selected Costs
			Fuel Costs	Power Costs		
Texas City, Texas	(1)	$1.38 to 2.17	$0.00	$0.00	$18.92	$20.30 to 21.09
Institute, W. Va.	(1)	1.16 to 1.69	0.00	0.00	17.36	18.52 to 19.05
Boston, Mass.	(1)	3.11 to 3.73	+1.56/2.04	+0.26/0.34	17.27	22.20 to 23.38
	(2)	2.78 to 3.40				21.87 to 23.05
	(3)	1.81 to 2.64				20.90 to 22.29
Memphis, Tenn.	(1)	2.57 to 3.05	+0.47/0.61	+0.08/0.10	17.27	20.38 to 21.03
	(2)	2.31 to 2.79				20.12 to 20.77
	(3)	1.35 to 1.83				19.16 to 19.81
Mobile, Ala.	(1)	2.50 to 2.97	+0.42/0.55	+0.07/0.09	17.27	20.27 to 20.88
	(2)	2.26 to 2.73				20.03 to 20.64
	(3)	1.28 to 1.75				19.05 to 19.66
Wilmington, N. C.	(1)	2.54 to 2.92	+1.03/1.35	+0.17/0.23	17.27	21.01 to 21.77
	(2)	2.28 to 2.66				20.79 to 21.51
	(3)	1.46 to 1.94				19.93 to 20.79
Chattanooga, Tenn.	(1)	2.42 to 2.81	+0.68/0.89	+0.11/0.15	17.27	20.48 to 21.12
	(2)	2.18 to 2.57				20.24 to 20.88
	(3)	1.43 to 1.82				19.49 to 20.13
Puerto Rico	(3)	3.22 to 3.62	+1.03/1.33	+0.17/0.22	14.81[b]	19.23 to 19.96
					12.74	17.16 to 17.91
					10.68	15.10 to 15.85

(1) Rail class rates.   (2) Rail commodity rates.   (3) Water transportation.
[b] See p. 109.   Alternatively at weighted average hourly wage rates of $1.52, $1.31, $1.10.

Index

199

Regional framework, raw material regions, 1–2, 7–8, 36, 92–94
  Texas-Gulf, 1–2, 7–8, 36, 89, 93
  West Virginia, 1–2, 88, 93–94
Regional impact, 1975 forecast, 4, 149–155, 155–159
  employment, 4, 157, 158
  by regions, 4, 157, 159
  investment, 4, 155–156
  by regions, 4, 157, 159
  summary findings, 4
  synthetic fibers, 1975, 149–155

Saran, 13, 15
Scope of study, 1, 6–7, 13, 120–121
  fibers included, 1, 6, 13
  limiting factors, 6–7, 13
  major objectives, 1, 6
Spinning, 64, 67, 68–69, 70, 71, 72
Steam costs, *see* Fuel costs
Substitution analysis, *see* Location theory
Synthetic-fiber production, 2, 4, 6, 19, 22, 23, 24–25, 29, 32–33, 34, 62–82, 83–84, 143–149, 155, 156, 183–198
  Acrilan, 71
  agglomeration economies, 34, 83, 143
  capacity, 25, 155, 156
  Dacron, 72
  Dynel, 70
  findings of study, 4, 143–149
  growth in market, 24–25
  location alternatives, 2, 6, 29, 143
  location factors, 83–84
  nylon 66, 66–68
  orientation, 4, 144
  Orlon, 68–70
  plant locations, future, 4, 145, 146–147, 148, 149
   present, 22, 23, 24, 25, 146–147, 148
  production functions, 32–33, 72–83
   continuous filament, 74
   electric power, 79–80
   labor, 81–83
   major chemicals, 74–77
   staple, 73
   steam, 77–79
   water, 80

Synthetic-fiber production, regional advantages and cost differences, 4, 143–149, 183–198
  fiber-market regions, 145–148
  Puerto Rico, 148–149
  raw-material regions, 144–145, 146–147
  schema of manufacturing process, 19
  stages of production, 2, 6
  technology, 19, 62–66
   filament processing, 19, 64–65
   polymerization, 19, 62–64
   spinning, 19, 64

Taxes, 3, 32
Teflon, 13, 15, 23, 147
Terylene, 24, 142
Texas-Gulf, as raw materials region, 1, 2, 7–8, 36, 89, 93
  findings of study, 4, 130, 134, 138, 142, 144–145, 157, 159
Textile industry, 2, 86–87, 90, 91, 92
Textile South, *see* Central, East, and West South
Transportation costs, 90–91, 95–102, 144–145, 146, 147–148, 148–149, 161–167, 170–171, 183–198

Verel, 13, 15, 23, 148
Vicara, 12, 14
Vinyl acetate or pyridine (Acrilan), 23, 46, 50, 63, 71, 76, 131
Vinyl chloride, *see* Acrylonitrile-vinyl chloride
Vinyon, 14, 21

Water, 37, 58, 80, 106, 145, 146, 147–148
West South, as fiber-market region, 2, 89, 90, 91
  findings of study, 3–4, 147–148, 157, 159
West Virginia, as fiber-market region, 88, 90, 91
  as raw materials region, 1, 2, 88, 93–94
  findings of study, 3–4, 130, 134, 138, 142, 146–147, 157, 159

Zefran, 13, 14, 23, 147